P9-DOE-321

OTHER BOOKS BY BRIAN D. McLAREN

Reinventing Your Church

The Church on the Other Side:
Doing Ministry in the Postmodern Matrix

Finding Faith

A NEW KIND
OF CHRISTIAN

A Tale of Two Friends on a Spiritual Journey

Brian D. McLaren

JOSSEY-BASS
A Wiley Company
San Francisco

Copyright © 2001 by Brian D. McLaren. All rights reserved.

Published by Jossey-Bass
A Wiley Imprint
989 Market Street, San Francisco, CA 94103-1741   www.josseybass.com

No part of this publication may be reproduced, stored in a retrieval system, or
transmitted in any form or by any means, electronic, mechanical, photocopying,
recording, scanning, or otherwise, except as permitted under Section 107 or 108
of the 1976 United States Copyright Act, without either the prior written
permission of the Publisher, or authorization through payment of the appropriate
per-copy fee to the Copyright Clearance Center, Inc., 222 Rosewood Drive,
Danvers, MA 01923, 978-750-8400, fax 978-750-4470, or on the web at
www.copyright.com. Requests to the Publisher for permission should be
addressed to the Permissions Department, John Wiley & Sons, Inc., 111 River
Street, Hoboken, NJ 07030, (201) 748-6011, fax (201) 748-6008, e-mail:
permcoordinator@wiley.com.

Excerpt from *The Discarded Image: An Introduction to Medieval and Renaissance
Literature*, by C. S. Lewis (Cambridge, England: Cambridge University Press, 1964).
Reprinted with the permission of Cambridge University Press.

Excerpt from *The Last Battle* by C. S. Lewis. Copyright © C. S. Lewis Pte. Ltd. 1956.
Extract reprinted by permission.

Jossey-Bass books and products are available through most bookstores. To
contact Jossey-Bass directly call our Customer Care Department within the U.S. at
800-956-7739, outside the U.S. at 317-572-3986 or fax 317-572-4002.

Jossey-Bass also publishes its books in a variety of electronic formats. Some
content that appears in print may not be available in electronic books.

Library of Congress Cataloging-in-Publication Data

McLaren, Brian D., date
  A new kind of Christian : a tale of two friends on a spiritual journey / Brian D.
McLaren.
      p. cm.
Includes bibliographical references.
  ISBN 0-7879-5599-X
  1. Christian life.   2. Spiritual life.   I. Title.
  BV4501.2 .M43577 2001
  248.4—dc21

                                                                      00-012490

Printed in the United States of America
FIRST EDITION
HB Printing   10 9

CONTENTS

This book is dedicated to Grace, my wife of twenty-one years. She has been a true partner and friend on this spiritual journey, and together we have enjoyed four of life's greatest privileges and pleasures . . . raising Rachel, Brett, Trevor, and Jodi.

ACKNOWLEDGMENTS

Of the many, many people deserving thanks for their role in the production of this book, four groups of people stand out.

First, my spiritual mentors from my early days engaged me in many conversations like the ones in this book. I am deeply grateful for the hours that Rod Conover, Rev. David Miller, Dave Rickert, Dr. David Dunbar, Tom Willett, and several others have invested answering my questions, sharpening my thoughts, challenging my blind spots, giving me good books, exposing me to ministry opportunities, and being my friends. Back in the 1970s, they believed in a thin, raggedy-looking, blue-jeaned, guitar-playing, long-haired and bearded young guy without standard credentials. They echoed to me Paul's words to Timothy: "Let no one despise your youth. . . ." Now, as a balding, unthin, and middle-aged guy (still blue-jeaned whenever possible), I realize that without their encouragement back then, I wouldn't have much to say, or the confidence to say it, today.

Second, my colleagues in the Terranova Project (including Jeff Bailey, Rudy Carrasco, Brad Cecil, Tim Conder, Mark Driscoll, Todd Hunter, Ron Johnson, Andrew Jones, Tony Jones, Jason Mitchell, Sally Morgenthaler, Doug Pagitt, Dr. Alan Roxburgh, Chris Seay, Danielle Shroyer, Molly Smallen, Brad Smith) have been "Neo" to me in many ways in recent years, as have many other conversation partners (including Dr. John Franke, Dr. Stan Grenz, Chuck Smith Jr., Brent Brooks, Dr. Skip Smith, Tim Ayers, Stephen Freed, Doug Koenigsburg, Neil and Renea Livingstone, Dr. Dallas Willard, Dr. Len Sweet, Robert Kang, Pamela Bateman, Stephen Shields, Doug Flather, Lisa Holloway). Special thanks to Dr. Dave Dunbar, Dr. Alan Roxburgh, Todd Hunter, and Chuck Smith Jr.; they read an early version of the manuscript and gave me needed and helpful feedback and encouragement. When friends and colleagues truly communicate and collaborate, it's hard to tell where one person's thinking ends and another's begins; I feel that these pages reflect *our* best thoughts, not just mine.

Third, the congregation I belong to and serve among, Cedar Ridge Community Church, deserves my deepest thanks. It can be scary having a pastor who asks questions like those found in this book. Some congregations would restrict their shepherd to tending them in familiar pastures in their own backyard. But the staff and members of Cedar Ridge have explored new territory with me far beyond the backyard fence, and they have accepted me not just as a pastor, but also as a growing Christian, a human being, a quirky and curious guy who is by nature (and perhaps calling) drawn to innovation. They've prayed for me, encouraged me, challenged me, and taught me more than I've taught them.

Finally, the people of Jossey-Bass and Leadership Network have been an unmitigated delight to work with on this project.

Of course, in naming these names, I want credit for any value this book has to be shared among all. But any blame (for faults, errors, episodes of ignorance or naiveté, and other reckless stupidities) belongs to the author alone.

Spencerville, Maryland   BRIAN D. McLAREN
February 2001

THE TRUE STORY BEHIND THIS STORY

SOMETIME IN 1994, at the age of thirty-eight, I got sick of being a pastor. Frankly, I was almost sick of being a Christian. My crisis of faith deteriorated to the point that one beautiful August afternoon a year later, in the Pennsylvania mountains—on a day with one of those high-pressure Canadian air masses coming in from the northwest on a cool breeze and with the humidity so low and air so clear the distant mountains looked touchable—on this perfect summer day I felt as gray, low, foggy, dismal, and miserable as I ever have felt. I was sitting in a rocking chair, on a porch overlooking a stunningly beautiful valley shining with light, and in the dazzling brightness I wrote in my journal, "One year from today I will not be in the ministry." I think that dark sentence was both despairing and hopeful.

My prediction was wrong. Now, seven years later, I am still a Christian, still in ministry, and enjoying both more than I ever have.

But at that low tide of faith, my soul was trying to tell me something important, something I needed to listen to. Just as feelings of suicide are often an exaggerated way for our soul to tell us something we have been denying, something like, "The life you're living is insupportable; you can't keep living this way," my ministry death wish and urge for spiritual escape were telling me something I needed to attend to.

Only Two Alternatives?

At the time I could only see two alternatives: (1) continue practicing and promoting a version of Christianity that I had deepening reservations about or (2) leave Christian ministry, and perhaps the Christian path, altogether. There was a third alternative that I hadn't yet considered: learn to be a Christian in a new way. That is the subject of this book. Beginning that August day, when the gloom inside my heart was so dark and the sunshine around me was so blazing and stark, a process of reevaluation was somehow set into motion. Perhaps I was like a person who spends a few days feeling suicidal and then decides, "If I could seriously ponder ending my life, then I can do anything. I can change anything in my life. So instead of ending my life altogether, I'll end my life as I've been living it and start a new kind of life. I can now see a third alternative to the status quo and suicide."

M. Scott Peck says that depression often accompanies the collapse of a mental map or paradigm; it is a natural and necessary expression of grief, grief over the loss of something perhaps as dear to us as a brother or mother: our worldview, our way of seeing life. Alan Roxburgh, a colleague in the Terranova Project (an initiative to explore how Christian faith will reconfigure in the postmodern matrix), teaches people that this painful process of letting go of life as we have known it and embracing a new life on new terms (the process of paradigm change) typically follows five phases:

1. Stability, when life is fine, current theories explain everything adequately, and questions are few—perhaps like Dorothy of *The Wizard of Oz* living happily in Kansas

2. Discontinuity, when the old system seems to be working less well—reflected socially in Dorothy's conflict with her witchy neighbor, psychologically in her ambivalent desire to run away from home, and physically in the approaching thunderstorm

3. Disembedding, when we begin feeling that the current system is insupportable and we begin to disconnect from it—like Dorothy being carried away from Kansas by the tornado

4. Transition, when we haven't fully left the old world and we haven't fully entered the new world—like Dorothy newly arrived in Oz, trying to get her bearings

5. Reformation, when we decide to make a go of it in the new world we have entered—like Dorothy setting out on her journey to see the wizard, invigorated with new hope and passion

This in many ways mirrors my experience through those shadowy times.

Andrew Jones, another colleague in the Terranova Project, once drew a diagram for me that created a similar scenario. It looked something like this:

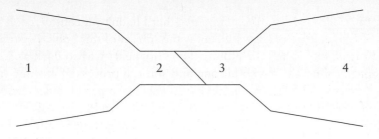

Area 1 refers to the old paradigm, the old mental map or way of seeing things. Over time, it becomes increasingly cramped and feels more like a prison than freedom. Area 2 describes the early transition period, where there is a high degree of frustration and reaction. An individual or group in this phase turns against the old paradigm and can't stop talking about how wrong, inhumane, or insupportable it is. In area 3, people gradually turn from deconstructing the past to constructing the future and begin the hard work of designing a new paradigm to take the place of the old one. This is a time of creative exhilaration, challenge, and perhaps anxiety—because the discovery of a new paradigm that will be superior to the old is by no means assured and because the wrath of the defenders of the old is likely to be unleashed on those who dare propose an alternative. If the creation of a new paradigm succeeds, the group moves into area 4, where the new era develops and expands freedom and possibilities. (Of course, one must anticipate a time when the new liberating paradigm itself becomes confining and old.)

Understanding My Frustration

These images and illustrations describe, at least in part, why I had grown frustrated with the way I was being a Christian and the way I was helping others to be Christians. The old way was, as an old Bob Dylan lyric puts it, "rapidly aging," and I needed to disembed and reevaluate and begin a journey toward a new home—for my sake, for the sake of the people I was called to lead, and perhaps even for God's sake. But the new way hadn't been created yet. We were barely into area 2, maybe sticking our toes into area 3. Hence the anxiety.

There is a dimension to this experience of disembedding from modern Christianity that none of us can fully understand or describe. That's the theological dimension. What if God is actually behind these disillusionments and disembeddings? What if God is trying to move us out of Egypt, so to speak, and into the wilderness, because it's time for the next chapter in our adventure? What if it's time for a new phase in the unfolding mission God intends for the people (or at least some of the people) who seek to know, love, and serve God? What if our personal experiences of frustration are surface manifestations of a deeper movement of God's Spirit? In other words, what if this experience of frustration that feels so bad and destructive is actually a good thing, a needed thing, a constructive thing in God's unfolding adventure with us?

Maybe Martin Luther felt this way in his life as a monk. Maybe when he was told to preach about indulgences or to make room for emissaries from Rome to do so, he thought to himself, "I can't take this anymore. Maybe I'll go back to being a lawyer." His experience seemed bad to him. (He must have been frightened: Am I losing my faith? Am I falling away from God?) But Protestants would agree, at least, that something good was afoot.

That August day, I felt miserable, and I continued to feel miserable for some months. But gradually, although giving up in despair remained tempting, hope started becoming more interesting.

On to Something

I began to feel like one of those rumpled detectives on TV who finds a clue that opens up a whole new twist in the plot. Or better, I began to feel like a scientist in a movie, doing a routine run of experiments. I'm looking over my data and this icy feeling starts back between my shoulder blades and crawls up my neck, and I think, "Something's not right here. This pattern in the data just doesn't make sense." The camera comes in over my shoulder, and all you see are rows of numbers, but I pull out my cell phone and call my partner and say, "Jack, you've got to get over here to the lab. No, now. We've got something major here." Or better yet, I felt like Eleanor Arroway in the movie *Contact*, at that moment when she is sitting on her car listening through headphones to the random noise of space picked up by the array of radiotelescopes that surround her. Suddenly comes this sound, like a clothes dryer with a really bad bearing that is drying a pair of rollerblades. "This is no random noise," she thinks. "There is a pattern to this noise. This noise is data, trying to tell me something."

Of course, my data isn't numbers. My data is my experience—my general experience as a committed Christian and my specific experience as a pastor. Experiences like these:

1. I drive my car and listen to the Christian radio station, something my wife always tells me I should stop doing ("because it only gets you upset"). There I hear preacher after preacher be so absolutely sure of his bombproof answers and his foolproof *biblical* interpretations (in spite of the fact that Preacher A at 9:30 A.M. usually contradicts Preacher B at 10:00 A.M. and so on throughout the day), his five easy steps (alliterated around the letter *P*), his crisis of the month (toward which you should give a "love gift . . . if the Lord so leads"). And the more sure he seems, the less I find myself wanting to be a Christian, because on this side of the microphone, antennas, and speaker, life isn't that simple, answers aren't that clear, and nothing is that sure. (Paradoxically, at that moment I might consider sending him money, hoping that by investing in his simpler vision of the world, I myself will be able to buy into it more. But eventually I will stop throwing good money after bad.)

2. I preach sermons that earn the approving nods of the lifelong churchgoers, because they repeat the expected vocabulary and formulations, words that generally convey little actual meaning after hearing them fifty-two times a year, year after year, but work like fingers, massaging the weary souls of earnest people. Meanwhile, as the initiated relax under this massage of familiar words, as they emit an almost audible "ahhh" to hear their cherished vocabulary again, these very massaging messages leave the uninitiated furrowing their brows, shaking their heads, and shifting in their seats. They do this sometimes because they don't understand but even more when they do understand—because the very formulations that sound so good and familiar to the "saved" sound downright weird or even wicked to the "seekers" and the skeptics. These people come to me and ask questions, and I give my best answers, my best defenses, and by the time they leave my office, I have convinced myself that their questions are better than my answers.

3. I do the reverse: I preach sermons that turn the lights on for spiritual seekers but earn me critical letters and phone calls from the "veterans" of the church often because the expected fingers didn't reach through my message to massage them as expected.

4. I have counseling sessions in my office, year after year, during which many wonderful people, people whom I love, people who have a lot of Bible knowledge, Christian background, theological astuteness, and "pew time," prove to have the same problems, make the same mistakes, harbor the same doubts (though more often unexpressed), indulge the same vices, and lack the same "spark" that unchurched people often do, the only major differences being that (a) the church people tend to use more religious language to define their problems, (b) their problems are further

complicated by guilt for having these problems in the first place, and (c) these religious people nevertheless consider themselves superior to their nonreligious counterparts. (I read recently that divorce rates among evangelical Christians—supposed guardians of traditional family values—are actually higher than those in the culture at large. What?) After these counseling sessions, I am left troubled, wondering, "Shouldn't the gospel of Jesus Christ make a bigger difference than this? And does pew time have to result in spiritual pride and inauthenticity?"

5. I realize that as people come into our church, everybody needs conversion. The not yet committed Christians need to be converted to a vibrant twenty-first-century faith, and the already committed twentieth-century (and nineteenth-century!) Christians need the same, myself included.

6. I realize, as I read and reread the Bible, that many passages don't fit any of the theological systems I have inherited or adapted. Sure, they can be squeezed in, but after a while my theology looks like a high school class trip's luggage—shoestrings hanging out here, zippers splitting apart there, latches snapping, clothes pouring out on the floor like a thrift store horn of plenty. My old systems—whether the Dispensationalism of my childhood, the Calvinism of my adolescence, the "charismaticism" of my early adulthood, or even my more mature, moderated, mainstream "evangelicalism"— can't seem to hold all the data in the Bible, not to mention the data of my own experience, at least not gracefully.

7. I read what other people who are having similar experiences are saying, including people writing outside of the religious context—like this from Peter Senge: "In any case, our Industrial Age management, our Industrial Age organization, our Industrial Age way of living will not continue. The Industrial Age is not sustainable. It's not sustainable in ecological terms, and it's not sustainable in human terms. It will change. The only question is how. Once we get out of our machine mind-set, we may discover new aptitudes for growth and change. Until then, change won't come easily."[1] As I read, I feel that "industrial age faith" faces the same fate.

8. I pick up most religious books, like the one you're holding, and know from somewhere midway through page one what the entire book will say, and I read on anyway and find out that I was right. I wonder: Doesn't the religious community see that the world is changing? Doesn't it have anything fresh and incisive to say? Isn't it even asking any new questions? Has it nothing to offer other than the stock formulas that it has been offering? Is there no Saint Francis or Søren Kierkegaard or C. S. Lewis in the house with some fresh ideas and energy? Has the "good *news*" been reduced to the "good same-old same-old?"

9. I meet people along the way who model for me, each in a different way, what a new kind of Christian might look like. They differ in many ways, but they generally agree that the old show is over, the modern jig is up, and it's time for something radically new.

Enough of this data accumulates (my list could go on and on) . . . and a pattern becomes perceptible, and a realization comes like a good cry: Either Christianity itself is flawed, failing, untrue, or our modern, Western, commercialized, industrial-strength version of it is in need of a fresh look, a serious revision.

Secrets and Sparks

You can't talk about this sort of thing with just anybody. People worry about you. They may think you're changing sides, turning traitor. They may talk about you as if you came down with some communicable disease. So you keep this sort of thing like a dirty secret, this doubt that is not really a doubt about God or Jesus or faith but about our take on God, our version of Jesus, our way of faith. You let it out only when you feel you have found someone you can trust.

And when you do, and the other person says, "I can't believe you're saying this. I have felt the same way, but I thought I was the only one"— that's a good moment. Relief. Company. Affirmation. It's like you're both pieces of flint, and when your secrets strike one another, a spark of hope flies: "Maybe we're not crazy. Maybe there's a better way. Maybe there's a new way of being a Christian." And then, over time, the two of you discover you're not the only two, that there are many more out there, including some respected people, "important" people, people with "names," who are wrestling with the same discontent, experiencing the same disembedding. You begin to wonder if maybe you're at the front edge of something—if your tentative and anxious steps "off the map" are actually the beginning of a new adventure into *terra nova*, new ground, fresh territory.

I've never been all that good at keeping my own secrets, so I've probably let my disillusionment out more than I should have. But as a result, I have seen a lot more sparks of hope fly than most people have, which has given me the courage and enthusiasm to write this book, which is a kind of bag of flints that when shaken together may produce a bunch of sparks that can catch fire in very hopeful ways.

In my first book, *Reinventing Your Church,* I hinted that a book like this might be rumbling around in the rear lobes of my brain. I said:

You see, if we have a new world, we will need a new church. We won't need a new religion per se, but a new framework for our theology. Not a new Spirit, but a new spirituality. Not a new Christ, but a new Christian. Not a new denomination, but a new kind of church in every denomination. . . .

I began to doubt that any of us Christians are actually Christians. I relate this experience simply to illustrate the importance of our challenge: to reopen the question of what makes a good Christian. . . . If need be, would we be willing to confess that we are hardly Christians at all and that we need to become as little children and start again?[2]

My second book, *Finding Faith,* was written to help people who are agnostics or atheists (or spiritual seekers wandering somewhere north of monotheism) in their journey to a good faith, which would open the door to a good relationship with God.[3] But I realized as I was writing it (and even more since it was published) that I was creating a problem. The kind of people who would come to faith along the path I was trying to clear for them would probably not end up just like the people waiting for them in church. They would be like a bunch of wild-eyed artists and excitable children and rugby players walking into a roomful of buttoned-down accountants and engineers. To be sure, that could be a great learning experience for all concerned but not the makings of a fun party.

And so in *A New Kind of Christian,* I explore, albeit indirectly, several questions:

1. Why am I not the same kind of Christian I used to be?

2. What might a new kind of Christian be like?

3. How might one become a new kind of Christian if one is so inclined?

An Apology

Before proceeding, I should say something about who I think you are. I'm assuming you're either a Christian of some sort ("hot" fundamentalist, "warm" evangelical, or "cool" liberal; charismatic or noncharismatic; denominational or nondenominational; Catholic, Protestant, or Orthodox; modern or postmodern, or amphibious) or else a non-Christian of some sort who is interested in Christianity (the kind of person who has perhaps read my second book, *Finding Faith,* and is interested in continuing the conversation we began there). If you are the latter, I must apologize because in several places I will, for the sake of my primary audience, have to belabor points that present little problem for you. The reverse may be true as well, but probably less often.

If you are a new kind of non-Christian considering becoming a new kind of Christian, you face different (and in many cases, I think, easier) issues than if you are an old kind of Christian becoming a new kind of Christian. Or if you are a postmodern non-Christian considering becoming a postmodern Christian, you face different (and in many cases, I think, easier) issues than if you are a modern Christian becoming a postmodern Christian. (Believe me, the previous two sentences will make more sense after a few more chapters.)

I should also add that my primary tribe has been the evangelical Protestant wing of the church. For readers from Roman Catholic, liberal Protestant, Orthodox, Jewish, or other backgrounds, at times you may feel like you've just tuned in Garrison Keillor's *Prairie Home Companion* and are listening to the news from Lake Wobegon, Keillor's fictitious largely Lutheran Minnesota town where all the men are good-looking, all the women are strong, and all the children are above average. Neither Minnesotan nor Lutheran, I'm still able to see myself in Keillor's characters and their "it was a quiet week in Lake Wobegon" stories. Similarly, even if your background is far different from mine, I hope you'll be able to see yourself in the stories and conversations that follow. If at times I seem to be addressing concerns of another part of my audience, I hope you'll take that as an opportunity to eavesdrop. (Eavesdropping can be a pretty interesting way to learn, sometimes more interesting than being addressed directly.)

I think that Christian leaders—pastors, priests, lay leaders, parachurch workers, missionaries—may have a special interest in this book. Many of them have experienced twinges of discontent similar to my own and, like me, are hopeful that we will find some new ways of being Christians as we enter the postmodern world. If you are in this category, I'm especially glad to have you along for the journey.

Beyond this, I'll try to assume as little as possible about you, except your basic sincerity, goodwill, intelligence, and desire to become a better person and help create a better world.

Three Points of Orientation

To prepare you for what you're about to step into, I can offer three additional introductory comments. First, as you'll see, I'm going to blur the line between fiction and nonfiction in the pages that follow. I think you will understand why I have done so as we proceed. This book started as a work of nonfiction but evolved steadily toward fiction with each revision. Knowing that I was not trying to commit a work of artistic fiction from the start will help lower your expectations about character development, plot, and other artistic concerns. Things will go much better for both of us if you consider this more in the category of a philosophical dialogue than a novel.

I am reminded of a man who was in a situation similar to ours, a man who lived at the boundary between the medieval and modern worlds. He had become convinced of some ideas that were in his time considered unorthodox, odd, crazy. He couldn't explain his new ideas in straight expository prose for a variety of reasons. So he resorted to an ancient form of writing. He said, "I have thought it most appropriate to explain these concepts in the form of dialogues, which, not being restricted to the rigorous observance of mathematical laws, make room also for digressions, which are sometimes no less interesting than the principal argument." I hope, as Galileo did, the dialogues that follow will be judged neither by the rigorous standards of mathematical laws nor by the equally rigorous standards of good novel-writing. And I hope that the digressions will prove no less interesting than the principal argument, as Galileo's were.

Second, you will soon meet Neil Edward Oliver, Dan and Carol Poole, and Casey B. Curtis. Please don't assume that any of these characters can be fully identified with the "I" who wrote this Introduction.

Third, this book is just a beginning. There are a number of other questions, important questions that follow on from these, that I will only nod toward in this book. Please don't be disappointed that you didn't get the last word. When you're on a really long voyage, you have to get beyond asking, "Are we there yet?" and instead start asking, "Are we making progress?" I hope that you will feel you have made real progress when you turn the last page, even though our destination will still be far ahead of us. The fact is, whatever a new kind of Christian will be, no one is one yet. At this point, we're more like caterpillars cocooning than butterflies in flight. But every transformation has to start somewhere. The sooner we start, the better.

It is my hope that these imaginary conversations will prompt you to engage in real-life ones and that those conversations will take you where these cannot. I'd be most happy if you share the book with a small group or maybe read it with one good friend. Then take some long walks or share a few meals together and see where those conversations lead you. If you'd like to engage with some other readers online, please go to www.findingfaith.org.

—B.D.M.

SOMETIME THE PEACOCK
WISH TO BE THE SEAGULL

"CAROL, I'M NOT SURE how long I'll last. I know this must be scary for you. I'm sorry." I was leaning against the counter, and Carol was sitting across the kitchen with her chair angled away from the table, her legs crossed, left elbow on the table behind her, facing me but not meeting my gaze.

She got up, turned her back to me, and began picking up the dinner dishes—quietly, deliberately, maybe a little more slowly than normal. Our twin ten-year-old sons, Corey and Trent, were at a birthday sleep-over (badly named—they stay up half the night and come home wired) at a friend's house, so there had been only three of us at the table. Carol put the dishes in the sink and stood beside me. She crossed her arms as mine were, and we stared at the same spot on the kitchen floor for a couple of seconds. "Well, Dan," she said, "if you quit, I'm sure we'll make it somehow. But I don't relish the thought of moving. I'd hate for the kids to have to change schools, especially Jess. But whatever damage moving would do would be a lot less than . . ."

"Than me being depressed all the time."

"Well, that too, but I was going to say it would be better than you getting embroiled in some big deal at the church. You know, heresy stuff or division stuff or getting fired. Lord knows we don't need that."

"No, I won't let that happen. I'll quit before I let that happen. I'll substitute-teach or something, maybe get certified. I wouldn't mind having my summers off, and . . . the pay wouldn't be that different."

"You just did it again," Carol said.

"What?"

"You sighed. You never used to sigh. In seventeen years of marriage, I never heard you sigh until these last few months."

"Yeah." We kept staring at that spot on the kitchen floor, not talking. Carol reached her arm around my waist and gave me a gentle squeeze. I said, "I keep thinking that there must be this ranch out in New Mexico somewhere. You know, we move out there, I get a horse . . ."

"And you ride the range all day and never have to talk to anybody. Cowboy Dan."

"Yeah. The thought of the quiet and the dry air and the big sky—shoot, I've never even been to New Mexico, but I'm ready to move tomorrow. . . . I just sighed again, didn't I?"

"You sure did. But look, if we have to move, let's move back near my folks. Atlanta's no Santa Fe, but the kids would love to be near their grandparents, and vice versa."

"Somehow dreaming of hot, humid, crowded Atlanta doesn't draw the same kind of sigh out of me," I said.

"Whatever," Carol replied. "Look, hon, it's almost seven. I'll get the dishes cleaned up if you'll take Jess to her concert, OK? You've got to pick up a couple of her friends from the youth group too. You know where it is, right?"

"It's at that rec center just off 95? Gosh, if it takes me forty-five minutes to get there and back, I might as well just stay."

"Better you than me. I hate that kind of music."

"OK. We'll probably be back by 11:30 or so by the time I drop the other kids off. Thanks, honey."

"For what?"

"For hanging in there with me. I wish I wasn't putting you through this."

"I wish you weren't putting yourself through this. You'd better get moving. Jess hates being late."

I think that conversation was the first time I'd put my plan into words. Not the New Mexico part—that was pure fantasy. The other part—about quitting my job as a pastor, becoming a high school teacher—I'd never put that into words before. I guess that's why I went out of my way to meet Dr. Oliver at the concert that night.

It was a Saturday, midsummer, 1999. Jessica wasn't yet sixteen, so even though she had her learner's permit, she needed me to drive her and a few friends to a concert. Some boys from her high school had put together a rock band called the Amish Jellies. (Quite a name, eh?) They'd rented out a community center for their first big gig. I'd played in a bunch of garage bands as a high school kid myself, so I didn't mind sticking around to hear them play. But they were a lot louder and worse than I thought they'd be, so about twenty minutes was all I could stand. I snuck out into the lobby, hoping it would be less painful out there.

Some parents of the boys in the band had put out some refreshments on an old blue card table (including coffee for the adults) so the kids could hang out and celebrate the band's debut after the concert. It turned out that a lot of the kids weren't interested in the music either, because the lobby was full of kids—all talking loud to be heard above the music. The other parents were holed up in the rec center's kitchen, so there I was, a thirty-nine-year-old guy trying to look coolly inconspicuous in a corner of a rec center lobby, a lone goose in a flock of animated ducks. I was just finishing a small Styrofoam cup of something vaguely resembling coffee when I heard Dr. Oliver's musical accent over the pulsing bass from the Jellies and the giggles and chatter of the kids.

I recognized his lilting voice from back-to-school nights. He was originally from Jamaica, I had been told, but his ethnic identity was mysterious for an American like me, used to two basic categories, black and white. He didn't seem to fit either of my standard categories. Part of his differentness was his style of dress, almost always a gray suit, a tie—more formal than American styles, yet the man himself was warm, engaging, enthusiastic, hardly a gray-suit kind of guy in my opinion. His features, his movement, his posture also defied easy categorization; I guess to me he looked African, but not African American. He was a science teacher, but I knew him more because he was the girls' soccer coach. Although he cut Jess her freshman year, he put her on first-string junior varsity as a sophomore. I'd missed most of her games though. Too many night meetings.

I'd heard lots of stories about Dr. Oliver over the years, even before Jess made the soccer team. Tall, articulate, and outspoken, the only Ph.D. on the Franklin Roosevelt High faculty, popular with the kids, survivor of a few controversies including a big textbook fight that had been in all the papers and on TV (that's how I originally heard about him)—he stood out in a lot of ways.

At first I couldn't see him because he was seated and surrounded by standing kids. After a few minutes, they left en masse, laughing and saying, "See you Monday, Dr. Oliver," and "Thanks for coming, Dr. Oliver." The crowd of teenagers parted like a motley curtain, and there he was, seated, smiling, shaking hands, giving high-fives, even in midsummer looking like it was any school day with his gray suit on. I went right over to say hello. He stood up as I approached. He made me think of Ed Bradley from *60 Minutes*—tall, bearded, salt-and-pepper hair, but thinner, darker-skinned, and a bit farther along in the receding hairline department. One other difference—where Bradley exudes TV newsmagazine seriousness, Dr. Oliver's whole face seemed wired to a smile that could appear at any moment, and his whole face seemed part of that smile—eyes, brows, cheeks. That's the smile I saw as I approached.

He shook my hand, with his peculiar mixture of formality and enthusiasm: "Ah, Mr. Poole—Daniel, isn't it? Father of the late-blooming soccer star? So *good* to see you, sir!" We exchanged a few flattering observations about Jess and then some complaints about the coffee, typical small-talk stuff, and then he asked how my summer was going. I didn't want to get into it, so I said, "Well, that's a long story." I was wondering how I could get some information on high school teaching from him without revealing that I was thinking about quitting my job at Potomac Community Church. That's not the kind of rumor I wanted my board to hear.

"And you, Dr. Oliver," I continued, "what brings you to an Amish Jellies concert?" He explained that the lead singer and drummer were students of his, and he liked to be supportive of his kids. "But listen, Dan," he said, "please don't call me Dr. Oliver. Only my students call me that. To my friends, I'm Neo. It's been my nickname since my freshmen year of college."

I cocked my head slightly, and that's all the cue he needed to continue with the story: "When I joined a fraternity at Rutgers, my roommate said I had three first names—Neil, Edward, and Oliver—and that confused him terribly. So he just started calling me by my initials, NEO. To tell you the truth, I think behind my back some of the others actually called me 'Negro.' They weren't used to having people of color around—especially ones like me with odd accents. But good friends we became anyway, and the nickname stuck. Now, if I recall correctly, I remember hearing that you are a minister. So how are things in the wonderful world of religion?"

Obviously, I didn't want to get into that either. I fumbled with my coffee cup and said, probably a little too quickly and cheerfully, "Well, I'm hanging in there. How's science?"

"Science," he said, finishing his last sip of coffee, "is a piece of cake compared to what you do. Our subject matter is mathematically definable, we're encouraged to experiment, and we're paid to be honest about our data. Somehow I don't think your cohort has any of those advantages. . . . Here, let me take your cup."

While he walked over to the trash can, I remember this strange feeling coming over me. The best word I can use for it was safety: *this guy is safe to talk to—he understands,* I thought. When he came back, I was surprised to hear myself saying, "Actually, Neo, things in church work are pretty rough sometimes. Pardon the pun, but it's not always a Sunday school picnic."

He rearranged the folding chairs and motioned for me to sit down, facing him, our knees only about two feet apart. He leaned forward, his forearms resting just above the knees. He looked a lot like a basketball coach

I had seen on TV, maybe conferring with a point guard in foul trouble. "Well, Reverend, it sounds like you could use a friend."

Out of nowhere, a wave of emotion rushed up my spine and caught in my throat. I'm a pretty "smooth" guy in public, not prone to extravagant expressions of emotion. But that simple sentence caused me to choke up. I tried to hide it, but I'll bet he saw my eyes brim. Without taking off my glasses, I quickly reached up under the rims and wiped my eyes and said, "Oh, you know, I guess every profession has some ups and downs."

"Yours more downs than many, I'm sure," he said. "Even with God's help it can still be brutal at times—or so Father Scott tells me. I'm an Episcopalian. Do you know St. Timothy's?"

I smiled politely and said, "Yes, over in Rockville," but I was afraid inside, thinking, "Don't do it! You can't pour out your heart to someone you hardly know." I forced a more cheerful look and said, "Thanks, Dr.—I mean Neo—for your concern." A polite put-off, gracefully done. I wanted to get the spotlight off me. I was comfortable in the role of listener, counselor, not revealer, counselee.

I perked up and said, "My daughter constantly tells stories about you, like about the time you brought a wild raccoon into class and he escaped in the storage room. Or the time your chemistry experiment caught fire and the whole school had to be evacuated. And then there was something about a tarantula having baby spiders that spread around the school. Did those legends really happen?"

He laughed: "Ah yes, I'm embarrassed to say yes, on all three counts, but it was an Amazonian bird-eating spider, which is actually much bigger than a tarantula. And I still have nightmares about that poor raccoon. . . . And the fire—Mr. Reedman at FDR will never let me forget about the fire. Actually, it was mostly smoke. . . ."

I said, "Well, you certainly make learning exciting—and memorable—for the kids, and I really respect that. The spider thing really gives me the creeps, though. I've never been much of an outdoors person. Well—I guess nobody will accuse you of being boring, which probably can't be said about that many science teachers . . . or pastors either." He smiled and shook his head, looking down, as if remembering something. Then I added, "I also remember admiring how you handled yourself in that big controversy about the textbooks a few years back. For a while you were a regular in the Howard County section of the *Sun*. I was really impressed how you handled the science-faith thing."

He made a whistling sound and then wiped his forehead with his hand, faking a sweaty brow: "Ah, 1996—don't make me think about 1996. A terrible year in my life, one I'd rather forget. I was caught between the fundamentalists, who didn't want me to teach about evolution, and the atheists, who didn't want me to admit that I believed in God! Nobody could accept that I would do both, so I became everybody's enemy. Mr. Reedman told me that the hard thing about being a bridge is that you get walked on from both ends. He was right about that!"

"Well," I said, "you certainly earned my respect through all that. I remember thinking that you were smarter and braver and more articulate than I would have been. When Channel 5 did that feature on you, you were brilliant. I never dreamed I'd actually get to meet you. Wow, some of those parents were ruthless, though. . . ."

"Indeed, ruthless is a good word for it, on both sides actually. But to me," he said, smiling, holding out his hands and shrugging his shoulders, "it was a simple matter of intellectual honesty. My faith has plenty of room for science, and my science only strengthens my faith—and I guess that just flows out of who I am."

I smiled and responded, "Well, I find that pretty remarkable."

He shook his head, and said, "No, no, no, I'm just . . ."

"You're not 'just' anything! Here you are, a Ph.D. scientist on the one hand, and on the other hand you come to an Amish Jellies concert—more for your love of your students than for love of their music, I'm sure!"

He replied, "Well, I think the auditory nerve damage will be temporary. . . ."

I joked back, "What's that? I can't quite hear you!" It was a dumb line, but we both laughed anyway.

Then he held up a finger and said, "One thing, Dan. My doctorate is not actually in science. It's in the philosophy of science. My undergraduate degree was in history. I came into high school science teaching completely by accident, only because Mr. Reedman couldn't find a real science teacher and because I couldn't find a college or university with an opening in philosophy of science. Actually, even though history and philosophy are my first loves, I've learned a lot of science these last few years. In fact, as a boy, I was incurably curious about the natural world—plants, animals, weather patterns. Jamaica's a great place for that, you know. So I love teaching science. And high school students are . . . the best. So I have no complaints. Say, would you like a cookie?"

I said sure, and we walked over to the blue card table and grabbed a few Oreos. "Would you like to step outside? A little quiet might help my nerve damage."

"Sure," I said, "although I imagine it's still pretty hot outside." By this time my daughter had left the auditorium too and was huddled with a few friends across the lobby. I caught her eye and motioned to her that I would be outside. She gave me a subtle wave and went back to her huddle.

As we walked down the rec center's front steps, Neo said, "I could be wrong, Dan, but I had the feeling in there that you really wanted to talk to me about something, and you were too polite to bother me with your problems."

"What? No. Well. No." He had caught me completely off guard.

"Dan, I'm not a pastor like you, but I am a Christian. I don't mean to sound too mystical, but I think I felt the Holy Spirit telling me that you need to talk about something." He sat down on the bottom step. I remained standing, leaning against a wrought-iron stair rail, staring across the parking lot, bouncing two Oreos in my hand.

"This is pretty weird. I really would like to talk, but . . ."

"But you're not sure I'm safe?" he asked.

"Actually, I feel you *are* safe. It's just that . . . well," I looked at my watch, "about an hour ago I was telling my wife that I'm thinking about quitting the pastorate. The reason I came over to talk to you in there was that I was thinking maybe I could get a job as a high school teacher—you know, when I leave. I was hoping you could give me some information about . . . about pay, getting certified, that sort of thing."

Then I sat down on the step next to Neo. He had his elbows on his knees again, and he turned toward me and said, "We had a saying in Jamaica: 'Sometime the peacock wish to be the seagull.' I guess it's a way of saying that sometimes important people, public people, wish they could just be regular people. It sounds like you could use a friend who will let you down off the pedestal, to just be a regular chap."

My eyes brimmed up again. I couldn't talk, even though now I wanted to.

Finally Neo spoke. Maybe he felt a little self-revelation of his own would make it easier for me. He wasn't speaking directly to me; he could have been talking to the parking lot. "I was born in a little town on the north coast, Port Maria. When I was ten, we moved to Kingston, where my daddy worked on the ships loading coffee, bananas, mangoes, all going to Miami and New York City. When my daddy's company wanted him to be a foreman in New York Harbor, we were so excited and proud! It was 1956; I was twelve. My parents rented an apartment in Elizabeth, New Jersey, where there were no other Jamaicans—mostly American blacks, Italian immigrants, and a few Puerto Ricans. All through school I felt that I was so different—I didn't really fit in anywhere; I could never just be one of the fellows. I still feel that way, I suppose—it's the curse of being an island person. But one thing I've learned: we're all the same, all men, all people, even you ministers." Then he turned toward me. "You don't have to tell me anything, but if you want to. . . ."

"No, I want to. It's just a little hard to get used to . . . being the one with the problem."

He quickly lightened up, almost joking, playing with me: "What is it? Do you have some fundamentalists after you? I've been there, in the 'textbook battles of '96.' If you've got some fundies after you, I can sympathize!" He made me smile, almost laugh, and after that it felt easier to talk.

"That's not my problem, Neo," I said. "I think I have the opposite problem. I think I *am* a fundamentalist, or was, or something." I was joking, but only half-joking.

"Oh, that's even worse!" he said, with such drama in his voice that we both laughed.

In spite of my laugh, I was still controlling—barely—an intense internal conflict. I wanted and needed to open up to someone, but I felt like a kid holding a balloon that he's blown up but hasn't tied yet. I was holding on, because if I let out all that was bursting inside me, I didn't know where things would go. So I held on.

"It's not so bad," I said. "Maybe we can talk about it some time." Not full disclosure—but a concession in that direction. It was all I could handle.

"No, don't minimize it. Just consider me someone you can talk to . . . anytime at all," Neo said. And then we just sat there for a full minute, neither of us talking.

It was hot outside, and humid, typical for a Maryland summer. But it was a quiet night, just crickets and the occasional swoosh of a passing car and the muffled bass guitar from the Jellies inside. I started eating another cookie.

Finally Neo said, "You know, I used to be a fundamentalist myself."

I couldn't tell if he was joking or serious. "Yeah? You? Right."

"No, in Port Maria, we belonged to the Brethren. You've heard of them? Wonderful people. Then, in Kingston my father joined a storefront Pentecostal church. My mother couldn't stand it; she would walk to a Presbyterian church in our neighborhood, but my brother and I would go with my dad. Ah, Dan, how those Pentecostal preachers could shout! They'd shout and we'd yell *amen, amen!* and they'd sweat and we'd sweat too, and they'd tell us we were *sinners* and that we needed to *repent* and we'd say *yes Lord, yes Lord,* and we'd wave our fans to cool ourselves off—those were the days before air conditioners—and when we'd leave, we all felt *wonderful*."

"So it worked for you?" I asked. "Then how, or why, did you become an Episcopalian? That's quite a change."

"Let's just say I've been through quite a few changes along the way."

"Apparently," I responded. "You even attend Amish Jellies concerts!" He laughed and said, "Well, believe me, the Jellies aren't typical storefront church material—or Episcopal concert material either." I half-joked, "You liberal Episcopalians prefer soft jazz, right?"

Neo looked over at me—I couldn't tell if he grew suddenly a little more serious or if he was playing with me: "Dan, may I ask what makes you so sure I'm *liberal?*" With his accent, that was a three-syllable word.

I noticed his change in tone and felt apologetic as I said, "Well, I guess I just assumed . . ."

"Because I'm Episcopalian or because I'm black?" he interrupted.

I wanted to say, "It was because of the textbook thing and the fact that you believe in evolution," but he continued before I could say anything: "Either way, Dan, I've found that liberals can be fundamentalists too. Liberals are often just fundamentalists with a different set of beliefs. Not all of them, but many. Anyway, I don't dislike fundamentalists, taken individually— they tend to be pretty nice folks. Get them together in a group though, and I get nervous. I start to twitch and break out in a rash."

I was still trying to mention the textbook controversy, but I was so struck by what he'd said about liberals being fundamentalists sometimes too that I sort of interrupted myself and said, "No, it was . . . wow . . . that's well put. I've felt the same way. Not bad taken individually, but as a group. . . . And I guess you're right, there could be fundamentalist liberals too. I never really heard it said that way before."

Neo said, "My pastor at Saint Tim's tells me that I have the spiritual gift of putting into words things people already know but didn't know they know—or didn't want to know. On several occasions I've offered to return the gift to the Lord. . . . It's not always a pleasant job. People often don't thank you for it."

"I can't imagine why they wouldn't appreciate it," I said. "I think you have a wonderful gift." We sat there for a few minutes, listening to crickets, watching the occasional car go by. I guess it was obvious that I didn't really want to talk about my situation any more than I had, so Neo changed the subject himself, quite graciously, really. He stood up and pointed out Orion and Cassiopeia, visible even through the wash of the parking lot lights. He told me how many light-years away they were (I've forgotten the number) and began telling me about the speed at which they were moving away from us but then stopped abruptly and apologized for giving me a science lecture. I told him I was interested, and so he went back to the science lesson. (He was obviously comfortable in the teaching mode. If he wasn't so interesting, it could have been annoying.) He talked about the red shift and cosmic background radiation and then something about muons, which I'd never heard of before.

After a few minutes, I interrupted and said, "You're better than one of those nature shows on cable TV."

He laughed and apologized again. "Those are my favorite shows! I watch them all! Ah, but I guess summers are hard on us extroverted teachers," he said. "By mid-July we'll walk up to people on the street and give them a lecture, we're so desperate to hear ourselves talk!"

I again said that I was intrigued, and meant it. But it was getting late and I had three kids to drop off and my sermon needed a bit more work, so I looked at my watch and said, "Tomorrow's a workday for me, so I need to find my daughter and hit the road. But I'm wondering, Neo . . . I don't know if you'd have time for this, but as I said, I'd like to find out a bit more about the teaching profession, you know, practicalities like certification and pay and benefits, that sort of thing. Might you have some time in the next couple of weeks to get together?"

He answered, still appearing embarrassed about being so talkative: "Well, my loquaciousness tonight suggests I am starved for human contact, so I would be most honored to get together."

I pulled out my pocket schedule book to write it down, and he pulled out his Palm Pilot. Like most PDA users, he couldn't resist showing his unit to me and telling me how wonderful it was. He entered my name and phone number, and we agreed to meet the following Saturday at a bagel place in Greenbelt, where he assured me the coffee was pretty good. He made me promise to say hello to Jess as we parted. I thanked him for the time, and when I shook his hand, he added some gesture with the fingers and a kind of knuckle-to-knuckle punch—something that I'd seen high school students do. I remember thinking, *Odd, he must look at me like one of the kids*.

I woke up Carol when I got home and told her the whole story about meeting Neo. She said, "Thank God. Maybe he can help you look into teaching." I lay in bed a long time without falling asleep. I think Carol was awake too.

2

ENTERING THAT AWKWARD AGE, OR DOES JONAH EAT BAGELS?

THE NEXT WEEKEND when I met Neo, we enjoyed a few bagels and cups of coffee (much better than the rec center brew), talked about my daughter's chances for a soccer scholarship, and reviewed our summer travel plans. (He had put on a lot of miles already that summer—including a trip to Seattle, where his parents now lived, and then a two-week stint escorting his church youth group to Guatemala for a short-term mission trip.)

When I turned the subject to life as a high school teacher, though, he put up his hand and said, "Just a minute, Dan. Before we go there, you must tell me more about why you're thinking of leaving ministry. I'd hate to be aiding and abetting a Jonah, you know, fleeing the work of the Lord. I think the church would be impoverished to lose yet another leader like you."

"'Yet another' leader? What do you mean?" I asked.

"It's just that, well, I have heard of quite a few pastors quitting in the last few years. It would be a shame if you left too, unless it was absolutely necessary," Neo replied. "Do you really feel you have no option but to leave your career, your calling?" He was looking right at me. We had both stopped eating.

I saw no way of getting the information I wanted without a partial disclosure, so I decided to let a little air out of the balloon I was holding inside. Just a little though. I told him I was tired, tired of all the church politics, tired of the constant criticism, tired of having to fight for every little change, tired of working for so many people who think they could do what I do better than me, who just don't understand. "I guess I sound like I'm feeling sorry for myself," I said.

"It's understandable. Your problems remind me of the story of Moses," Neo replied. "Leadership is hard. But I think there must be even more to it than that."

Neo apparently saw through my partial disclosure. At that moment, I remember deciding, "OK, I'll just let go. . . . I'll just let the pent-up balloon of emotion inside me escape." I leaned forward and spoke quietly, almost whispering: "You're right. Leadership is hard, but it's next to impossible when the leader isn't sure of where he's going."

"Yes?" he said, intoning a question.

I answered his question with a question. "What does a pastor do when he's having questions and doubts of his own? Can he stand up in his pulpit and say, 'Brothers and sisters, for the past three months, God hasn't seemed real to me. I have faith that God will seem real to me again in the future, but to be honest, God doesn't seem real to me today'? What does a pastor do when he questions the stock answers he's supposed to be convincing others of?"

Neo pressed his lips together, squinted his eyes, and nodded his head, as if to say, "Go on."

And then it all flowed out: "Remember when I told you—at the concert, out on the front step—that I felt like a fundamentalist? Well, I feel like a fundamentalist who's losing his grip—whose fundamentals are cracking and fraying and falling apart and slipping through my fingers. It's like I thought I was building my house on rock, but it turned out to be ice, and now global warming has hit, and the ice is melting and everything is crumbling. That's scary, you know? I went to seminary right out of college, and it was great, and I thought I was getting the truth, you know, the whole truth and nothing but the truth. Now I've been a pastor for fourteen years, and for this last year or so I feel like I'm running out of gas. It's not just burnout. It's more like I'm losing my faith—well, not exactly that, but I feel that I'm losing the whole framework for my faith. You know, I keep pushing everything into these little cubbyholes, these little boxes, the little systems I got in seminary and even before that—in Sunday school and summer camp and from my parents. But life is too messy to fit. And I'm supposed to be preaching the truth, but I'm not even sure what the truth is anymore, and—that's it, really—I just feel dishonest whenever I try to preach. I used to love to preach, but now every time—well, maybe not every time, but quite often—when I start to prepare a sermon, it's agonizing and . . . and people come to me with their problems and I used to be so sure of what to say but now I try to act confident but I don't know. The only thing I'm confident about is that I don't have all the answers anymore. I'm sorry. I'm not making any sense."

"No, you're making more sense than you realize," he said, and then he started working on me. I felt like I did when I'd gone to a chiropractor a few years before. He was probing here, pushing there, poking, stretching. *Are you feeling depressed, maybe suicidal?* Not seriously, not at all. *Is your marriage OK? Are you having moral problems?* No real problems there, thank God. *Are you working too many hours? How many?* Maybe fifty, fifty-five—that's not really it. *Are you afraid to tell your people what you're really thinking?* Yes, I feel that all the time. *Do you feel trapped by your profession, like you have to choose between your own personal pursuit of truth and the requirement to give an orthodox sermon every Sunday?* Yes, yes, exactly. *Do you sometimes feel that your seminary professors are looking over your shoulder and scolding you?* Every day. *Are you struggling with some specific doctrines or theological positions?* Yes, several. *Do you have anyone to talk to about all this?* Well, there's my wife, Carol. But it really upsets her to see me questioning. *Anyone else?* No. Nobody.

After about ten minutes of this kind of rapid-fire questioning, he said, "I think I understand your problem."

"What is it, doc?" I asked, half-referring to the chiropractor in my memory.

"Daniel, I think you're suffering from an immigration problem, something I have a bit of experience with, you know? You have a modern faith, a faith you developed in your homeland of modernity. But you're immigrating to a new land, a postmodern world. You feel like you don't fit in either world. You can't decide whether to settle in a little ghetto or to move out into the new land. But you can't make the transition to the other side alone. You need a sponsor—someone who has already settled and acclimated, who can help you do the same."

Neo was holding out his hands, as if to say, "There it is! Plain and simple!" But I had no idea what Neo's little analogy meant. Modern faith . . . I took that as a compliment, the opposite of archaic or outdated. Postmodern world, transition, immigration, ghetto—what? I'd read an article on postmodern architecture in an airplane once, and I'd heard some radio preachers using the term as a synonym for *bad*. (Lately, I was reacting to radio preachers in a kind of inverse proportion, so that association made me more interested.) "You lost me." I said. "New land? Immigration?"

Neo reached into his sports jacket pocket looking for a pen. (Before that day, I had only seen him in that gray suit, so a sports jacket seemed like a major step toward informality.) There was no pen to be found in any of his pockets. "Since I started using my Palm," he said, "I don't even carry a pen anymore. . . ."

"Here's one," I said, and he took it.

"Dan, I think I told you my first love is history. Do you mind if I give you a little history lesson?" I said no, and he cleared away the paper plate and crumbs from his placemat and wrote one word: *history*. What follows is my best recollection of what he said (with a few of my interruptions in brackets), scribbling notes on his restaurant place mat, and when it was filled, on mine too. If this sounds a little too much like a lecture (I remember feeling that I was being given an entertaining performance, actually), a little less than fully spontaneous, just remember that Neo is an educator to the bone. It's hard to turn that teacherly style off, even during summer vacation (we pastors have that problem too, between Sundays). At any rate, even though I can't fully convey the animated way he presented what he called his "little history lesson," I think you'll see why this breakfast meeting captured my interest and set the stage for some of the most stimulating conversations of my life.

Dan, you know I teach high school, but let's imagine we're back in fifth-grade social studies class. We're sitting in the back row, and the teacher is up front pointing to an outline on the chalkboard with an official pointer—remember those? I still actually use one—maple stick, black rubber tip. "History began," she says, "with the ability to write history." [Neo would click into a full-blown Jamaican accent whenever he quoted the teacher.] We have no idea what she means, but that isn't unusual.

"Before history," she says—and we wonder, *How can there be anything before history?*—"there was prehistory, the time before man could write his story. Man was an illiterate, uncivilized, hunter-gatherer, stalking saber-toothed tigers and giant ground sloths with crude spears, killing mastodons with rough clubs." Then she writes words like *Paleolithic* and *Neolithic* on the chalkboard, and we copy them into our tablets, knowing nothing more about them than that they'll probably be on the spelling test.

[As Neo created this scenario, he was gesturing with his long, thin arms, acting it all out, like a stand-up comic. I was cracking up. I thought to myself, *This guy would make a great actor or comedian . . . or preacher.*]

The teacher continues, "The first great period in human history, the Ancient World"—hear two taps of maple pointer on chalkboard—"stretched from 2500 B.C. to about A.D. 500. It was the age of the first historic civilizations: the Sumerian, Egyptian, Babylonian, Assyrian, Greek, and Roman empires." She draws a horizontal line on the board [which Neo drew on the placemat], scribbles up a few words, and continues.

"Then came the second great period, the Medieval World, from about A.D. 500 with the collapse of the Roman Empire, to about 1500, with the collapse of feudalism." Having no idea what *feudalism* means, we copy it from the board anyway because it looks like another spelling-test word for sure. Our teacher explains, "During this time, the church and Christianity dominated Western Europe. It was the age of castles and monasteries, lords and serfs. Then, from A.D. 1500 to the present, we have the Modern World, the age of reason and science." By now, her line looks like this:

	2500 B.C.	+	A.D. 500		A.D. 1500
Prehistory	Ancient World		Medieval World		Modern World

That's where our teacher stops, but that is where I must begin. I raise my hand, and the teacher says, "Yes, Neil," and I ask permission to come to the board. [Neo really seemed to be enjoying this. I could imagine him acting this scenario out in front of an audience and really hamming it up more than the confines of our corner of the bagel shop would allow.] "May I?" I ask her. And I hold out my hands. She drops a piece of chalk in one hand and puts the maple pointer in the other. The first thing I do is extend her timeline toward the right, like this. . . . Then I have to tell our class something even more nonsensical at first glance than "prehistory": namely, that there is something after the modern world—a *postmodern* world. To speak this way, we have to stop thinking of modern as "now," and we have to distance ourselves from the "now" we have grown up in and think of it as a "then," a period in the past. I add to her diagram so that it looks like this:

	2500 B.C.	+	A.D. 500		A.D. 1500		A.D. 2000
Prehistory	Ancient World		Medieval World		Modern World		Postmodern World

[At this point, Neo dropped the classroom simulation and spoke directly to me.] Now Dan, this is where the prefix *post-* is so helpful. Think of *post-* as applied to the word *pubescent*—something you as a parent and I as a teacher deal with a lot. Puberty is a period of life children experience, and after it, they are never children again (at least, not biologically). To be postpubescent means to have passed through puberty, to have been changed by it, and by virtue of having experienced it, to be now different, to be postpubescent: no longer a child; now an adolescent.

Similarly, to be postmodern doesn't imply being antimodern or nonmodern, and it is certainly different from being premodern (though it is similar in some ways). To be postmodern means to have experienced the modern world and to have been changed by the experience—changed to such a degree that one is no longer modern. I guess if you think of hormones as what change a child into a teenager, you could think of modernity bathing us in its hormones too.

[At this point, without a word, Neo scribbled out ten phrases—which I have italicized—on my placemat; it was as if he had them memorized, although I think he was actually making them up on the spot. I asked him if this was a lecture he had given somewhere, and he said no, but it was a lecture he had imagined giving many times and was just waiting for a chance like this to test it out. "You're my trial run," he said. After writing the sentences, he went back and explained them.]

Now this is a gross oversimplification, Dan. If my professors from graduate school heard me telling you this, they would probably strip me of my degrees. And it's a completely Eurocentric version of the story as well, but I guess that's part of the point. Anyway, you must understand that I'm painting with very broad strokes here, speaking very broadly, OK? [I said of course, no problem.]

1. First, modernity was an era of *conquest and control*. From Columbus and his fellow Western European explorers (in Spanish, they were called *conquistadores*, "conquerors") in 1492, the modern era meant conquest of the entire world by Western European philosophy, Western European culture, Western European languages, Western European economies, Western European religions, and Western European technology. Nature was conquered, native peoples were conquered—especially people of color like my ancestors—and a thousand problems (from bad breath to syphilis) were eventually conquered too. Of course, once you've conquered something, you need to keep it conquered, which means controlled. As a result, modern people have dedicated themselves to controlling people, results, risks, economies, experiments, profit margins, variables, nature, even weather. Got it? [I nodded my head and he moved on.]

2. It was the age of the *machine*. Mechanization has been the unspoken goal of the modern world. Not surprisingly, for modern folk, the universe itself came to be seen as a vast machine, controlled by an engineer-God, and ultimately, modern folk themselves became small cogs in the machine, machines themselves.

3. It was an age of *analysis*. If the universe is an intelligible machine—and science is the master screwdriver to take it apart—then analysis is the ultimate form of thought, the universal screwdriver. By taking wholes or effects apart into smaller and smaller parts or causes, each of which becomes understandable, analysis renders the universe both knowable and

controllable. The fact that to us *thinking* and *analyzing* seem to be synonymous suggests how successful modernity has been at marginalizing all other forms of thought—imagination, intuition, pattern recognition, systems thinking, and so on. [I was still nodding my head, but the new ideas were coming slightly faster than I could process them.]

4. It was the age of *secular science*. We can hardly conceive of a nonscientific worldview, which tells us how pervasive and invasive modern science has become; in fact, you can't say "nonscientific" without it sounding like an insult. With mechanistic and scientific views of the universe gaining hegemony and analytical minds swearing unyielding antipathy toward any invincible mystery that couldn't be broken down into controllable parts (God, for instance), nation-states and their cultures rose above ecclesiastical influence. It's no wonder that religion was scurrying in retreat in the modern era, fleeing the exterminating gas of modern science and secularism, like cockroaches from an apartment building. Perhaps religion could survive in the hidden corners of the private sector, but in the public sector it was seen by the scientific establishment as a dirty embarrassment, unsanitary, unwelcome, gauche. Do you follow me? [I nodded my head and said, partly lying, "Yes, this makes sense."]

5. It was an age aspiring to absolute *objectivity*, which, we believed, would yield absolute certainty and knowledge. In modernity, the ultimate intelligibility of the universe was assumed. What was still unknown was ultimately knowable. Also assumed was the highest faith in human reason to replace all mysteries with comprehension, superstition with fact, ignorance with information, and subjective religious faith with objective truth. As a result, in modern times, narrative, poetry, and the arts in general (which yield softer, more impressionistic returns than science, math, or engineering) took a back seat, or else they were asked to leave the car entirely to hitchhike on their own. Or they were brought along for their entertainment value but generally not as serious "front-seat" colleagues in the search for truth.

6. It was a *critical age*. If you believe that you absolutely, objectively know the absolute, objective truth, and you know this with absolute certainty, then of course you must debunk anyone who sees differently from you. Besides, in an age of conquest, if your ideas don't win, they lose. So the modern age was an age of debate, dialectic, argument, and discussion. Have you read Peter Senge's book *The Fifth Discipline*? No? Great book. He says that *discussion*, as opposed to dialogue or conversation, suggests a more aggressive, win-lose style of communication, more closely related (etymologically) to *percussion* and *concussion*. As a result, the views of others must be critically relativized, debunked, and reduced by one's own

views.[1] One of the most critically satisfying phrases in the modern era was the reductionist phrase "nothing but," as in "That's nothing but a Freudian Electra complex at work" or "That's nothing but a typical Marxist class struggle" or "That's nothing but a result of Darwinian evolution" or "His beliefs are nothing but superstition." Ah, how we moderns love to eviscerate our opponents with a verbal slash like that!

7. It was the age of the *modern nation-state and organization*. Since the collapse of the medieval world, modernity has been the story of organization and reorganization, from the assembly line to the picket line to the party line. Organization grew hand in hand with urbanism, since larger and larger aggregations of human beings required more and more organizing. "Man" himself became "organization man."

8. It was the age of *individualism*. As mechanistic organizations pursued conquest and control, communities were disintegrated, leaving their smallest constituent parts—individuals—disconnected and hanging in midair. The modern era moved inexorably from a focus on "we" to a focus on "me." Never have individuals been so "free" of all social constraint and connection as they are in late modernity. Not surprisingly, never have they felt so alienated and isolated.

9. It was the age of *Protestantism and institutional religion*. Where religion most thrived in the modern world, it was in its most institutional forms and its most Protestant forms (protesting not just Catholicism but medievalism and premodernism in general).

10. It was the age of *consumerism,* an age when people often quoted the maxim "Money can't buy happiness" but seldom acted as if they believed it. The market economy led to freedom from the feudal system, but it has become a powerful lord in its own right. [Neo leaned toward me now and spoke in a lowered voice.] I mean, just look at all the people in this shop. Most of them are wearing T-shirts with corporate logos on them. That always amazes me: people pay companies for the privilege of advertising their products!

Now, Dan, can you imagine how a society could bathe in these ten hormones long enough for it to reach a state where it couldn't continue on in its current form but would transform itself into something new? And can you imagine what happens to the church, the whole Christian enterprise, when it has so thoroughly accommodated to modernity—so much so that it has no idea of any way Christianity could exist other than a modern way? Do you follow me?

I said I thought so, but I was lying. Really, my head was swimming. I think he'd lost me with his second or third statement. Anyway, Neo then wrote the prefix *post-* sideways on the edge of the placemat and drew an arrow from it to each word or phrase. He then said, "In the postmodern world, we become postconquest, postmechanistic, postanalytical, post-secular, postobjective, postcritical, postorganizational, postindividualistic, post-Protestant, and postconsumerist." Then he asked, "Do you see what this means for us as modern Western Christians?"

Again, I felt overwhelmed with all this, but I don't like looking stupid, so I responded: "Let me see if I'm following you up to this point. You're saying that back in fifth grade, we couldn't conceive of anything before history: to us, history was the past. These days, it's hard for us to conceive of anything after modernity: to us, modernity is simply the present, now. But if you're right, Neo, modernity isn't 'now' for many of us, and it won't be 'now' for any of us much longer. You're saying that modernity has worked on us as a civilization (and the world) for long enough to propel us into something postmodern, just as puberty propels us into something new, different in many ways, exciting, and even a little scary at times. It sounds like I really have to understand postmodernism. I've heard people talk about it, mostly to say that it's something evil on the horizon that must be opposed at all costs. Can you explain postmodernism as a philosophy to me?"

Neo replied: "I could, but I'm not sure it's necessary. We could go there if you want. You may have already noticed, perhaps with relief, that I've tried here to describe postmodernity without once mentioning Foucault, Derrida, Rorty, Fish, Baudrillard, or any of the other great philosophical lights of postmodernism. That omission is intentional: I believe it possible to describe *postmodernity*—the broad culture defined by its having moved beyond modernity—without having to go too deeply into *postmodernism* as a philosophy. That's not to say that understanding postmodernism is unimportant or uninteresting. It's just that [Neo looked over at my watch] it's almost lunchtime already, and I don't want to keep you all day."

Neo said that if I were interested, he could recommend a few books on the more philosophical side of things.

He also offered his personal opinion—that whatever postmodern philosophy is, it is still in its infancy. Defining it is premature. Just as modernity took nearly two centuries to find its full expression in Enlightenment rationalism, Neo thought we're at least a few decades from anything close to a mature expression of postmodern philosophy. He said that in a new philosophy's early stages, it tends to be negative—to focus on what's wrong with the prevailing school of thought. It takes some time for the phase that deconstructs the prevailing view to give way to a phase where a new view is articulated, a new vision is proposed. He said we aren't in that phase yet, as far as he could see.

Then he added this: "My personal hunch is that there may not ever be a single dominating, monolithic postmodern philosophy, but rather that postmodern philosophy itself may be a pluralistic umbrella making room for many diverse philosophical voices within it. But that's just a hunch.

"Well, I must have exhausted you with this Saturday morning lecture. So much terminology, too many big words. I usually have a bell ringing to shut me up, but not today. I'm so sorry for carrying on like this. . . ."

I told him that no apology was necessary. I wondered, though, how he had learned all of this. He answered, "When I went for my doctorate in the late eighties, I had little interest in science. I meant to study philosophy, the philosophy of religion, actually, but in my first graduate seminar I came across a Hungarian philosopher named Michael Polanyi. He had been a chemist just after World War II, and before I knew it, Polanyi had captivated me and led me into the philosophy of science. From Polanyi I went to Heidegger, and from Heidegger I found myself reading the postmodernists. Through Polanyi I stumbled into this fascinating frontier where philosophy, history, theology, and science meet."

I had heard of Heidegger but not Polanyi. I told him I was fascinated by all this and hoped we could talk more about this in the future. But I still wanted to ask my questions about high school teaching, which he had completely pushed aside. He said he would be delighted to get together again and pulled out his PDA. After fooling with it for a few minutes he was ready, and we set up our next appointment. I had to do some traveling, and he had a lot of duties getting ready for the new school year—especially the soccer season—so it would be about a month before we could meet again. He recommended we take a walk along the old C&O Canal near the Potomac River, less than an hour's drive from each of our homes.

When I got home it was about noon. Carol was obviously trying to restrain her curiosity and enthusiasm about my meeting with Neo, but I could hardly finish a sentence before she had another question. She felt that Neo was a godsend, quite literally. Whether or not he would help me work through my theological problems or help me get a job as a teacher, I shared Carol's feeling that something good was at hand.

"Do you think," I asked her, "that maybe this is why I've felt so burned out for this last year or so? Could it be because I've been feeling what Neo's talking about but just didn't have the words for it?"

I cut the lawn that afternoon. As I went back and forth pushing the mower, I was also going back and forth in my mind—staying in the pastorate, leaving to become a teacher . . . modern, postmodern . . . Atlanta, New Mexico.

3

DAN DISCOVERS WHERE THE CROSS MEETS THE DREAM CATCHER

SINCE MY COLLEGE DAYS, I've kept a journal, a rough mix of prayers, thoughts, quotes, and reflections. It's become a kind of tradition for me to use those classic drugstore composition books with the cheap marbled black-and-white cardboard covers. I think I have an archive of thirty of them stowed in a box in my basement. When I got home from the bagel shop, I taped the placemats with Neo's scribbles on them into my current journal, folded so that I could open them for future reference. In the days and weeks that followed, I kept going back to that breakfast conversation and Neo's notes and diagrams.

○

AUGUST 22

Still processing yesterday's breakfast. If Neo is right, all that we currently understand being a Christian to be has been conditioned by our being modern. All of our theologies (at least, all of our Roman Catholic and Protestant ones) are basically modern, having been created in the modern world. I can imagine that my Catholic friends would say that their theology predates modernity. But couldn't they agree that while their medieval and even ancient structures may have been maintained (for better or worse), Catholic theology took a turn for the modern with the Counter-Reformation and the Council of Trent and hasn't turned back since? True, they may in many ways be less modern than their Protestant counterparts, but they're probably more modern than they think.

And I guess my Protestant friends would be livid right about now, saying things like "We're not modern—we're biblical! We believe in 'sola Scriptura'! We follow the New Testament!" But couldn't they agree that the way they read the Bible, the way they feel the need to put a *sola* in front of *Scriptura*, the way they follow the New Testament may possibly themselves be modern ways? The very terms of their protest against the medieval version of Roman Catholicism—could they imagine this?—could be themselves an engine of modernity inherent in their identity. That would be especially true if "modern" really means "postmedieval." God, help me, because I'm not sure where this thinking leads. Please guide me, Lord. It was hard to preach this morning with all this going on in my mind!

AUGUST 25

I have to keep reminding myself: it's not that modern is bad and postmodern is good. No doubt there are seeds of evil in postmodernity just as there are in modernity. I remember hearing a saying somewhere that he who marries the spirit of the age is sure to be a widow in the next. Give us a century or two of postmodernity, and we'll see its fatal flaws as clearly as those of modernity are becoming to us now. It's not a matter of good versus bad. It's a matter of appropriate versus inappropriate. This is especially true in our mission as Christians. I think of Paul in 1 Corinthians 9, saying that he'll become whatever he has to—Jewish or Gentile, educated or simple—in order to effectively convey the good news. Today maybe he'd say, "To the moderns I became modern, and to the postmoderns I became postmodern, so that by all appropriate means I could help people find Christ." But would he pretend to be postmodern to then try to convert non-Christians to a modern version of Christianity? Can there even be such a thing as a postmodern version? Is it possible to have a faith that transcends the historical situation we find ourselves in?

Reading over what I just wrote, I wonder if what I said about "it's a matter of appropriate versus inappropriate" is really the whole story. I wonder if I'm underemphasizing the ways that modernity twisted and deformed the Christian message. This is complicated. God, this is a little scary. Help me figure this out.

AUGUST 31

Lord, I've been thinking more about how my version of Christianity is modern. I wonder how its modernity is distorting my understanding of you. For example, I was thinking about the statement

"God is in control." I know that the question of what that statement means has been under hot debate in recent years, with the
"openness of God" camp suggesting new interpretations and tradi-
tionalists crying "heresy" in response. Now I realize that this debate really reflects some thinking people questioning their own
modernity, not your ultimate power. At any rate, what does "God
is in control" really mean to people today? I am almost certain
that we cannot consider the word *control* without thinking of it
mechanistically. In other words, for you to be in control means to
make something happen your way, the way an operator operates a
machine, flipping switches, turning gears, pressing buttons, causing
effects that cause other effects. I think it is almost impossible for us
to consider *control* meaning anything else.

But then I consider this: before the modern world, there were no
complex machines. There were no switches to flip, buttons to
push, or gears to grind. If I recall correctly, some of the first complex machines, clocks, were beginning to be developed in the
1300s, but it wasn't until the harnessing of the pendulum for clock
technology in the early 1600s that modern machines really became
commonplace. So God, whatever a person in ancient biblical times
would have meant by saying "God is in control" (if he would have
said such a thing at all) it is almost certainly very different from
what we mean today. For him, your control was associated with
farmers controlling animals or parents controlling children or perhaps a king controlling subjects—all very different from an operator controlling a machine "like clockwork." So if we say the Bible
speaks of you being in *control* (a word that doesn't even appear in
the old King James Version, according to my concordance), we run
the risk of importing and imposing all our modern conceptions of
clockwork, operation, mechanism onto you. We end up thinking
of you in a way that may really distort both your nature and our
situation in relation to you. In one way, Lord, this makes me want
to praise you, because many of our intellectual problems with
faith, like the whole issue of how evil can exist in your universe,
seem to disappear or shrink when we step outside the mechanistic
model. In other words, if a company designs a plane and it crashes
due to design failure, we hold the designer liable. Or if a person
drives a car drunk and kills a pedestrian, we hold the driver responsible. In both cases, the machine designer or operator is the
only sentient being capable of being held responsible. But if a parent raises a child with all appropriate guidance and the child grows
up and rejects his parents' teaching and commits a crime, we don't

hold the parent responsible in the same way. So I can see how limiting ourselves as moderns to a mechanistic view of the universe—
and of you—really creates problems for us. Forgive us, Lord, for
judging you according to our own incomplete paradigms.

SEPTEMBER 1
Neo's thinking is really infecting me. I feel like I've been invaded
by a computer virus that's corrupting all my data—or at least re-
organizing my data. The last day or two I've been thinking of another example of how our whole approach to Christianity is so
conditioned by modernity. What do we think of when we think of
theology? We think of Latinate terms like *omnipotence, omnipres-
ence,* and *immutability*. We think of an analytical outline, where
theology is divided up into many other "ologies": soteriology,
hamartiology, eschatology, and so on. It's a dissection of God—
a "theosection." It strikes me how rare these kinds of words, outlines, and dissective ways of thinking are in the Bible, which preoc-
cupies itself with earthy stories rather than airy abstractions, wild
poetry rather than tidy systems, personal and contextual letters
rather than timeless, absolute pronouncements or propositions. I
have often wondered, Why doesn't the Bible consist of an ordered
schema, like the average curriculum of a seminary? Of course, I'm
not against our systematic theologies. I'm beginning to see them as
an artifact of worship from the modern era, no less sincere or mag-
nificent than medieval cathedrals—in fact, you could call them
modern conceptual cathedrals. Rather than condemning, I am simply noticing that our systematic theologies are themselves a modern phenomenon. Medieval theologians had different questions,
concerns, and approaches; so did ancient ones and biblical writers
and characters. (I was tempted to write "biblical theologians," but
I'm not sure there were any, at least not as we conceive of them—
again, I seek not to criticize but simply to observe.)

SEPTEMBER 7
After rereading the last few entries, this thought strikes me: it's not
only our ways of thinking about God and Christianity and life that
show the DNA of modernity. All of our "Christian" institutions—
seminaries, radio stations, denominations, Bible studies, and so
on—are in fact modern inventions. Within the world of the
church, almost every influence is a modern one.

Meanwhile, step outside the church, and more and more
cultural influences are postmodern. To Christians steeped in
modernity, to move toward postmodernity can only look like

"worldliness," declension, decline, sliding away from the truth as they know it. If people start accepting this new way of thinking, I wonder if they'll be tried as heretics by the existing Christian institutions. God, as I write that sentence, I feel a chill of cowardice creep up my neck. I can't tell if I'm being insubordinate in exploring these thoughts or if I need courage to go farther. I feel that I may be falling away from my faith. But then again, if I hold back from honestly pursuing the truth, wouldn't that be pulling away from you—even worse? If I let go of or loosen my grip on some things I've never before doubted, will I fall away from you? Or could I actually find myself falling into you? Guide me, please, Holy Spirit. Jesus said you would guide us into all truth.

○

Between journal entries, I was asked to speak at a Christian education conference in Virginia Beach, about four hours away (at least five with traffic). It was an annual early September weekend gathering of highly committed Sunday school teachers and small group leaders, mostly laypeople, who wanted to sharpen their skills as teachers and leaders—a kind of kickoff for the new school year. While there, I realized how much Neo's thinking had already affected (or infected) me.

I was asked to be on a panel with a Christian author-educator whom I respect a great deal. ("Respect" is an understatement: a recent book of his was one of the best books I've ever read.) I felt outclassed just to be on the same platform as this fellow. The panel was called "Ministry in the New Millennium," a trendy topic in 1999.

The moderator's first question went something like this: "What do you foresee in the new century for us as committed Christians? Are you optimistic or pessimistic?" The author-educator responded first with something like this: "I see dark days ahead. We stand at the brink of a pagan revival. It will be harder than ever to be a Christian."

When my turn came to answer, I was bursting inside. I had to say that I saw it very differently; I felt that we were potentially on the verge of a genuine spiritual awakening and that God was every bit as active as any darker forces. I saw the collapse of modernity as opening the door for fresh spiritual explorations. True, I said, the spiritual resurgence that I see brewing is unconventional and even irreverent at times, largely developing outside the boundaries of our institutional religion. But that to me says more about the rigidity of our institutions than the darkness of the current spiritual resurgence; it says more about our old wineskins than about the quality of the new wine fermenting around us. I said that I felt the modern, mechanistic view of the universe was cracking, and in those cracks, some seeds of faith could grow.

My panel partner replied by giving anecdotal evidence for his concern: he had been sitting in traffic at a red light recently in his hometown of Wheaton, Illinois, and saw two objects hanging from the rear-view mirror in the car next to his: a Christian crucifix and a Native American dream catcher. To my colleague, this represented syncretism, a Samaritan mix of Christianity with a pagan religion, a slide away from true Christianity, a portent of dark days ahead, a sure sign of pagan revival.

I responded, "I would interpret that scene very differently. My guess would be that this driver respects Christianity but finds something lacking in the modern version that we have presented him with. If he is a postmodern person, the modern version of Christianity he has seen seems to him isolated from creation, narrow and fragmented rather than holistic, and rigidly rational rather than open to the mystical. Native American spirituality, represented by the dream catcher, is more connected to creation. It's more holistic, more mystical; it fulfills what he feels is missing in modern Christianity. So rather than a repudiation of Christianity, I see hanging from his mirror a diagnosis and perhaps the hint of a prescription for us modern Christians. The two items hanging from the mirror could be a figurative mirror to help us see ourselves and recognize that our modern version of the faith is missing something important and needed."

That's where I ended, but if I could go back, I would explore that last sentence further. I don't know how convincing any of this was for my colleague on the panel, as the conversation quickly turned down other paths. Perhaps I had misunderstood him. Perhaps I was just reacting to his use of the word *pagan*, which has both a clinical meaning and a connotation-laden meaning that I take exception to. I hope I'll get a chance to talk with him again sometime. At any rate, my energy and boldness in disagreeing with someone I greatly respected unnerved me a little. I wondered if Neo's ideas were "corrupting" me after all, turning me into some sort of wild-eyed radical. After returning from the conference, my discomfort continued showing up in my journal.

○

SEPTEMBER 17

I'm scared. The kinds of things I'm thinking will surely be considered heresy. How many Christians do I know who could accept that there is a difference between "our version of Christianity" and any other version of Christianity that could possibly be "right"? Even harder to accept might be the idea that while the modern version was right (by "right," of course, I mean appropriate, not perfect) for five hundred years (just as the medieval version had been appropriate for a thousand years), the modern version might not be right for the next leg of the journey. Wow, that sounds relativistic.

But maybe I'm still not going far enough. Maybe talking about our version of Christianity being appropriate to modernity is a cop-out. I can't get the thought out of my mind that our modern version of Christianity may have been so shaped by modernity's pressures as to be severely deformed, distorted. But we can't even see it.

Every adolescent boy and girl has to make adjustments to being postpubescent, since the toys and clothes and activities that were right for childhood are no longer right for adolescence. Maybe we're entering "that awkward age" as a culture? Or maybe I'm losing my faith or my mind—or both? At this moment, that old verse from Proverbs 3 comes to mind: "Trust in the Lord with all your heart, and do not lean on your understanding. In all your ways acknowledge him, and he will direct your paths." Lord, can I trust in you beyond my own theological understanding? Can I acknowledge you even in the midst of what feels a lot like doubt?

○

That puberty analogy of Neo's kept coming back to me. It described exactly how I felt that whole month—like a kid who is growing up but is scared because things are happening inside him that he can't fully understand. It was exciting but unnerving at the same time. I kept wishing I could talk with Neo immediately. The waiting was killing me.

4

WHAT A DIFFERENCE
A WORLDVIEW MAKES

THE WEEK BEFORE our next meeting was scheduled—I believe it was September 17, the same day as the last journal entry I included in Chapter Three—Neo called (at the last minute) to invite me to a lecture he was giving at a nearby college. "You might enjoy this," he said. He was speaking to a joint gathering of Christian students from several campus ministries—Intervarsity, Campus Crusade, the Navigators, the Baptist Student Union, and one or two others. We met in the parking lot and sat together during the opening singing, which was enthusiastic, with lots of hand-clapping and strumming guitars. During a song, he leaned over and said something about the Amish Jellies, and we both laughed. I noticed he was the only person of color in the room, but he never seemed particularly self-conscious.

Neo's lecture had a kind of scholarly feel to it, complete with visuals on an old overhead projector (which, by the way, drove me crazy; it had a bad fan that interrupted his lecture randomly with an ugly grinding screech, the kind of metal-on-metal sound that makes your skin crawl). He was much less animated and much more serious than he had been with me in the bagel shop. He explained that his purpose was to make clear the current transition from modernity to postmodernity by comparing it to the last major historical transition. His love of history really came through.

I taped his lecture at Carol's request, although the tape was incomplete and was interrupted on several occasions by the stupid overhead projector fan. (Carol's curiosity about Neo continued to grow. She told me repeatedly how relieved she felt that finally I had someone other than her to talk to about my struggles.) I'll summarize the tape as best I can, skipping a few less interesting parts and interrupting Neo's flow of thought as little as possible.

Neo was introduced by a very polished young woman who was president of one of the groups. He made some introductory comments (which rambled on too long, I thought). Then he launched into his theme.

"One of the best ways to get perspective on the scope and significance of the current postmodern transition," Neo said, "is to go back to our last major transition, the medieval-to-modern transition that occurred around 1500. I know that picking dates like this can be rather arbitrary. I also know that many people mark the beginning of modernity with the beginning of the Enlightenment, well over a century later. For our purposes, I propose the sixteenth century as the approximate time of modernity's conception, followed by a long period of gestation and then birth in the seventeenth century. Enlightenment thought has been maturing ever since into the middle-aged modernity of the present. (And remember, although the middle years seem dull and monotonous, it's during the middle years of life when one's children grow up and move out to start new lives of their own. The new generation starts spreading its wings while the old generation is routinely humming along in the prime of life.)

"The year 1500 works as a transition point to the modern era for a number of reasons. Consider the confluence of world-changing events that occurred around 1500." Neo fiddled with the projector for a few seconds and then, after getting it to work without screeching, had to chase his transparency—which had slid gracefully off the projector and under a desk. Finally he got his visual centered on the screen. It looked like this:

GENERAL CATEGORY	SPECIFIC EVENT
1. New communication technology, with profound effects on how people learn, think, and live.	The printing press revolutionizes human culture.
2. New scientific worldview, with staggering implications for humanity.	Copernicus asserts that the earth is not the center of the universe, toppling the medieval model of the universe.
3. A new intellectual elite emerges, challenging church authority and introducing a new epistemology (way of knowing).	Galileo, Newton, Bacon, and others give birth to modern science.

4. New transportation technologies increase the interaction of world cultures around the globe, making the world seem smaller.	The development of the caravel (sailing ship) for long voyages makes possible the explorations of the late thirteenth to early sixteenth centuries.
5. Decay of an old economic system and rise of a new one.	Market capitalism replaces feudalism.
6. New military technology.	Development of modern guns leads to the development of the modern infantry and rise of modern nation-state.
7. New attack on dominant authorities, with defensive reaction.	Protestant Reformation denies the authority of the Roman Catholic Church; Counter-Reformation develops in response.

Neo read it out to the group without much elaboration. Then he said, "Now think of the similar confluence of changes clustering around the year 2000." This time he managed to switch transparencies without mishap. Notice that the items in the left-hand columns are exactly the same as before.

GENERAL CATEGORY	SPECIFIC EVENT
1. New communication technology, with profound effects on how people learn, think, and live.	Radio and television, and then the computer and the Internet, revolutionize human culture.
2. New scientific worldview, with staggering implications for humanity.	Post-Einsteinian theories of relativity, quantum mechanics, indeterminacy, and the expanding universe unsettle the stable, mechanistic worldview of modern science; psychology, psychiatry, neuropsychology, and psychopharmacology create new ways of seeing ourselves and new crises in epistemology.

3. A new intellectual elite emerges, challenging church authority and introducing a new epistemology (way of knowing).	Postmodern philosophy challenges all existing elites and deconstructs existing epistemologies.
4. New transportation technologies increase the interaction of world cultures around the globe, making the world seem smaller.	The development of air travel leads to the trivialization of national borders and intensifies the interaction of world cultures.
5. Decay of an old economic system and rise of a new one.	The global economy transforms both communism and capitalism, and the development of e-commerce suggests further market revolution.
6. New military technology.	Air warfare and nuclear weapons change the face of warfare, and the new threats of terrorism (especially chemical and biological), power-grid sabotage, and cybercrime begin to revolutionize the role of governments in keeping the peace.
7. New attack on dominant authorities, with defensive reaction.	Secularism, materialism, and urbanism contribute to the decline of institutional religion worldwide; fundamentalist movements arise in reaction and self-defense.

Again Neo read his chart to the group before driving his point home. "Obviously, our whole view of the medieval world flows from our perspective as moderns—the word *medieval* itself simply meaning 'middle period,' what came between the ancient world and now. And obviously, medieval people never thought of themselves as medieval, any more than Plato thought of himself as an ancient. Thus the very term *medieval* reminds us that our modern perspective is only that: a perspective, a point of view, not the ultimate perspective, not *the* point of view. But it's hard for us to really feel the impact of that obvious truth, immersed as we are in our own modern worldview."

As some audience members looks puzzled and others nodded, Neo's enthusiasm quickened. "Sometimes, the best way to see what it means to be modern is to try to reverse the perspective and put ourselves into the shoes and minds of medieval people—instead of seeing them through our eyes, to try to see the world through their eyes, thus creating a vantage point from which to get a new view of ourselves. C. S. Lewis takes on this extraordinary challenge in one of his least-appreciated books *The Discarded Image*.[1] He explains that medieval European Christians had developed a sophisticated worldview that was so intertwined with their faith that to them it was an essential part of their faith. In this worldview, the universe consisted of a series of concentric spheres, the smallest of which was the earth. As spheres ascended from the earth, they held objects of increasing perfection—the moon, then the planets, then the stars, the angels, and so on. The spheres moved around the earth in a beautiful kind of cosmic dance, and it was thought that as they moved, they produced a beautiful music, symbolic of the harmony of God's creation.

"Near the end of the book, Lewis notes how new developments— especially new observations in the field of astronomy, which are of special interest to me as a science teacher—forced the medieval model of the universe to be 'adjusted,' and the adjustments were becoming increasingly complex. Here's how Lewis explains this tinkering with the model." Neo placed the following quotation on the overhead and read it with exaggerated distinctness:

> The old scheme . . . had been tinkered a good deal to keep up with observations. How far, by endless tinkerings, it could have kept up with them till even now, I do not know. But the human mind will not long endure such ever-increasing complications if once it has seen that some simpler conception can "save the appearances" [account for the data]. Neither theological prejudice nor vested interests can permanently keep in favor a Model which is seen to be grossly uneconomical.[2]

"In other words," Neo explained, "the medieval world had developed a working worldview, a working model of reality—a paradigm, a mental map—that could not account for or adapt to increasing amounts of new data (like the scientific findings of Copernicus and later Galileo and of course later still Darwin). Perhaps like a contract or constitution that is updated with more and more footnotes, fine print, and other amendments, people try to keep the old contract alive, but eventually the amendments outweigh the original document, and someone says, 'Why don't we just start over from scratch on a new one?'

"But it's not that easy. Trading in an old model of reality for a new one has real costs associated with it. True, something may be gained, but a lot is lost too. Let me put on the overhead this quote from Lewis, where he starts making clear what was at stake in trading in the old worldview for a newer one." Neo put on the next transparency and stood silently for a moment. The bright projector made his face shine as he prepared to read the quote aloud:

> In our universe [the earth] is small, no doubt; but so are the galaxies, so is everything—and so what? But in theirs there was an absolute standard of comparison. The furthest sphere, Dante's *maggio corpo,* is, quite simply and finally, the largest object in existence. . . . Hence to look out on the night sky with modern eyes is like looking out over a sea that fades away into mist, or looking about one in a trackless forest—trees forever and no horizon. To look up at the towering medieval universe is much more like looking at a great building. The "space" of modern astronomy may arouse terror or bewilderment or vague reverie; the spheres of the old present us with an object in which the mind can rest, overwhelming in its greatness but satisfying in its harmony. . . . Pascal's terror at *le silence éternel de ces espaces infinis* [the eternal silence of the infinite spaces] never entered his mind. He is like a man being conducted through an immense cathedral, not like one lost in a shoreless sea.[3]

"So," Neo intoned, "it was not comfortable, it was not easy, being pushed out of the medieval world by the hard data of the new emerging science. One became, in a sense, spiritually homeless. But as we know, eventually the trade was made. We gave up the medieval worldview with its harmonious, concentric spheres, its absolute up and down, its ultimate finite boundaries. We accepted a model that was less personal, to be sure, and also less orderly in some ways, but even more rigidly controlled in others. As part of the trade, we gave up the idea that some people simply had the God-given right to rule over others, and we gave up our corresponding respect for 'the authorities.' As a result, authoritative tradition lost much of its value, and we unleashed five centuries of a kind of change that the medievals wouldn't have understood very well—we call it 'progress' or 'evolution,' but to them it would have sounded like chaos and insanity. To them, change was considered ungodly, since God was changeless. Their conservatism was perhaps further bolstered by the belief that the best days on earth—back in the Garden of Eden—were behind them, not ahead of them. Changing that static and past-oriented worldview to a dynamic and future-oriented one wouldn't come easy."

Neo stepped away from the projector and walked down an aisle so that he stood in the middle of the lecture hall. "To really get the impact of how different the medieval model was, we could imagine what would happen if we could take two of you students—let's say you, there, and you, over there—and send you back into the fifteenth century. Nobody could possibly believe that you could be Christians. Of course, first there would be the obvious cultural issues—for example, even a medieval prostitute wouldn't have been seen in public dressed like you"—there was a ripple of laughter here—"and your fine haircut would have made people either laugh at you or fear you were a witch of some sort"—even more laughter erupted here. "But on a deeper level, if you told them you didn't believe in the pope and you didn't accept that kings ruled by divine right and you didn't believe that God created a universe consisting of concentric spheres of ascending perfection, and if you let it slip that you agreed with Copernicus that the earth rotated around the sun, you would surely be tried as heretics and perhaps burned at the stake."

Neo walked slowly back to the front of the room. There wasn't a sound except for his black leather wing tips scuffing the dusty tile floor. Then he continued, "Now take a moment and let this really sink in. To the Christian culture of medieval Europe, none of you today could be considered real Christians. True, you might say that you believe in Jesus and that you follow the Bible—but that would sound like nonsense to them if at the same time you denied what to them was essential for any reasonable person to accept: the medieval worldview, which was the context for their faith.

"That brings me to an important question for you to think about: Is it possible that we as moderns have similarly intertwined a different but equally contingent worldview with our eternal faith? And another question: What if we live at the end of the modern period, at a time when our modern worldview is crumbling, just as the medieval one began to do in the sixteenth century?"

Neo paused at this point. He put his hands together, prayer-like, thumbs under his chin, index fingers touching his nose. He looked down at the floor and said, "I wonder if . . . well . . . Let me go back to C. S. Lewis again." Neo's pace began to quicken. "Lewis seemed to anticipate these kinds of questions with his characteristic brilliance. At the end of

The Discarded Image, he does something quite astounding for a some-what conservative writer in the early 1960s: he begins to suggest that our modern view itself is not the absolute, ultimate truth, that it is not the ul-timate viewpoint but rather just a 'view from a point.' It is as if his suc-cess at entering the medieval world has enabled him to see his own modern model of the universe in the same way we might look at a model of a car: maybe the best model so far, but not the absolute best model that will ever exist. Lewis, usually thoroughly modern, writing late in life sounds himself almost postmodern.

"Most modern people love to relativize the viewpoints of the others against the unquestioned superiority of their own modern viewpoint. But in a way, you cross the threshold into postmodernity the moment you turn your critical scrutiny from others to yourself, when you relativize your own modern viewpoint. When you do this, everything changes. It is like a con-version. You can't go back. You begin to see that what seemed like pure, objective certainty really depends heavily on a subjective preference for your personal viewpoint. In this next quote, Lewis makes exactly these very postmodern moves and emphasizes how one's subjective posture af-fects what one sees and 'knows objectively.'" He slipped a new trans-parency onto the overhead and said, "Listen to Lewis in his own words:"

It would . . . be subtly misleading to say, "The medievals thought the universe to be like that, but we know it to be like this." Part of what we now know is that we cannot, in the old sense, "know what the universe is like" and that no model we can build will be, in that old sense, "like" it. . . . There is no question here of the old Model's being shattered by the inrush of new phenomena. The truth would seem to be the reverse; that when changes in the human mind pro-duce a sufficient disrelish of the old Model and a sufficient hanker-ing for some new one, phenomena to support that new one will obediently turn up. I do not at all mean that these new phenomena are illusory. Nature has all sorts of phenomena in stock and can suit many different tastes.[4]

Neo slid a new transparency onto the projector, saying, "Lewis then continues with these reflections not on the medieval model of the world but on our modern one and on models in general." As he read the fol-lowing quote, he leaned over the projector and ran his index finger under each word as he read it.

I hope no one will think that I am recommending a return to the Medieval Model. I am only suggesting considerations that may induce us to regard all Models in the right way, respecting all and idolizing none. We are all, very properly, familiar with the idea that in every age the human mind is deeply influenced by the accepted Model of the universe. But there is a two-way traffic; the Model is also influenced by the prevailing temper of mind. We must recognize that what has been called "a taste in universes" is not only pardonable but inevitable. We can no longer dismiss the change of Models as a simple progress from error to truth. No Model is a catalogue of ultimate realities, and none is a mere fantasy. Each is a serious attempt to get in all the phenomena known at a given period, and each succeeds in getting in a great many. But also, no less surely, each reflects the prevalent psychology of an age almost as much as it reflects the state of that age's knowledge. Hardly any battery of new facts could have persuaded a Greek that the universe had an attribute so repugnant to him as infinity; hardly any such battery could persuade a modern that it is hierarchical.[5]

I must apologize: I lost concentration at this point in Neo's lecture, and the tape ran out without my noticing it. My mind had wandered into a long-forgotten memory from my own days as a college student in the early 1980s. The memory was triggered, maybe, by the quotes from C. S. Lewis, since it involved a particular moment at a seminar at the C. S. Lewis Institute at Baylor University in Texas, where I graduated in 1982. I remember that one of the speakers (someone whom I had respected until that particular moment) shocked us by making some rather critical comments about the writings of Dr. Francis Schaeffer, a Christian writer who had helped me and most of my fellow students immensely. Someone asked him how he could possibly criticize Schaeffer—our hero, who was to us the most intelligent and articulate Christian alive.

He said something like this: "One complaint would be all of his talk about the Christian worldview." I think we all must have looked quite puzzled, because in our understanding, "the Christian worldview" was exactly what we were attending the seminar to learn. Someone asked him what he meant, and he said something to this effect: "Well, there really isn't such a thing as *the* Christian worldview." I was scandalized. He was speaking nonsense—or else heresy. Now, twenty-some years later, I was so glad he wasn't afraid to stretch my thinking. No model—no matter how resplendent with biblical quotations—can claim to be *the* ultimate Christian worldview, because every model is at the least limited by the limitations of the contemporary human mind, not to mention the "taste in universes" of that particular age. (I'm aware that you may now be feeling about me exactly as I felt about that speaker back in the 1980s.)

I was jolted back into the present by the screeching fan on the overhead, and I immediately noticed the tape had stopped recording, so I quickly flipped it over. Neo was concluding his lecture, again quoting C. S. Lewis.

"Lewis concludes his book with a fascinating prediction." Neo slipped a new transparency onto the overhead.

> It is not impossible that our own Model will die a violent death, ruthlessly smashed by an unprovoked assault of new facts—unprovoked as the nova of 1572. But I think it is more likely to change when, and because, far-reaching changes in the mental temper of our descendants demand that it should. The new Model will not be set up without evidence, but the evidence will turn up when the inner need for it becomes sufficiently great. It will be true evidence. But nature gives most of her evidence in answer to the questions we ask her. Here, as in the courts, the character of the evidence depends on the shape of the examination, and a good cross-examiner can do wonders. He will not indeed elicit falsehoods from an honest witness. But, in relation to the total truth in the witness's mind, the structure of the examination is like a stencil. It determines how much of that total truth will appear and what pattern it will suggest.[6]

"What Lewis imagined to be 'not impossible' some generations away— the death of the modern model or worldview—turns out to be happening just a single generation after he wrote." Here Neo paused and looked up from his notes and gave the students a long gaze, making eye contact with nearly every one. Then he began walking down one row, up another, talking as he walked.

"The modern worldview, including the modern version of Christianity that you follow, bears ominous resemblances to the medieval worldview that Lewis so crisply described, the worldview that was celebrated and embodied in the medieval cathedral. The ornateness, grand construction, and sheer size of medieval cathedrals mirrored the complexity and expansiveness of the medieval worldview itself. However, both the cathedrals and the worldview they expressed reached a point where they permitted no new development and where they threatened to collapse under their own weight. Not only that, but over time they were nearly as difficult to maintain as they were to build. Ironically, the very stone buildings that expressed the belief that their medieval version of Christendom would last forever now mock that belief because today, when we visit them in Europe, they seem to us like museums—or mausoleums. They tell a story of a world that is over, a world that is . . . "

Suddenly the overhead projector screeched again, startling Neo and several students too. Neo rushed to the machine and turned if off this time. He seemed a little shaken, as if he had been interrupted at the worst possible moment. He took a few seconds to regain composure and looked at the old-fashioned round clock behind him, at the front of the classroom.

"Well, I see that my time is also up. In fact, I've gone a bit overtime already, which unfortunately is quite common with me. But there was one last thing that I wanted to say to you before I finish. This is the real point of my whole talk, actually. You are college students, with a long life ahead of you, so full of potential and promise. You may disagree with me, but I believe that the modern version of Christianity that you have learned from your parents, your Sunday school teachers, and even your campus ministries is destined to be a medieval cathedral. It's over, or almost over.

"Most of your peers live in a different world from you. They have already crossed the line into the postmodern world. But few of you have. Why? Because you want to be faithful to the Christian upbringing you have received, which is so thoroughly enmeshed with modernity. One of the most important choices you will make in your whole lives will be made in these few years at this university. Will you continue to live loyally in the fading world, in the waning light of the setting sun of modernity? Or will you venture ahead in faith, to practice your faith and devotion to Christ in the new emerging culture of postmodernity?

"I don't think you'll hear many people my age urging you to do what I'm about to urge you to do. But I will say it boldly: I want you to invest your lives not in keeping the old ship afloat but in designing and building and sailing a new ship for new adventures in a new time in history, as intrepid followers of Jesus Christ. Thank you."

Frankly, I expected some applause. It had been a good lecture, if a little long and overly philosophical in the middle. I found the ending downright inspiring. But there was nothing. Just silence. A tense silence.

5

NEO WORRIES ABOUT KEEPING UP WITH JESUS

I WISHED THE STUDENT LEADER would come forward and say something. But she just sat there, expressionless. I was tempted to get up and say something myself.

Neo himself looked uncomfortable and started to go sit down but then moved back to the lectern and said, "Well, I'll close in prayer." His prayer seemed to reduce the tension a bit, and as he returned to his seat, the young woman leader exchanged whispers with him and then came forward and said, "We've gone about ten minutes overtime, so we'll dismiss. But if any of you would like to stay and ask questions, Dr. Oliver just told me he would be willing to stay as long as anyone is interested in talking. Good night, everyone."

Two or three students left, but everyone else—maybe seventy-five or eighty others—stayed. What a night! The silence at the end of Neo's lecture didn't signal boredom or disapproval; for the most part, the students were stunned with the brilliance and candor of Neo's talk, and his ending had more than inspired them; it had nailed them to their seats. They hadn't applauded because they didn't want the talk to end. True, a few students were ready to brand Neo a heretic, and they grilled him with some questions in a tone bordering on rude. I was embarrassed by their aggressiveness. But the other questions sounded cordial, respectful, and sincere. Neo was careful to require each student who asked a question to state his or her name and major. I'll summarize just a few of them here.

QUINN: Dr. Oliver, my name is Quinn, and I'm a general studies major. Doesn't every age think of itself as the pivotal age? I mean, don't all generations think of themselves as the most important generation, when all the biggest changes in history are taking place?

NEO: First of all, Quinn, that's a very good question. Second, please just call me Neo. I know it's an unusual name, but only my high school students call me Dr. Oliver. And now for your question. You're right—change is ever-present, and nearly all generations see themselves as generations of change. And they're right. But let me make a distinction between *change* and *transition*. Let's say I'm making an omelet. I mix the eggs with a little milk and put them on the griddle. A good omelet is cooked slowly, so I keep stirring the egg with my fork as it cooks, slowly stirring, stirring, stirring, like this. But at some point, something happens. The egg that has been *changing* from raw to cooked rather suddenly *transitions* from a liquid to a solid. At that point, if I keep stirring with the fork, I will ruin the omelet. The tool that succeeded in helping me bring the omelet to this point now threatens to destroy it. The tool that I need now is not a fork but rather a spatula, so the omelet can be gently folded and then served, like this. Here's what I'm trying to say tonight: yes, all ages are ages of change, but not all ages involve transition. You young men and women happen to have been born at a time of transition. If you keep on doing the same old things with the same old tools—the tools you have inherited from my generation and [here Neo pointed to me] my friend Mr. Poole's generation—you'll make a mess of things.

ALEXIS: I'm Alexis, and I'm a history major, and so your analysis makes a lot of sense to me, although I think a few of your details are debatable. But as a Christian, I'm wondering what we're supposed to do with a talk like this. You talked about a new adventure. I mean, what do you think we should do, practically, with what you've said tonight?

NEO: Well, I wouldn't rush out and do anything, really. But I would expect that little by little, you'll begin doing just about everything you currently do in a different way, if you do it at all, and I'd expect you'll begin doing some things you've never even thought of doing before.

ALEXIS: Could you give some examples?

NEO: I hesitate to do so, Alexis, because I really think you need to come to these things yourselves. But let me ask you a few questions that might get you thinking. How many groups are represented here? [Somebody said six.] Why aren't there any students from the Catholic Student Union here? Were they invited, and if not, why not? And isn't there a Methodist fellowship on this campus? And how about Christians like myself of, shall we say, a darker complexion? Where are they? And what about the United Campus Ministries group? Why weren't they invited? I know some of you are thinking, "Because they're too liberal, and we're all evangelical." Well, if I'm right, those distinctions are about to become inconsequential. So I'd imagine that when you plan a joint activity among your various groups in the future, you'd be wise to broaden the invitation. That's just one example, and a rather tame one, but it's a start.

CARL: Please, Dr. Oliver—I mean, Dr. Neo—I mean Neo. Please give us a little more than that. We need specifics. Oh, and my name is Carl. Business.

NEO: Well, let me suggest a little thought experiment for those of you who know something about history. Imagine that we had a time machine and you could go back in time to about 1507, just before the crest of the last historic transition. Wycliff has had his effect, and Hus has stirred things up, and now there's a young German monk by the name of Martin Luther beginning to think some radical thoughts. The world is about to change. Let's imagine you go back in our time machine and meet a young monk, a sincere young medieval Christian who wants his life to count for God. He has no idea of the turmoil that will be unleashed in the next few years. What practical advice would you give him?

At this point, a number of hands went up, and Neo elicited several answers:

Don't put your confidence in the institution of the church; put your confidence in God.

Be open to new ideas and new interpretations of the faith.

Don't be too quick to criticize.

Expect things to be messy.

Don't resist the change. Go with it. It's like a tidal wave is coming, and you can either run or drown or grab your surfboard. I'd say, "Cowabunga!"

Keep going back to the Bible, but not with the standard interpretations blinding you to new interpretations.

Try to sort out tradition from the real essentials of the gospel.

Get with it, get out of the way, or get counseling!

Then another student spoke up:

STELLA: My name is Stella, and I'm a dance major. Aren't you scared by this kind of talk, Neo? I mean, it seems to me that you could be preparing us for a new, like, revival or something, or else you're sending us down the road to some sort of, like, major heresy. For me, I can totally relate to what you're saying, but if my pastor from back home in Louisville were here, you'd be toast. [laughter]

NEO: Am I scared? Sometimes I'm terrified. Especially when I think of meeting your pastor from Louisville! But seriously, you're right—the dangers of transition are real. But are the dangers of the status quo less real? People often call me a risk taker, but really, I consider myself a risk avoider. To me, Stella, the risk of digging in our heels and resisting change is so high—I think it's the highest risk. The second-highest risk is to just let go and go with the flow, whatever happens. You know, this would mean reinterpreting the faith so it fits in with whatever "taste in universes" the culture around us has. History tells me that that is a terrible risk too. The lowest available risk that I see is the risk of journeying on in faith. You see, I believe in the Holy Spirit. I believe Jesus meant it when he said the Spirit of God would be with us, guiding us, to the very end. So I believe that he will guide us through these winds and currents of change, no matter what storms come. In fact, I believe that he is the wind in our sails, leading us into the change, because that's his way. He always moves ahead. He's not about taking us back into the past, some beautiful illusion of good old days. He has a purpose he is working toward, and I want to keep up with him. I suppose that's my greatest fear, not that I'll go too fast or too far but that I'll lag behind.

COLBY: My name is Colby, and I'm a senior in computer science, although I've also been thinking about going to seminary. Neo, I find it hard to believe that modern evangelical Christianity, of which I am glad to be part, is dying, as you suggest. I mean, aren't evangelicals the fastest-growing segment of the church? Look at all our Christian colleges and radio stations and TV programs and seminaries. I think you're a little premature in writing an obituary for modern Christianity. It looks alive and well to me.

NEO: I would agree that the contemporary church is rich, somewhat powerful (though that's waning), and outwardly successful in many ways. And I would agree that the evangelical church is the fastest-growing sector of the church at large, especially the charismatic wing, both domestically and globally. But that simply means that it has more to offer than the alternatives, which may not be saying much. It may also mean that the church is growing fastest where premodern people are coming to terms with modernity, and so the modern version of the faith offered by conservative Christianity is more up-to-date than their own medieval worldview. Remember, Colby, the whole world doesn't progress at the same pace, and in many places in the world, people still live in a medieval or even ancient and in a few cases prehistoric mind-set. Just because people perceive something is a step up from what they already have does not mean that it is the final step, the top step.

But also remember—the medieval church was never more powerful, large, rich, or outwardly successful than it was around 1500. And dinosaurs were never more big and powerful and dominant than they were at the end of the Jurassic period. Think of it like this: if it were 1910, what kind of transportation would you buy? What would be the most reliable form of transportation available to you in 1910?

COLBY: I guess it would have been the automobile. It had been invented not long before that, right?

NEO: If you were looking for a good stock investment, Colby, I'd wholeheartedly agree: the Ford Motor Company would have been a great investment. You're right—automobiles had been invented only a decade or two before. But in 1910, they were still notoriously undependable. Not only that, there weren't good roads for them to ride on, and there weren't any gas stations around. So if you needed good, reliable transportation, you would not have bought a car in 1910. What about airplanes? They were still seen pretty much as a joke, an impractical dreamer's machine— it had only been a few short years since the first one got off the ground. So if you wanted good, reliable transportation in 1910, you would have bought a horse and buggy. Why, never in history had better buggies been built! Do you see the point? We would expect that the best modern churches in history would exist today, right at the time when the modern world is passing, much like the world of the horse and buggy in 1910. The smartest modern churches see this and are building in flexibility so that they can "convert" to postmodern effectiveness in the future— perhaps like a foresighted buggy manufacturer who realizes he's not just in the buggy business but rather in the transportation business. He would continue building fine buggies but would be preparing to build automobiles too.

MIKE: I'm Mike, and I'm an art major. I just have one question. How did an older gentleman—I hope you don't mind me saying that—how did you figure this out? I mean, everything you've said tonight is exactly the way I think, but I have never heard anyone older than maybe twenty-five talk or think like this.

NEO: Well, much as it might surprise you, I think a lot of my peers when I was in college were going in this direction. I think that maybe 30 to 40 percent of my baby boom cohorts were leaning into postmodernity. The majority were thoroughly modern. I think the great economy of the 1980s managed to convert most of my secular postmodern friends from my generation back to modernity; money has a lot of power to influence the way people think, right? As for those in the church, well, as you say, one just can't talk about this sort of thing among most older folks, so if there are any older people thinking this way, they tend to keep quiet about it. But I brought a friend with me who is well over 30 [Neo winked in my direction], and I know he's thinking about these issues too, so there are some of us dinosaurs out there who want to learn to dance.

For your generation, I think the statistics are reversed: I'd say that 30 to 40 percent of your generation is modern, with the majority being postmodern. That's why it's so important—if you're going to have any impact at all on your generation for Christ—for you to deal with these issues, as lonely a road as it can be in the church at times. If you were a missionary going to Spain, you'd have to learn to think and speak Spanish. If you are a missionary going to any educated culture on earth today, I think you need to learn to think and speak postmodern.

RUTH: I'm Ruth, and I'm a secondary ed major, and I'll definitely be contacting you when it's time for my student teaching assignment. [laughter] I don't really have a question, but I just wanted to say that everywhere in my life except here and at church, I think I *am* postmodern. But I think when I go anyplace religious or Christian, I just sort of switch. It's like I click into my parents' way of thinking for an hour, and then I switch back. It's really cool to think that I might not have to keep switching back and forth and could just be one person all the time.

NEO: Yes, that is really cool indeed.

When the night was over, Neo looked exhausted (and a bit overheated—I couldn't believe he kept his gray suit jacket on the whole evening) but happy. He was an educator to the bone and had just hit an educator's version of a home run. We chatted briefly on the way to the parking lot and confirmed our plans to meet the next Saturday. Neo again suggested we walk along the C&O Canal, on the old historic towpath where teams of oxen once pulled barges full of goods. Neo said it was one of his favorite places—a level path between the old canal (empty of water in many places, but always full of history) and the ever-changing river. I had been in the picnic area at Great Falls once but had never walked the towpath. (I'm not really much of an outdoor guy.)

The last thing Neo said to me as we got into our cars was this: "Can you believe what that one fellow called me? An 'older gentleman'? That almost killed me!" We both laughed, got into our cars, his a Dodge Spirit and mine a Honda Accord, and drove away. As I pulled out of my parking space, a stupid pun hit me. I rolled down my window, and motioned to Neo to do the same: "Hey, my friend, we're leaving in one Spirit and one Accord!" He groaned and shook his head. "See you Saturday!" he said, with a wave.

6

HOT WORDS ABOUT
BIBLICAL INTERPRETATION

CAROL KINDLY PACKED A LUNCH for our hike, but as I pulled into the parking lot at Great Falls, I realized I'd left it sitting on the kitchen counter back home. I hoped my mistake wouldn't spoil our day. My mind was buzzing with questions for Neo.

Neo was leaning against his car when I pulled up. I had never seen him in anything but a suit or a sport jacket before that Saturday, but for our hike he had dressed down considerably: jeans (clean and pressed), a blue button-down Oxford shirt (also neatly pressed), running shoes, and—completely out of character—a rather shabby red baseball cap, the kind you'd expect to see on a farmer riding a tractor somewhere. I remember thinking, *If my kids saw me in that hat, they'd be embarrassed to be seen with me.*

We were about a half mile into our walk when Neo started to seem a little perturbed. I had been asking him to distinguish between postmodern Christians and traditional Christians: How would a postmodern Christian respond to this or this or that?

"Look, Dan," he said, "I'm really uncomfortable with the way you're asking your questions. The last thing we need to do is insert yet another division into the church. Your language is reminding me—pardon another history lesson—of your First Great Awakening here in the United States, when Jonathon Edwards was leading a renewal movement that came to be called the 'New Lights,' and before you knew it there were the 'Old Lights' fighting against him. I don't want to divide 'New Christians' from 'Traditional Christians' or 'Postmodern Christians' from 'Modern Christians.' I don't have time for that kind of foolishness, so I think we have to be very careful about the language we use. Please help me try to avoid any 'us-and-them' kind of thinking, and if you see me going in that direction, by all means tell me, OK? We're talking about *a* new kind of Christian, not *the* new kind or a *better* kind or *the* superior kind, just a new kind. Right?"

I told him I agreed with him, but I was trying to sort things through, and making a clear distinction would help me.

"But Dan, the need to put everything into nice neat categories is part of the problem. Modern people believed that they could create a nice framework that would pigeonhole everything. So if you succeed in creating a postmodern framework, I think you've just sabotaged it. At the very least, you have to be ironic or ambivalent about your pigeonholes. Remember that the Pharisees were the great pigeonholers and that Jesus told them that many who came out last in their framework would come out first in his. So you'd better doubt and deconstruct your boxes as fast as you construct them. Does that make sense?"

I told him that it did but that I was incurably a pigeonholer and needed some sort of recovery group for my addiction. Neo chuckled and then said, "Look at this. This might help cure you." He knelt down on the path, cleared away some fallen leaves, and drew a line in the dust. I stooped down next to him.

"This might help you. Very often," he explained, "debates in the church occur on this level. There are all kinds of positions on an issue, along this line, with the most extreme positions being here and here."

I offered a couple of examples: "OK. So Catholics are over here, and Protestants over there. Calvinists are over here, and Arminians are over there. And charismatics are here and anticharismatics over there. And we could do the same on the issues of pacifism, inerrancy of the Bible, women in leadership, how the church should treat homosexuals, and—"

"Exactly," he interrupted. "Now, almost all debate in the church takes place on this line. The issue is where the *right* point on the line is. So people pick and defend their points. Each person's point becomes *the* point in his or her mind. Here's what I'm suggesting: What if the point-defending approach is, pardon the pun, pointless? In other words, what if the position God wants us to take isn't on that line at all but somewhere up here?" He was moving his hand in a small circle, palm down, about a foot above the line he had drawn in the dust.

"So you're saying," I replied, "that we have to transcend the normal level of discourse. That makes sense to me. I mean, Jesus did that sort of thing all the time. Like with the woman at the well in John 4. The big debate is over where people should worship, on this mountain or that mountain. Jesus doesn't choose one point or the other; he says that the answer is on this higher level, that what God wants is for us to worship him in spirit and truth, wherever we are. Both mountains are good places to worship, so in that way both sides are right. But where you worship isn't the point at all, so in that way both sides are wrong."

"Well put, Dan. Amen! You're preaching now!" Neo said, grinning and winking, and good naturedly gave me a high-five. Then he added, "Be careful, Daniel. You may be too good a preacher for God to let you quit."

"Oh, thanks, but no . . . ," I said. I pushed off his compliment, but inside I glowed. "Too good a preacher"—those words and that moment are so vivid in my memory. Most of the leaves around us were just beginning to change and show their fall colors. I looked over at Neo, his smile lingering on his face. Then I looked past him, to the river sparkling in the sunlight, and beyond the river, to the Virginia shoreline. Oranges, yellows, and reds were just beginning to erupt from deep, end-of-summer green, all reflecting in the shimmering silver and blue of the river. Within a few minutes, we were so thoroughly engrossed in conversation that we are almost oblivious to the beauty around us. But for that moment, I was breathing it in, through my eyes, my ears, my skin.

We covered at least six miles in our walk that day. Our conversation covered even more ground, though its course wasn't nearly as linear or as smooth as the towpath beneath our feet. Let me share with you part of our conversation.

"One of the biggest debates," I said, "and maybe the most important, is the whole Bible thing. In the conservative evangelical churches that I grew up in, our view of the Bible was the most important element in our identity. Many of our churches were in fact called 'Bible Church' or 'Bible Chapel,' and our summer camps were 'Bible camps,' our higher education institutions were 'Bible colleges,' and our experiences of fellowship took place in 'Bible studies.' Our arch-opponents were 'the liberals,' the people on the other end of your line, whom we fought against because they didn't take the Bible 'literally,' as we felt they should. How do you see us transcending that level of discourse, Neo?"

"You like to start with the tough ones, don't you, Dan?" he quipped. "One of my mottoes in life is that people are often *against* something worth being *against* but in the process find themselves *for* some things that aren't worth being *for*. I think that's the case with both sides of the battle about the Bible. The conservatives are against reinterpreting ancient wisdom in light of contemporary fads or moods, and they're against in any way weakening the strong, unchanging backbone of the faith, fearing that we'll be left with a kind of jellyfish spirituality if the liberals have their way. Meanwhile, the liberals are against pitting faith against honest scientific investigation and turning faith into an anti-intellectual enterprise. They're against the obscurantism—the resistance to free inquiry—that is so common in conservative circles. And they're against the privatization of faith. They feel that conservatives have retreated to the private sphere, worrying only about their own personal salvation, leaving the world at large to go to hell ecologically, culturally, in terms of social justice, that sort of thing. So I think we have to begin by saying that both sides are against something worth being against. They both have a point."

I interrupted. "OK, Neo, but still, the issue is pretty important. I don't think you can just kind of wish-wash around in the middle and say nice things about both sides. There's a lot at stake. Evangelicals would say that the Bible is the foundation for everything, so if you tamper with the foundation, the whole structure is in danger of crashing down. It seems to us evangelicals that liberals kind of sort through the Bible and throw out anything that doesn't appeal to them."

"Yes, and you evangelicals tend to be unaware that evangelicals themselves do the same thing. But I won't get into that . . ."

I interrupted, "No, I'd be interested in what you'd say about that."

"OK," Neo continued. "Fortunately, evangelicals don't say that people who disobey their parents should be stoned, as the Bible teaches in Leviticus, or that people whose genitals are mutilated should be excluded from worship, as the Bible also teaches in Leviticus, or that it's a sin for women to wear jewelry or have a short haircut, as the Bible teaches in some of Paul's writings. They don't justify killing infidels, even though Moses ordered the faithful to do so in Exodus. They don't practice polygamy, even though David and Solomon did. They don't recommend dashing the infants of their enemies against stones, as one of the Psalms celebrated. No, they have a grid of decency that keeps them from applying the Bible literally in these situations. But they seem generally unaware of this grid; they think they rigorously apply the Bible literally, and no one else is as faithful as they are. Their grid is like their own retina—they see by it, so they can't see it. As you said, the liberals do this sifting and sorting too, but they just have a different grid. So when evangelicals say they're arguing about the Bible's absolute authority, too often they are arguing about the superiority of the traditional grid through which they read and interpret the Bible. Of course, I'd not recommend you say that to any of them, because they'll get pretty upset with you. They really can't see it. They'll think you're a fool or a troublemaker."

I responded: "I think you're being unfair there, Neo. It's not some arbitrary grid. We avoid applying some passages literally because other passages teach us not to. For example, Jesus set up a kind of revolution in how the Old Testament law would be read and applied, and the early apostles clarified the difference between living under grace as opposed to law."

Neo stopped walking and faced me. "Well, let me ask you a question. You're aware of how conservative Christians in the United States just 150 years ago used the Bible to defend slavery, just as they did in Jamaica? And now you'd say that those chaps were dead wrong, would you not?" I was nodding my head slowly, realizing that this issue affected us in very different ways. "How can you be sure that some of your ironclad interpretations today aren't similarly fueling injustice?"

I protested: "Neo, I never said that my interpretations were infallible. I'm just saying that the Bible itself is." He responded, "Well, I'm wondering, if you have an infallible text, but all your interpretations of it are admittedly fallible, then you at least have to always be open to being corrected about your interpretations, right?" I was nodding again. Yes. Of course. Neo kept talking: "So the authoritative text is never what I say about the text or even what I understand the text to say but rather what God means the text to say, right? So the real authority does not reside in the text itself, in the ink on paper, which is always open to misinterpretation—sometimes, history tells us, horrific and dangerous misinterpretation. Instead, the real authority lies in God, who is there behind the text or beyond it or above it, right? In other words, the authority is not in what I say the text says but in what God says the text says."

At this point, I wasn't sure what to say. Neo continued, "Our interpretations reveal less about God or the Bible than they do about ourselves. They reveal what we want to defend, what we want to attack, what we want to ignore, what we're unwilling to question. When Judgment Day comes, God might ask a lot of us how we interpreted the Bible—not to judge if our interpretations are right or wrong but to let our interpretations reveal our hearts. That will be telling enough."

Does Neo believe in a literal Judgment Day? I wondered to myself. I was shaking my head, more out of confusion than clear disagreement. Neo stooped down and drew his line in the dirt. "Over here you have the conservatives, who look at the Bible the same way medieval Catholics looked at the church and pope: infallible, inerrant, absolutely authoritative. Then over here you have the liberals, who see the Bible more or less as a collection of artifacts, reflections of the religious life of the Jewish and early Christian people—inspiring, perhaps even inspired in places, but not authoritative. I know this is a caricature, but are you with me?"

I said I was.

He continued, "What if the real issue is not the authority of the text down on this line but rather the authority of God, moving mysteriously up here on a higher level, a foot above the ground? What if the issue isn't a book that we can misinterpret with amazing creativity but rather the will of God, the intent of God, the desire of God, the wisdom of God—maybe we could say the kingdom of God?

I just raised my eyebrows, as if to say "OK, go on." He did. "If that's the case, both sides have to wake up and take notice. Conservatives may have gotten terribly comfortable perpetuating slavery or the extermination of the Indians or the subjugation of women or the marginalization of minorities or the exploitation of the environment because they can use the text to justify it, and liberals may have become terribly complacent because they've kind of dispensed with any clear word from God other than 'be nice modern American consumers and citizens of liberal democracies.' But if there is a real, living, active, relevant desire of God and wisdom from God that needs to be brought to bear on our concrete life situation, then both sides had better move to the edge of their seats, start praying, start listening to each other, and start reading the Bible in fresh ways for all the new wisdom they can mine from it, don't you think?" Neo was jabbing his right forefinger into his left palm and pretty agitated, about as close to angry as I had yet seen him.

I didn't know what I thought, so I let out a long whistle, as if to say, "Wow, you're pretty worked up, and you just said a mouthful." On the one hand, he didn't seem to be giving the Bible the same place of absolute reverence and authority I had been trained to give it. On the other hand, he wasn't simply giving up on the Bible, nor was he shopping it, picking and choosing what he would buy and what he wouldn't. He really seemed to care about what God's will was, and I wondered, isn't that all that really matters?

This thought really disturbed me. *Oh no. I'm becoming liberal!* I said to myself, with an almost physical shiver of fear. (Looking back, I'm amazed by how much fear the label "liberal" elicited in me. I have to wonder if there are others out there who are equally frightened by the label "conservative.")

We started walking again. I was quiet for a few minutes, tending my own thoughts. I remember this question presenting itself to me: Wouldn't I rather be a "liberal" who really cared about God's will than a good conservative evangelical who was smug in my understanding, who had perhaps stopped "hungering and thirsting after righteousness"? Another chill crawled up the back of my neck; I was scaring myself.

Neo probably could tell I needed time to think, so he didn't speak either.

Finally, he spoke up. He seemed to have been having his own internal conversation: "Besides, the whole notion of authority as so many people conceive it is thoroughly modern." Now, I must have looked even more confused, because Neo gently hit me on the shoulder, smiled, and winked. "Relax, Dan, I'm only saying what the Bible says. That oft-quoted passage in Second Timothy doesn't say, 'All Scripture is inspired by God and is *authoritative*.' It says that Scripture is inspired and *useful*—useful to teach, rebuke, correct, instruct us to live justly, and equip us for our mission as the people of God. That's a very different job description than we moderns want to give it. We want it to be God's encyclopedia, God's rule book, God's answer book, God's scientific text, God's easy-steps instruction book, God's little book of morals for all occasions. The only people in Jesus' day who would have had anything close to these expectations of the Bible would have been the scribes and Pharisees. Right?"

All I could say was, "Wait a minute. Wait a minute." Then I said, "What—do you want to throw out the Bible, then?" Neo said, "Daniel, Daniel, a little defensive, aren't you? I never said anything like that. I think that when you let go of the Bible as God's answer book, you get it back as something so much better." I asked what that would be, and he said, "It becomes the family story. Look, you have kids. You must give them some idea of what the Poole family name means. You tell them stories about their great-grandparents and grandparents. You give them the idea that to be a Poole means something, right?" I nodded.

"Well, the Bible does the same thing. It tells the family story—the story of the people who have been called by the one true God to be his agents in the world, to be his servants to the rest of the world. It's absolutely essential—to give the family a sense of identity, so we know who we are and why we're here and where we're going. And not only that, it's wonderfully honest about our weaknesses and mistakes. I mean, there's no mistaking who the hero is in this story—it's certainly not any of us humans! So I think we need to let go of the Bible as a modern book, but that doesn't mean we discard it. Not at all! When we let it go as a modern answer book, we get to rediscover it for what it really is: an ancient book of incredible spiritual value for us, a kind of universal and cosmic history, a book that tells us who we are and what story we find ourselves in so that we know what to do and how to live. That letting go is going to be hard for you evangelicals."

"What are you saying?" I asked. "That the Bible doesn't have any answers?"

"Sure it has answers, but I don't think that's the point. Think of a math book, Dan. Is it valuable because it has the answers in the back? No, it's valuable because by working through it, by doing the problems, by struggling with it, you become a wiser person, a person capable of solving problems and building bridges and balancing your checkbook and targeting the trajectory of a rocket to Mars. That's one way I see the Bible as being valuable. The whole answer-book approach is what modern people want the Bible to be, but it's not necessarily what the Bible really is. Of course, the Bible is even more than a book of wisdom and wisdom development. It's a book that calls together and helps create a community, a community that is a catalyst for God's work in our world."

I protested, "But Neo, you can talk all you want about wisdom and community. We need something more than wisdom and community. We need some rock-solid answers—some hard facts to be the foundation for our Christian worldview. Every building needs a foundation, right?"

He replied, "The Bible never speaks of itself this way. You're the pastor, you should know—there are only two places I know of where the New Testament speaks of foundations—no three. In one case, the church is the foundation of the truth, and in the second, Jesus is the foundation of the church, and then there's a third, when Jesus told Peter he was the foundation. But unless I'm mistaken, the Bible never calls itself the foundation."

"Well, you've got me there," I said.

He looked at me, perturbed, and said, "I'm not trying to 'get you,' man! Just a minute." Then, with no explanation of where he was going, he adjusted his faded red baseball cap and stepped off the path and in a second vanished into the forest undergrowth. I walked over to the edge of the path and strained my eyes to try to see him. A minute passed. Then two. I could hear the snap of breaking twigs moving toward the river but still couldn't see him. What was going on?

I called his name once, twice, three times. No answer.

7

LETTING THE BIBLE READ US

AFTER THE FOURTH TIME I called his name, he called mine: "Dan, over here, come here!"

I'm a bit nervous about poison ivy and snakes, but I gingerly pushed through the bushes toward his voice. When I saw him, my first thought was that he was relieving himself. He was standing perfectly erect, with his back toward me.

Then he turned and motioned me to come closer. When I came up beside him, he pulled a branch aside to reveal a perfect web made by a huge yellow and black spider. "That's exactly what I was looking for, a common garden spider, *Argiope aurantia,*" he said, always the science teacher. "But in spite of the 'common' in their name, they aren't all that common. Beautiful, isn't she?" That wasn't the word that had leapt to my mind. "Let me ask you a question, Daniel. Where is the foundation for the home of this spider?" I replied, "Well, I guess it doesn't exactly have one. But it does have anchor points—like where the web attaches to that leaf and that branch and that branch there. . . ."

"OK," Neo said, "I think you can see where I'm going. What if faith isn't best compared to a building, but rather to a spiderweb? Instead of one foundation, it has several anchor points. Those points might be spiritual experiences, exemplary people and institutions whom one has come to trust, that sort of thing." "But where does the Bible fit in?" I asked.

"Well," Neo replied, "it could be seen as one of the anchor points. Or perhaps every passage in the Bible that has affected your life could be seen as an anchor point. Or perhaps the Bible isn't only in the anchor points. Perhaps it is part of every thread of the web."

I wasn't satisfied. "But I think you're stretching things, Neo. I mean, why just pick a spiderweb as your model for faith? That seems kind of arbitrary, doesn't it?"

"No more than a building with a foundation, really. When you think about it, a spiderweb has some real advantages over a building. It's flexible. It can be repaired when it's damaged. It functions as both a home and a tool for catching food. But if you don't like spiderwebs, let's use a different model altogether. Let's take the earth. What's the foundation of the earth? What keeps the earth stable?"

"Well, it's not that simple," I said. "The earth seems to get its stability from a combination of things—its own momentum, the gravity of the sun; maybe even the moon and other planets play some role, I'm not sure."

"What if faith were more like the earth than a building? What if faith could never be stable in the way God intends it to be if it didn't have forward momentum and if that momentum weren't in the field of the gravity of God himself? And if you don't like that metaphor, think of a bird in flight or a bicycle or a ship on the sea. In each case, there's movement in relation to some larger forces and realities. Stability comes through an interplay of those factors. Stability is not always as simple as a static building sitting on a solid foundation. John Wesley—he was an Anglican, you know—understood this very well: he talked about the church deriving its stability from a dynamic interplay of four forces—what were they? Scripture, tradition, reason, and . . . what was the fourth? Oh yes, spiritual experience. Maybe"—and here he backed away from the spiderweb, knelt down again, and drew his line on the ground—"maybe both liberals and conservatives are working from a static model of authority and both need to be called to a higher point of view to see that our situation is much more dynamic, much more predicamental, moving up here instead of down in the dust."

Neo took a last look at the spider. I overheard him saying, probably to himself, "First frost and she'll be gone. Absolutely beautiful." Then we climbed back to the path and continued walking for a few minutes in silence. I think Neo was waiting for me to say something, but I couldn't think of anything to say, except to ask him what he had meant by "predicamental," but I thought it was something I should already know, so I let the question go. My mind was beginning to feel kind of frozen, paralyzed. Finally, he stopped, and I turned around and walked back toward him, and he said, "Maybe neither liberals nor conservatives take the Bible seriously enough."

I almost laughed. "That's a good one."

"No, I'm serious," Neo said. "One thing that both modern liberals and conservatives have in common is that they read the Bible in very modern ways. Modern conservatives treat the Bible as if it were a modern book. They're used to reading modern history texts and modern encyclopedias and modern science articles and modern legal codes, and so they assume that the Bible will yield its resources if they approach it like one of those texts. But none of those categories even existed when the Bible was written. Sure, there was history, but not with all of the modern trimmings like a concern for factual accuracy, corroborating evidence, or absolute objectivity. Sure there was law, but I'm not sure there is a one-to-one correspondence between an ancient Near Eastern concept of law and our modern concept. The conservatives seem somewhat blind to these kinds of differences, I think."

He continued, "The modern liberals seem to make a corresponding mistake. They acknowledge that the Bible is a different kind of text from our modern texts, but then they in a sense judge it by modern standards. If something doesn't fit in with a modern Western mind-set that reveres objectivity, science, democracy, individualism, that sort of thing, it is dismissed as primitive and irrelevant.

"There's a third option neither of them takes, and that's the option I think we should take. Can you see what it is? I don't want to tell you, Dan. I want you to try to get it yourself."

We started walking again, Neo shuffling through the leaves with his hands in his pockets and his eyes scanning the trees, and me looking down at the tops of my shoes, engrossed in thought. After a few minutes we came to a place where the park service had installed a picnic table and an old-fashioned water pump. In the absence of lunch, we took turns pumping for one another and drinking from cupped hands, then washing our faces, cooling off. It was late September, but it felt hot like August. We sat on the picnic table to rest awhile.

Finally I was ready to try to "get" what Neo was leading me to: "Neo, maybe the third alternative is to . . . to loosen up and approach the Bible on less defined terms. Instead of approaching it with our modern assumptions and expectations and our aggressive analysis, maybe we need to read it less like scholars and more like humble seekers trying to learn whatever we can from it, in the context of our sincere desire to live for God and do what he wants. I guess that would be the momentum you were talking about before—the desire to do God's will. Maybe we need to read it with more of that desire and less of our critical analysis, whether of the liberal or conservative variety. Maybe postmodern is postanalytical and postcritical. Is that what you're getting at?"

Neo replied, "Good! Good! I think that's a very good start. But I wonder if we could even take it a step further. What if instead of reading the Bible, you let the Bible read you?" I gave him a kind of queer look, and he responded to my puzzlement: "OK. Dan, think of a scientist preparing to dissect a northern leopard frog, *Rana pipiens*. How would you describe his attitude, his posture, toward the frog?" I said that the scientist would be objective. He wouldn't have any feelings for the frog. It's just a routine dissection; it's objective science.

"OK. Tell me more."

"Well, I guess he would be curious. He would be looking for something. He would be trying to compare the frog's anatomy with a fetal pig's anatomy or a rat's anatomy. Maybe he would be looking for some abnormality, some tumor or something."

Neo replied, "OK, Dan, good. Now think of a detective at a crime scene. How would you describe his approach?" I said something about the detective wanting to prove something, looking for evidence for or against innocence, and wanting to avoid contaminating any of the evidence by his own presence.

Neo said, "Good. Now think of a teenage boy meeting a girl at the mall. How does his attitude or posture differ from the scientist's or the detective's?"

I was starting to get it. "Whoa, Neo—you really are a good teacher. I see where you're going. It's not so analytical or objective. There's some fun in it, a sense of personal investment, a feeling of adventure. There's less caution, less holding back. But in another way, there is holding back, because he wants to make his move and then leave room for her to make her move. It's less aggressive, less controlling, and more . . . relational. So—I get it. You're saying we need to approach the Bible more that way. You're saying we need to flirt with it, romance it—or maybe let its message romance us."

Neo replied, "Yes, good, that's one way of saying it. But let's keep thinking. Let's say you're a patient and you know you have cancer, and you're meeting your new oncologist for the first time. What would your posture be like then, and how would it differ from the scientist's, the detective's, or even the teenage boy's? Do you see what I'm getting at? Our modern age has predisposed us to only a limited range of postures with the Bible. It's all objective analysis and forensic science, always trying to prove something. It's all about a kind of aggressive conquest of the text—reducing it to something explainable by our preconceptions, turning it into moralisms or principles or outlines or conclusions or proofs or whatever.

"I wonder," he continued, "what would happen if we approached the text less aggressively but even more energetically and passionately. I wonder what would happen if we honestly listened to the story and put ourselves under its spell, so to speak, not using it to get all of our questions about God answered but instead trusting God to use it to pose questions to us about us. See the difference? What would happen if we just trusted ourselves to it—the way a boy opens his heart to a girl, the way a patient trusts herself to an oncologist. Actually, I think the Catholics know more about this than we Protestants. The Benedictines still practice something very like this; they call it *lectio divina*. Anyhow, I don't claim to have this all figured out. I only know that our modern approaches aren't working very well."

I thought for a second and then came back: "Neo, I just have one question. A minute ago you said something about listening to the story, but that makes me wonder: What is the story? And what's the difference between getting the story and getting answers? And wouldn't the answer I'm looking for sometimes be the story? Is there really such a big difference between a story and an answer?"

"Hold on! You said you had one question, and I think I counted three, maybe four. That's cheating!" he said. We both laughed, and I zeroed in on the question about the story: How would he articulate it? He told me he needed some time to think about that. "Could we save this for another time?" he asked. "I really think that might be the most important question you have asked me yet, and I want to do it justice."

About then we both hauled ourselves off the picnic table to begin walking back to where our cars were parked. I'm not in the best shape, but Neo looked even more tired and sore than I. We walked without talking for a while, resting our minds now that our bodies had rested for at least a few minutes. Eventually I broke the silence.

"Neo, how are you so knowledgeable about all of this theology? You told me that you studied history in college and the philosophy of science in graduate school, but you know too much about theology—unless they're doing a better job of training Episcopal laypeople than I've ever heard about!"

"Well," he responded, "I actually have a secret." He took off his old baseball cap and held it behind his back, slowing down and looking directly at me. "Daniel, this is something nobody at FDR knows about, something I very seldom tell anyone." My mind was racing. For some reason, I got the odd feeling he was about to tell me he was gay. "Ready? Before I became a teacher, and before I got my Ph.D., I was a pastor—for seventeen years, even longer than you. I was a pastor far longer than I've been a science teacher."

I stopped walking, stunned, shook my head, and turned to him with wide eyes. "I knew it! No, I didn't know it, but I knew there must be some reason why you are . . . different."

"Well, now you know."

"Where did you go to seminary?" I asked. For some reason that was important for me to know.

"I went to Princeton. They had a lot of scholarship money for minority students like me back in the sixties."

"Princeton? A *Pentecostal* at Princeton?" I didn't mean to be rude, but I guess my question revealed a kind of low opinion of Pentecostals.

"No, no, no. I went to Pentecostal church with my dad as a boy back in Kingston. But here in the States, I started going to the Presbyterian church with my mom. I was ordained Presbyterian, in fact."

"Well, why did you leave ministry?" I asked.

He replied, "I'm surprised at you, Dan. I thought you'd realize that I can be in ministry just as much as a high school teacher as I was as a pastor. Sometimes I think more so."

"Mmmm, point well taken," I said. "Then why did you leave the pastorate?"

"That's a story," he said, "for some other time. There were personal issues. But a big part of it was that I was asking the same questions you are, and I found the pastorate a pretty hard place to be a growing, thinking, honest Christian. Too many people want you to spout the party line, never question, never think. In the end, it was a matter of integrity and compassion. If I had been honest in the pulpit about what was going on in my mind and heart—my questioning, my reevaluating—I would have either split the church or been fired. I decided they were all bad options— risking splitting the church or at least traumatizing it or being inauthentic and just going through the motions. So I left. Maybe you think I was a coward."

"Not at all," I said. He had no idea how well I understood.

"Now you can see why I went out of my way to get beneath the surface with you when I met you at the Amish Jellies concert," he said. "I saw too much of myself in you, Daniel."

"Yeah," I said. Beyond that, I was speechless.

8

YEAH, BUT WHAT ABOUT THE OTHER GUYS?

WE KEPT WALKING. It was hot enough now that Neo had taken off his shirt and was walking in his white T-shirt, with the blue button-down draped over one shoulder.

After ten minutes or so, we came to a place along the towpath where the river was easily accessible. We walked down to the bank and sat on a couple of large rocks there. "Neo, what does a guy like you say about other religions? I mean, do you believe Jesus is the only way? Do you believe good Buddhists and Muslims will be in heaven?"

Neo stood up and found a couple of flat stones and started skipping them across the water. Two skips, four, seven . . . Before long I had joined him. "Dan," he said, "I feel that my goal in life is to help people love God and to know Jesus, not to hate the Buddha or disrespect Muhammad. The fact is, to have some televangelist with erect hair make snide comments about the Buddha—that isn't my idea of Christian maturity."

For some reason, his answer angered me. Not that I am overly fond of televangelists or that I have anything against the Buddha. I suppose I felt . . . betrayed. "So," I responded, with something like cynicism in my voice, "you're more or less a pluralist, then. Whatever people believe is OK, as long as they're sincere. That's certainly a popular and convenient attitude."

Neo squirmed. He plunked his last rock into the water and looked down. "Dan, I don't know what you intended, but the tone of your voice brings back some pretty bad memories for me. It seems like we just switched gears from two friends talking sincerely and openly to . . . a kind of inquisition. Did you mean to sound that way? Are you testing me? Is that what this conversation is all about?"

I instantly knew what he meant. I had felt the same thing more times than I wanted to remember—people who were church-shopping, asking, "Are you Spirit-filled?" or "Do you believe in inerrancy?" or "What's your position on homosexuality?" It's a cheap feeling to answer a test question of that sort, like you're selling yourself.

So I apologized. I told him I hated that feeling of being under inquisition, and I was sincerely sorry I made him feel that way. Looking back, I think the discomfort Neo was causing me, just by making me think, was beginning to stir up a bit of hostility in me. I'm not proud of that, but there it is. I hoped it wouldn't get worse.

"It's OK," Neo said. "Apology accepted."

I dropped my last stone on the shore and walked over to the edge of the water, where some driftwood had accumulated. I found two sticks and broke them to the right length for walking sticks. I gave one to Neo, and without a word we climbed up the bank and back onto the towpath. For a long time the only sound was the leaves crunching under our feet. After a few minutes, as if nothing had happened, Neo plunged right back into our conversation: "Dan, when it comes to other religions, the challenge in modernity was to prove that we're right and they're wrong. But I think we have a different challenge in postmodernity. The question isn't so much whether we're right but whether we're good. And it strikes me that goodness, not just rightness, is what Jesus said the real issue was—you know, good trees produce good fruit, that sort of thing. If we Christians would take all the energy we put into proving we're right and others are wrong and invested that energy in pursuing and doing good, somehow I think that more people would believe we are right."

I was intrigued but not satisfied. "Of course I agree with you that goodness is important, Neo, but I wonder . . . Are you saying that questions of truth are passé?"

He responded, "No, it's just that the old notions of truth and knowledge are being, hmm, I was going to say 'deconstructed,' but we don't need to get into all that vocabulary. The old notions are being questioned. New understandings of truth and knowledge that might improve on them haven't been fully developed yet. So Dan, I'm not in any way saying truth isn't important. But I am saying that truth means more than factual accuracy. It means being in sync with God."

Looking back, I wish I would have waited and pondered that last statement a good bit more before pressing ahead. But I just skated over it and moved on. "Well, how do you evangelize, then, if you don't try to convince people of truth? I remember that old quote from Saint Francis, about telling his followers to go everywhere and preach the gospel, and if necessary, use words. Is that what you mean—let your good deeds preach?"

"Sure, that's part of it. An important part of it. Demonstration must accompany proclamation, I guess you could say. But there's more. Instead of saying, 'Hey, they're wrong and we're right, so follow us,' I think we say, 'Here's what I've found. Here's what I've experienced. Here's what makes sense to me. I'll be glad to share it with you, if you're interested.'

"Instead of conquest, instead of a coercive rational argument or an emotionally intimidating sales pitch or an imposing crusade or an aggressive debating contest where we hope to 'win' them to Christ, I think of it like a dance. You know, in a dance, nobody wins and nobody loses. Both parties listen to the music and try to move with it. In this case, I hear the music of the gospel, and my friend doesn't, so I try to help him hear it and move with it. And like a dance, I have to ask if the other person wants to participate. There's a term for pulling someone who doesn't want to dance into a dance: assault. But if you pull someone in who wants to learn, and if you're good with the music yourself, it can be a lot of fun!"

With that, Neo turned his cap backward and pretended to be waltzing along the path with an imaginary partner, looking about as much like a ten-year-old boy as a middle-aged Jamaican guy in a perfectly white T-shirt can look. He pulled his blue dress shirt off his shoulder, took the cuff of one sleeve in his left hand and flung the other sleeve over his right shoulder, giving substance to his invisible partner. At one point he pretended to trip and managed to catch himself by grabbing onto a tree, and then he made a great show of pretending to help his fallen partner up off the ground, dusting off the shirt with great courtesy and concern. He said, "Of course, sometimes the best of us get tripped up, and in so doing, we trip others up too." I laughed for a brief moment—at his little act and at his boyish freedom. But for some reason, I couldn't loosen up myself and really laugh with him. I had to get right back to my heavy questions.

"But don't you want to critique other religions? I mean, there's so much that's false there. Are you saying that just any dance will do? It doesn't matter whether it's the right dance?" We had started walking again.

"Yes, Dan, I believe it must be God's dance. And you're right, there is so much that is false in other religions. But you know, there's a lot that is false in here," he said, pointing to his head and then his heart, "and in here too. My knowledge of Buddhism is rudimentary, but I have to tell you that much of what I understand strikes me as wonderful and insightful, and the same can be said of the teachings of Muhammad, though of course I have my disagreements. And before you mention conversion with the sword and violent fundamentalism and that sort of thing, just re-member that Christianity has had the same problems. We have a lot of our own embarrassments to face. In the long run, I'd have to say that the world is better off for having these religions than having no religions at all, or just one, even if it were ours. I wonder if these other religions might have a role much like Paul described for the Old Testament law back in Galatians—they serve as tutors or caretakers that preserve a culture until Christ can come to it with his good news. They aren't the enemy of the gospel, in my mind, any more than Christianity is the enemy—though of course, sometimes it is."

I heard him say this, but it didn't register. Christianity as the enemy of the gospel? What could he possibly mean? He picked up my confusion and stopped walking. He motioned for me to come over and sit on a mossy old fallen tree parallel to the path. I looked back—we had come a long way—and then I leaned and looked forward—we still had a long way to go. I was getting tired of both walking and thinking. As we caught our breath, Neo said, "I hope I'm not upsetting you too much. I think that last bit about Christianity too often being the enemy of the gospel really threw you."

I said yes, it had. To explain, he told me a story about his summer va-cation, back in June. He had gone to Seattle, where his parents lived. One day he took the ferry out to Bainbridge Island, just to look around. On the way back he got talking to a man who was, like him, enjoying the beautiful Seattle skyline from the rail on the top level of the ferry. They got talking, and somehow the subject of religion came up. When Neo identified himself as a Christian, the man identified himself as Jewish and then added, with no malice, "I watched one of your cable TV stations re-cently. To be honest with you, it made Christians look pretty stupid." Neo said that he hoped the man wouldn't judge all Christians by a few kooks with a cable station. The man said, again, with no malice, "Actually, I've thought about it a good deal. On the whole, I think Christianity is a force for evil in the world."

Then the man added, "I grew up in a small town in Indiana. We were the only Jewish family surrounded by Christians. It was a terrible way to grow up. We were never accepted; we were always outsiders. The only contact beyond superficialities was when some of the fundamentalists would tell me I was going to hell; they hoped to convert me. Obviously, they had the opposite effect. I travel a lot, and wherever I go, it seems that Christians are creating in-groups and putting everybody else in out-groups. Of course, the Holocaust is the most extreme example of that. It's too bad, really, because I've studied Jesus, and I think he was a great Jewish prophet, maybe the greatest who ever lived. But Christianity and Jesus don't seem to have too much in common, as far as I can see."

I asked Neo how he replied to the man. "What could I say? I told him, sadly, that there was too much truth to his statement." That's all? I asked. "Yes. But when he said goodbye, he was genuinely warm to me. He walked with me down the gangplank and all the way to the street. He was catching a plane to Hawaii, and so I helped him carry his bags and accompanied him across the street from the ferry to the taxi stand. When he said goodbye, it felt like we were old friends already. So I hope I represented a different kind of Christianity to him."

"Didn't you feel obligated to in some way defend the faith to him?" I asked.

"Why, Daniel? Why defend the indefensible? The man already thought well of Jesus—that's the important thing. I just wanted to give him further evidence that the Spirit of Jesus is not behind the craziness he saw on TV or the exclusionism he experienced as a child or the horror he saw in the Holocaust. Sure, he made something of an overstatement, but there was too much truth in it to brush it away. The best thing I felt I could do was simply to agree with him. After all, in the gospel itself, Jesus had to rebuke the disciples on several occasions, telling them they weren't of the right spirit. If it happened then, why be surprised that it happens down through history? Christianity isn't salvation, that's for sure! The good news is."

I responded, "As you say that, I think of Jesus telling Peter to 'get behind me, Satan.' I guess that should tell us that we Christians will sometimes be walking with Jesus and at the same time working against him. Wow. I never thought of that before."

We were walking again. I kept wishing I had brought along a snack of some sort, because we were both getting hungry.

"But getting back to other religions," I continued, "didn't Jesus say that all who came before him were thieves and robbers? And didn't he warn his followers about false Christs who would come after him? That doesn't sound like he's so positive or neutral about other religions."

"Well, to whom do you think Jesus was referring when he talked about those who came before? Was he referring to Plato? Aristotle? The Buddha? Was he referring to the Old Testament prophets—they came before him? My guess is that he was referring to the false messiahs of his own era, maybe even people like Barabbas, insurrectionists, zealots. I don't know. And as for those who came after, did he mean David Koresh or Joseph Smith types, or Hitler or Stalin types, or what? Whomever he was referring to, I'm sure they *were* thieves and robbers. And I'm sure *he* wasn't—because he came to give, not take. You know, Dan, he could have meant the cable TV types my Jewish friend on the ferry referred to!"

I came back: "But Jesus said, 'I am the way, the truth, and the life. No one comes to the Father but by me.' What do you do with that?" I was pretty tense, but my tone was sincere; I wasn't putting him through "inquisition" this time.

"I'll tell you what I do with that. I agree with it. One hundred percent. I am in no way saying that the Buddha, Muhammad, or anybody else is the way. I'm not saying they're alternatives to Jesus. Dan, I'm a Christian! I love Jesus! I'm just saying that it's pathetic for some ignorant preacher to mock the Buddha and Muhammad—neither of whom he has ever seriously studied, much less understood—as if he's smarter, wiser, and better just because he believes in Jesus. He might be blessed for believing in Jesus, but that doesn't make him smart."

Then Neo said something that I will always remember: "I think some Christians use Jesus as a shortcut to being right. In the process they bypass becoming humble or wise. They figure if they say 'Jesus' enough, it guarantees they won't be stupid. I agree with the guy I met on the ferry—that doesn't seem to be working! If people reject Jesus when they hear some half-baked would-be evangelist strutting his stuff and mocking the Buddha or Muhammad, I don't think they're really rejecting Jesus. They're rejecting the arrogance, ignorance, and bad taste of the preacher."

"OK, Neo. But I never said anything about mocking anybody."

"I know. But I've heard so much of that sort of thing—and unfortunately, now, thanks to the miracle of television, people around the world can see and hear Christians being stupid. I think it's very ugly. Look, I believe that Jesus is the savior of the world. I believe that someday every knee will bow to him and every tongue will confess he is Lord. I believe that he is truly the way, that if we believe in him and follow him, he will bring us to the Father. Too often, when we quote the verse about him being the way, it sounds like we're saying he's *in* the way—as if people are trying to come to God and Jesus is blocking the path, saying, 'Oh no, you don't! You have to get by me first.' I really don't think that's what he meant when he said he was the way.

"And Dan, I really believe he is the truth. He is reality; he is authentic; he is genuine and real and not fake or false in any way. And I really believe that he is the life, that fullness of life is in him. And I really believe that not one person will be in real contact with God the Father apart from the work and wisdom and love of Jesus. If I didn't believe that, I don't think I could call myself a Christian."

"Now you're confusing me," I said. "A few minutes ago you seemed to be defending other religions. Now you're agreeing that people of other religions are lost."

"That's not exactly what I said, Dan. Look, I believe that to be a just person means I should defend others when they're falsely accused. And I think that too often Christians falsely accuse other religions of things that just aren't true. That injustice on our part is an ugly blemish. It brings shame on the gospel and on Christ. Can you blame me for wanting to stand up for justice even in regard to people I may not agree with?"

I nodded my head and said I could see what he meant, and he continued. "Look, my understanding of the gospel tells me that religion is always a mixed bag, whether it's Judaism, Christianity, Islam, or Buddhism. Some of it reflects people's sincere attempts to find the truth, and some of it represents people's attempts to evade the truth through hypocrisy. Some of it reflects glimpses of God that people get through nature, through experience, through the fingerprint of God in their own design and the design of the universe—like Paul talked about in Romans 1 or in Acts 19. And some of it represents our own ego, our own pride, as we try to suppress the truth and look holy while we do it. As you said, even Peter had to be told that he was a mouthpiece of Satan once! So I don't think Christianity has, on the whole, proved itself much better than Peter. But isn't that the point of the gospel—that we're all a mess, whatever our religion, in need of God's grace?"

I came back fast: "So you don't think Christianity is better than any other religion? You can't mean that!"

I stopped walking, and he walked on a few paces and then turned around and waited for me to catch up. He said, quite firmly, "Look, Dan, I believe Jesus is the Savior, not Christianity. Is that so bad? Why do you think I left the pastorate?"

Something at that moment broke loose in me. It felt like a rope that was holding me up suddenly snapped and I was falling. Why was there this reservoir of fear or aggression (or both) seething inside me, waiting for a moment like this to erupt? "Damn you!" I shouted, surprising myself, because I'm not habitually a "cusser." "Damn you! You are so damn hard to figure out! And if you think you're helping me"—now I was yelling—"you're not! You're just making things worse!" My hands were clenched, and my face was trembling. I was beside myself. Was I about to start crying? Where was this guy coming from? What was he doing to me?

Neo looked shocked, completely speechless. He held out his hands. "I didn't mean to . . ."

"I don't care! I don't care!" I shouted. "If I were to think like you, if I voiced one-tenth of what you're saying to me, I'd be fired in a second. I won't put my wife through that. I won't put my children through that. I won't put my church through that either. Why the hell don't you just tell me about becoming a high school teacher and forget all this theological crap? This is crazy! You're not helping things!"

Not only am I not normally a cusser, but I've never hit anyone or anything in my adult life. I'm just not by nature a violent person. So what happened next surprised—and still embarrasses—me. I took my walking stick and swung it with all my might, swung it like a baseball bat, swung it at nothing in particular but maybe at everything in general. I heard the swoosh, and I swung it again, this time against the trunk of a tree. Half of it snapped and flew off into the woods, whirling like a helicopter blade. "Damn it all!" I shouted. Then I sent the other half of my stick flying into the woods, flying end over end, and turned my back on Neo as the stick bounced off one rock and then another and landed on the fallen leaves. A full second of silence ensued, and then I stormed away, back in the direction we'd come from, away from our destination, with no thought about where I was going.

9

REDEEMING OUR CULTURE
OVER DINNER

NEO CAME AFTER ME, calling "Dan, Dan, I'm sorry, I'm sorry for upsetting you. I'm *so* sorry." I kept walking—stomping was more like it—
but I hadn't gone twenty paces before I felt like a fool. I was a kid
throwing a temper tantrum. What an idiot I was. I turned back, and we
met in the middle of the path. I couldn't look at him. There were no birds
singing, no insects, nothing.

We both said it at the same second: "I'm sorry."

We walked back to the parking lot without saying another word. I
don't know what Neo was thinking, but I was hardly capable of thinking
anything. I was feeling a lot though—embarrassment, frustration, fear, regret, and more embarrassment for my outburst.

When we got to our cars, Neo leaned his walking stick against a "No
Parking" sign and came over and grabbed me by the arm. "Look," he
said, "neither of us wanted this to happen. We're both tired, in more ways
than one. Let's let this settle for a few days. Then why don't you give me
a call if you'd like to talk again. OK?"

I nodded my head. I began to apologize, but he interrupted: "No apology is necessary. I have a way of pushing too hard sometimes. The fault
is all mine. I'll wait to hear from you." He took off his hat, got in his car,
and drove away. I stood leaning against my car for a few minutes and then
did the same.

I was hoping to avoid Carol when I got home, but no such luck. She
took one look at me and asked, "What happened? What's wrong?"

"Nothing, nothing. I'm just right back to where I started." I walked
right past her, no hug, nothing, and continued, "I had some hope there—

for a few weeks I had some hope. But this isn't going to work." I slammed the door and went up and took a shower.

When I came downstairs, Carol's eyes were red and there was a box of tissues on her lap. I came over to the couch and sat next to her. I tried to give her a hug, but she was stiff. "I'm worried about you," she said. "It was so good to see you happier for the last few weeks. Meeting Neo really seemed to light something up again in you. But like a bubble, now it's burst again. I'm worried and afraid for you, Dan—for us. I've tried to be strong, but . . . I'm tired of being married to . . . to . . ."

She didn't know how to finish the sentence. I helped her: "to an unstable person. I can't blame you. I'm tired of being an unstable person."

Carol said, "I've been praying for you, Dan. Just this morning, I thought of all your sadness, all your thinking, all your struggle, and I prayed: *God, do you see how much he loves you? If he didn't love you, if he didn't love the truth so much, he would just play the game, just fulfill the role. But God, he is suffering because he really wants the truth. He really cares.* I hope God notices, Dan. I hope God pulls you through this."

Carol and I have a kind of repetitive pattern in our marriage. It's an ongoing fight, really. She asks me how my day was or how my week away at a conference was, and I say fine. She asks for more details, and I try to give them, but my mind goes blank. Then she acts hurt, as if I'm trying to hold something from her. And then I get mad, because I honestly can't think of anything to tell her and I just want her to let it go.

Fortunately, this time I not only *could* remember all the details, but I *wanted* to share them. I told her everything I remembered about my walk with Neo, our talk, and my snapping on the way back. She listened, with tears in her eyes, and when I finally finished and asked her, kind of pathetically, "What should I do?" She said, "You've got to keep talking to that man. I don't know what it is, Dan, but he seems to have what you need. I think God sent him into your life, but not just to tell you about teaching. And maybe he needs you too. I hope you didn't scare him away."

"But Carol," I said, "when I talk to him, sometimes I feel like I'm going to fall away from God."

"Maybe," she said. "But maybe that's a risk you have to take. It's not like you're in such a great place now. Besides, maybe you'll fall into God instead." I smiled and looked down, remembering that I had written something very similar in my journal a few weeks earlier.

I got through my Sunday duties as best I could, and I managed to hold off calling Neo until Monday afternoon. It was odd. I expected to feel awkward. When he answered the phone, I said, rather gravely, "Dr.

Oliver, Dan Poole here." He said, "Reverend Poole . . . it's *damn* good to hear from you!"

And I couldn't help it—I just started laughing. He mocked my cussing and in one sentence dispelled the tension.

"Neo, my wife suggested that I ask you if you'd be so kind as to come over to dinner," I said. "I'll cook something simple—and I promise, no poison!"

"As long as you don't have any sharp objects in your hand. I saw what you did with that walking stick!" he joked. "Seriously, Dan, I'd love to come over. I'm free Thursday and Friday."

"Thursday it is, then," I said. I gave him directions, and I was off the phone in less than thirty seconds.

On Tuesday, I worked for over an hour on a long letter of apology to Neo for my outburst. On Wednesday, I threw it out and started over again. Both versions tried to say the same thing, but with a lot of somewhat tortured introspection and analysis: *I don't know what came over me Saturday. I think I felt torn between my honest curiosity and desire to pursue the truth and the practical realities of being a pastor—which means living in a role where changes in theology have serious ramifications. I have been vacillating so long between hope and despair about continuing in ministry. Our conversations had been rekindling my hope that maybe I could make it, but then I think reality set in and despair resurfaced. When hope and despair collided at that moment, it was like an explosion. I vented that explosion on you, Neo, and I'm sorry.*

On Thursday, I threw out version two of the letter and instead wrote this short note on a sympathy card we normally send to people who have lost a loved one. I hoped my attempt at humor would come through: *Neo, I think you probably understand my outburst last Saturday better than I do. I've never acted like that or spoken like that with anyone. I ask your forgiveness, and your prayers. Dan.* The lack of long and involved explanation seemed to honor Neo's intelligence and our friendship.

When Neo arrived, he gave me a warm greeting, a hug this time instead of a handshake. I hadn't gotten a chance to give him the letter before Corey and Trent ran in and introduced themselves. They were in their soccer uniforms (they had a scrimmage right after dinner), and within seconds Neo was out in the backyard with them, kicking a soccer ball. I watched him out the window, his tie flying back over his shoulder, his gray suit jacket flapping as he turned and dodged and dribbled. He was laughing, and so were the twins. I felt bad breaking things up for dinner. "That's the best sport in the world," he said as he came in, catching his breath, straightening his tie. "And there's one of the world's best midfielders!" he said as he saw Jess, who ran over and shook his hand—with the added knuckle-to-knuckle punch—before we all sat down for the meal. I said a prayer, and then Neo and Jess talked about some of her teammates, none of whose names I recognized, I'm embarrassed to say.

Carol is normally a bit shy, but shortly after we sat down to dinner (I cooked my specialty, red beans and rice with spicy chicken), Neo had her telling all kinds of stories about her childhood in Atlanta, how we met at Baylor, her work as a graphic artist before our kids were born. She got him to recount the outlines of his own story, which he had shared with me in our first few conversations. I stayed pretty quiet. I was physically conscious of the envelope in my jacket pocket; I wanted to give it to Neo but wanted to find the right moment after the kids left the table.

The boys needed to be driven over to the middle school for their soccer scrimmage, just a few miles away, so the three of us excused ourselves after the main course. Jess must have excused herself shortly after the boys and I left—probably to talk to some friends on the phone, her after-dinner ritual. That left Carol and Neo alone at the table for about twenty minutes until I got back.

It was clear they had gotten into some serious conversation while I was gone. When I brought in dessert and coffee and sat down, Neo was telling Carol about his divorce—a surprise to me, as I had assumed he was a life-long bachelor.

He was saying, "No, Carol, we had no children. I always wanted children, but first it was seminary for me, and then college for her, and then . . . then we began splitting up. These things take time." I didn't know how to take that last sentence.

"Maybe that's why you enjoy teaching so much then, Neo. Maybe all these kids are like your kids," Carol said.

"Ah, yes, I'm sure that's true," he said. "Welcome back, Dan!"

Carol didn't acknowledge my reentry into the conversation, but she didn't waste any time involving me: "Neo, my husband tells me he totally freaked out with you the other day. What do you think got him so upset?"

"As I recall, Carol, I said something unfair and disparaging about organized religion. I imagine that Dan suddenly felt that I was not taking seriously the complexities of his life, as someone who has devoted his life to organized religion and has a family to support and a mortgage to pay. And he was right—I was insensitive and completely out of line. It's so easy for an outsider to take cheap shots, and so he had every right to get upset with me. I was grossly oversimplifying a complex—"

Looking back, that would have been my chance to take out my letter and apologize, because the whole mess was my fault, not his. But for some reason I missed the opportunity entirely and instead interrupted with this: "But you're Episcopalian, Neo. That hardly makes you an outsider to organized religion."

He replied, "Good point, Dan. Good point." He thought for a moment and then said, "You know, 'organized religion' is a terribly troublesome term, two terribly troublesome terms, really. I mean—would we prefer 'disorganized irreligion'?" Carol smiled at that, and he continued, "Overorganization or underorganization would be problematic, but I don't think organization itself is the problem."

Carol said, "Then religion is the problem?"

Neo replied, "The old Latin roots of the word simply mean 'reconnecting,' you know—broken ligaments, severed connections, being reconnected and defragmented. That sounds like exactly what we need, don't you think? We're 'deligamented,' disconnected, fragmented people who need to be 'religamented,' reconnected, put back together with God, with one another, reintegrated within ourselves, reconnected to the world we are part of."

Carol's mild south Georgia accent struck a noticeable contrast to Neo's Jamaican lilt: "That's truly fascinating, Neo. I don't tend to think of religion in those positive terms. Actually, I think I've seen religion as part of the problem. Being a pastor's wife, of course, you see a lot, and it's easy to get cynical. But even as when I was growing up, I think I felt that way. Where I come from, with the religious right and all, religion tends to get wrapped up in city politics, state politics, national politics—as if the world's secular power is the real prize. But up here—and to me, Maryland is still definitely *up north*—it's very different."

"What do you mean?" Neo asked.

"Well," she continued, "the religious right is certainly strong up here too. But in general—you know, among the people of our neighborhood here, for example—religion seems to be more about the private world. It's about my needs, my comfort, my feelings, my preferences. You know how people say religion is a private matter. Either way, I've always had mixed feelings about the word *religion*."

"I see what you mean, Carol," he said. "You're quite right. On the one hand, there are plenty of people everywhere who want to impose their religion on others through legislation, as if values and beliefs could be imposed any better by law than by sword. And on the other hand, there are plenty of people for whom religion has become little more than a hobby, or maybe a way of talking to yourself, like the 'positive self-talk' you hear about sometimes—maybe like a child singing songs to herself in the darkness of her bedroom, to help her fall asleep without imagining ghosts in her closet and monsters under her bed."

I'm not good at just listening to a conversation, so I interrupted: "Hey, Neo, I know what you're thinking." He asked what. I said, "That political and private are two poles on a line down here"—I ran my finger along the condensation on my glass of ice water and then drew a line of water on the table—"but that there's another answer up here," moving my other hand in a circling motion above the line.

Neo was stirring his coffee and flashed me a warm smile. "Actually, Dan, I was thinking no such thing. But now that you mention it . . ."

I said to Carol, "Get ready, honey. Here it comes!"

He smiled and spoke slowly. "I think what Jesus was about, and really, what all the apostles were about at their best moments, up here on this higher level"—he was moving his hand in an oval—"was a global, *public* movement or *revolution* to bring holistic reconciliation, a reconnection with God, with others, with ourselves, with our environment. *True* religion, *revolutionary* religion. That's what got them in such trouble."

Carol responded, "How could anybody be against that? How could anybody not want that?"

Neo ignored her question, or missed a step in the conversation, or else was reverting to something earlier, because I wasn't sure how what he said next related to what Carol was asking: "I think what people really mean when they say they are against organized religion is that they're against hypocritical religion, misguided religion, blind or unthinking religion, religion of rules and laws rather than love, religion that comes diced and preprocessed and shrink-wrapped like ground beef. And that's what I'm against, whether it's in Hindu garb or Buddhist or Christian—especially Christian! So it's not a matter of private comfort or political power. It's a matter of revolutionary mission, wouldn't you agree, Dan?"

His question was obviously rhetorical, so I didn't try to answer it. Instead, I asked, "Neo, how would you tell the difference between authentic religion and misguided religion?"

He said, "I don't think you can. It's not that simple. Remember what Jesus said? The wheat and the tares are always mixed together. There are good Catholics, good Greek Orthodox, good Pentecostals, and good Episcopalians, believe it or not. And there are plenty of bad ones too."

At that point we all got serious about the dessert I had brought out. It was a store-bought pumpkin pie, but Neo made a big deal about it. A few minutes later we took our coffee mugs out onto the deck. It was cool, but not too cool, and we resumed our more serious conversation.

Neo spoke, but not in his usual direct manner. He was kind of rambling. "Back to your question, Dan. I remember a couple of years ago, when I was in Paris as a chaperone for a senior-class field trip—which I don't recommend, by the way. I remember hearing that the word for 'a religion' in French was *culte*. And it got me thinking about the relationship between their *culte* and our *cult* and the relationship between a cult and a religion in English. And then that got me thinking about the relationship between the words *cult* and *culture*."

Carol and I were holding our coffee cups, anticipating the rest of his story, but he just kept staring, looking down at his shoes. Finally I said, "OK, well, what?" He laughed. "Gosh, it's funny. It struck me as a really great insight at the time, but I don't have many people to talk to about all this, and so I think I've forgotten. . . . Oh, yes. Now I remember. I got to thinking about the different ways religion tends to relate to the culture around it, the way the *culte* interacts with the *culture*. I wish I could remember. . . . I guess for starters, *culte* can simply try to serve culture—you know, kind of like civil religion. I would even include your religious right in this category, Carol. Sometimes your radio preachers seem so concerned about "saving America" that you'd think the gospel existed for the sake of American *culture*. Sometimes, I think, religion loses its soul in this way, and *culte* simply becomes a facet of *culture*. It gains a certain kind of power and respectability at the cost of its soul."

Neo continued, "Religion can also try to withdraw from culture—isolate itself and create its own subculture. I suppose the most extreme groups we call 'cults' do this most notoriously; they completely separate themselves and develop their own insider language, their own conspiracy theories, their alternative histories, and as a result we call them cultic. But there's a whole range of isolation, from mild to extreme. Jesus, it seems to me, had a different way—radically different. He wanted to send his people into the culture with a mission—not in service to the culture in the sense of helping the culture achieve its own ends but in a kind of divinely subversive way, *culte* infiltrating *culture* with the kingdom of God, not trying just to serve it as a civil religion would, but more like trying to redeem it for a higher agenda, God's agenda."

For Carol, that word *redeem* brought back a memory from several years back, which she shared with Neo. We had been at a conference in Washington, D.C., about Christianity and the arts, and performing at this event was a dance troupe from Uganda. The leader of the group gave a little speech in between two dance performances. Carol said, "I still remember the sound of his accent and the passion of his words. He said, 'When the missionaries came to my country, at first they tried to drive the culture from the people. They tried to replace it with their own European culture, and they almost succeeded. But even though we believed the gospel, we resisted their efforts to eradicate our culture, because we came to realize that Jesus came not to drive the culture from the people but the sin from the culture. He came not to condemn our culture but to redeem it.'"

Neo said, "That's good. That's very good. Uganda . . ." After a long, thoughtful pause, he continued, winking at me, "That's why, in my mind, it should be possible to be a Christian and yet be culturally Buddhist, Muslim, or Navajo."

He anticipated a reaction from me, and he got one. "You mean, they would still be Buddhist?" I asked.

He answered, "We have to realize that Buddhism is more than a religion, more than a *culte*. It is also a *culture*. So I can't see why Jesus couldn't invade Buddhist culture, just as he invaded Jewish and Greco-Roman culture in the first millennium and European cultures in the second. If in the third millennium Christ enters Buddhist culture, he will spark an outbreak of real Christianity—just not Western European Christianity. And if Christ enters Islamic culture, he will spark an outbreak of real Christianity, but again, it won't be Western European Christianity. That to me is the missionary challenge of the third millennium: not eradicating Buddhist or Islamic or tribal cultures but blessing them with Christ—letting Christ enter them and drive the evil from them, as that dance troupe leader said, and in that way redeem them. And my guess is that each will bring something that will enrich our Christian heritage too, just as the African dances enriched you that day. And in the process, maybe we'll let Christ enter our own Western culture in a new way too. That's a nice thought!"

Two or three times I started to say something, but each time I anticipated what Neo would say, so I stopped myself. I finished my coffee and then went inside and poured myself another cup, and then another memory came to mind, which I shared with Neo when I came back out on the deck: "You're making me remember another really fascinating moment from a couple of years ago. I got a call one Friday morning saying that a group of Native American pastors was coming to D.C. for some special meetings and their accommodations fell through. Would I be willing to host them? I said sure (after checking with Carol—I have learned that much through the years!), and that evening I picked up seven of them at the airport. I'll never forget the crowded ride home in the van—I don't think I've ever been around such happy, fun-loving men. The jokes and puns and laughter just flowed. When we got home and they saw my guitars and mandolin, they immediately started to play and sing. I never would have guessed that Indians like cowboy music!"

Neo chuckled at this, and then I continued. "On Saturday they had their meetings downtown, and then they did some sightseeing. On Sunday we sang an old country-and-western gospel song together at my church, with me playing the mandolin. It was a riot—the people just loved it. The guys had to leave on Monday morning, so we stayed up well after midnight that Sunday night, singing and talking. When the music quieted down, I asked them a question: 'Do any of you use Native American culture in your church services back home?' There was this awkward silence, and they looked around at each other—no joking now; everyone was very serious.

"Finally one of them said, 'No, we don't.' And then, all around the room, they started to admit that they didn't use any Native culture in their services, that the missionaries had told them it was all of the devil, that sort of thing. Then one of the men made a confession. I could tell that it took some courage for him to say this. He said, 'Actually, I do still go to "the sweats," and for me it is part of my worship.' He then explained the ritual of the sweat lodge: 'I take off my clothes—which is like getting honest before God. Then I go down into the sweat, which is like going down deep into my heart. I am there, naked, with all my brothers, which is a reminder that I am part of a community and I can have no pride or pretense in front of them. Then we pour water on hot rocks over a fire, and the rocks make steam. This is like prayer, and as I pour the water, I confess my sins to God. The more I confess, the hotter it gets, and the hotter it gets, the more I sweat. The sweat is like purification. So for me this is a meaningful part of my worship now that I'm a Christian. I've never told anyone this—you might think that this is terrible.'

"Then," I continued, "one of the other pastors spoke up and said it really did concern him. It sounded to him like syncretism, like adulterating pure Christianity with pagan elements. He said that we shouldn't mix worship of the One True God with elements from other religions. The silence became uncomfortable until this same fellow started to speak again, with tears now streaming down his face. 'I'm sorry,' he said. 'That wasn't me speaking. That was my seminary speaking through me. Please forgive me. I really think what you just said about the sweats was beautiful.'

"It took him a couple of minutes to finish speaking, he was so choked up—it was really quite moving to see how emotional this was, not just for the two men who had spoken but for all of them. Then this man continued, 'I am Hopi, and one of the most meaningful memories in my life is being a boy, before our family became Christians, and being at the powwow. We would dance and dance for hours each day. You see, in Hopi culture, dance isn't just symbolic. Dance is actually a form of prayer. Every time my foot stamps on the ground, I'm saying something to the Great

Spirit that I could never put into words. My whole body is praying as I move around the circle.'

"By this time, he was standing and demonstrating the movements. Then he sat down again and put his head in his hands. 'One of my greatest dreams,' he said, 'would be someday to lead my congregation in a Hopi dance of worship to my Savior.' Then he really started to weep, and the other men went around him and put their hands on his shoulders, and one of them prayed for him. What a moment that was. I'll never forget it."

I went on to tell how the conversation ended. After everyone sat down again, I asked how they could begin to reintegrate native customs into their worship, and one of the pastors responded, "It's not that simple, Dan. It may be too late. You see, I travel all around the country doing antidrug talks at reservation high schools. I probably see more Indian kids than just about anybody else in any given year. Wherever I go, I see kids who are ashamed to be known as Indians. My own daughters refuse to register as Indians, even though by doing so they could get free college tuition. If you go into any high school on any reservation, you would think you were in Philadelphia or Chicago, because the kids have totally embraced African American urban culture—rap music, baggy pants, whatever is in style on MTV. They are almost all ashamed of their culture; they don't want to be different from the 'teen mainstream.' So I think if we want to reach the younger generation, we have to become even less Indian than we are now. It's sad, really."

This engendered some lively discussion, and I remember adding, "Wouldn't it be ironic if, in the name of Christ, we try to conserve and preserve the very same native cultures in the twenty-first century that we tried to wipe out in the nineteenth and twentieth centuries?"

I looked over at Neo to see his response to all of this, and he was just staring at me, his fingertips pressed together and touching his lips. He was smiling faintly. At the time, I didn't realize why he seemed so interested in and moved by these stories. Later I realized that as a black man, for him these stories had a meaning and an impact that went beyond anything Carol or I, as Caucasians, could grasp. Maybe he was being kind by not saying what he was thinking about my people, my ancestors. I don't know.

Since we were on the topic of culture, and since Neo seemed so interested, Carol said, "Dan, you should tell him about that Indian wedding you performed last summer." I looked at Neo to see if he wanted to hear the story. He looked at my watch and said he needed to leave shortly but would like to hear the story. It was also getting quite cool, so I promised I'd give him the short version.

I had been asked to perform a wedding for a Native American woman and an Anglo man. They decided to bring marriage customs from both cultures into their wedding. The wedding began with loud yip-yip-yip shouts, and it included having the couple smoke a peace pipe and blow sage smoke in the four directions of the compass and several other customs that were new to me. I remember thinking that some of the people from my church must think I'm really over the edge to be participating in this event. But then we came to the part of the wedding where they exchanged rings, and I realized that gold rings were simply part of European culture—no better or worse than smoking a pipe or blowing sage smoke. And I realized that organs and flowers and white dresses were no better or worse than yelling yip-yip-yip. I was simply more used to customs that came from my own culture.

When I finished this story, Neo didn't get up to leave. I wish I had been more sensitive to what he must have been thinking, but at the time I was focused only on my own questions and issues. I said, "But it made me wonder, wouldn't it flow the other way too? I mean, Christ would influence the culture, but wouldn't the culture influence Christianity too?" I guess that concern about syncretism that the Hopi pastor expressed was also a concern of mine.

Neo's voice sounded a little sharp as he responded, "Well, syncretism is usually what Christians who are thoroughly immersed in one culture talk about when Christianity is being influenced by other cultures. So, for example, modern Western Christians are very sensitive to a potential syncretism with postmodernity, but they are for the most part pretty oblivious to how enmeshed their version of the faith is with modernity. To some degree I think syncretism is unavoidable. For example, when the gospel came to the Greco-Roman world, the Greeks and Romans got the gospel, but Christianity got Plato and Aristotle and Socrates too, for better or for worse. Or take democracy—we certainly didn't get that from the Bible alone; the Athenians had something to do with it. But most of us hold it pretty dear—just as medieval folks held to the idea of monarchy as being God's sanctioned form of government. So syncretism is pretty hard to avoid."

Carol said, "I guess that worries me—or concerns me. How do we know that we are really getting the gospel at all, instead of a tossed salad form of it, with a little of this, a little of that?"

Neo paused a moment and then said, "That's a good question. I guess the first protection that comes to mind is the Bible. This is why I think we must always keep coming back to the Bible and doing our best to let it form and unsettle us when necessary. A friend of mine who now pastors back in Jamaica once told me that the parts of the Bible that bother you most are the ones that have the most to teach you. He said that instead of minimizing your discomfort and trying to explain those parts away, you should bear down on those passages and maximize how different they are, really wrestle with those parts. That sort of wrestling is good for us. It would have been nice if American and Jamaican Christians in the eighteenth century had wrestled a little harder with Paul's letter to Philemon, for example, while they were importing my ancestors from Africa and enslaving them on plantations and—"

I interrupted, "Yes, but I'm thinking about what you've taught me about postmodernity, Neo. The Bible didn't seem to save the Western church from getting in bed with modernity. It seems like we see the Bible through whatever lens we get from our culture."

Neo said, "No doubt, no doubt. That's why we need the church itself—not just our little local church or our denomination, although it starts there, but more, the whole church, now and through history. If we've sincerely and honestly wrestled with Scripture—not just as individuals but as a community—and if we're really listening to one another—especially the minority voices, the ones we might try to marginalize and ignore—we have to believe that we'll be better off, more in tune with God's plans for us, less beguiled by our own culture and its subtle ways of tricking us into reinterpreting the faith—exaggerating some things, minimizing others, and totally missing still others. That's why the black church and the Hispanic church, the South American, Asian, and African churches, and also the medieval and ancient churches all have voices that the dominant modern European-culture churches really need to listen to."

Then he added, "Something else comes to mind. If we're trying to not let the gospel get diluted or polluted with all kinds of other influences, at the end of the day we have to trust that the Holy Spirit will guide us. As we wrestle with Scripture and listen to one another, we have to believe that God will guide us too, don't you think?"

Carol came in with a loud "amen" and then said, "You know, Neo, Dan just preached about that a few weeks ago. He's going through the book of Acts in his sermons, and he got to that big debate in Acts 15. Dan talked about how dramatic it was. Who could have imagined that within a few decades of Jesus' life on earth, Christians would be making some of their most sacred traditions optional—like circumcision and . . . what was the other one, Dan? Oh, yes, all the dietary laws. But here they are, feeling that God was guiding them to do something that must have seemed very dangerous, very compromising. They argued and listened and probably prayed a lot too, and in the end they said, 'It seems good to the Holy

Spirit and to us.' So I agree with you, Neo. We have to interact with the Bible and the whole church and listen to the Holy Spirit and wrestle it out. I reckon we'll still make our share of mistakes—but I guess the mistakes can go either way, you know? I mean, it would have been a terrible mistake to try to keep the dietary laws and impose circumcision on everyone, even though that might have seemed 'safer.'"

Neo pointed his finger at Carol and gave her a big smile. "You, Carol, must give your husband plenty of competition when it comes to good theological thinking. Do you preach too? You'd be pretty tough competition for Dan, I would think!"

Before I could say anything, Carol smiled at me, half-joking (but only half), and said, "Dan, I don't see what's so radical and outlandish about Dr. Oliver's ideas. He makes perfect sense to me." We all laughed.

With that, Neo thanked us and got up to leave. Before he left, he and I agreed to get together for lunch on Saturday, just two days away. He drew me a map to a favorite restaurant of his in Takoma Park. I'd never been there, never even heard of it.

Carol and I walked Neo out to his car. As he drove away, I realized I had forgotten to give him my letter. I guess it didn't matter. The conversation was flowing again. Our friendship had survived my meltdown.

When I came back inside, I saw an envelope leaning against a pitcher on the kitchen table. It had my name printed on it. I opened it. Of course, it was from Neo. Oddly, the message was written in pencil on graph paper. Here's all it said:

> Daniel, please accept my apology for pushing you so hard. I have some feeling for what I was putting you through intellectually and spiritually on our long walk.
>
> When I was very young, my grandmother used to point to the mountain ranges that stretched from east to west just inland from Port Maria. She would say, "If you find you-self on one mountain peak and you wanna get to anodda higher one, den dey is only one way up, and dat is to go down fust." I am confident that the low point in our conversation was simply a necessary descent in our journey to a higher peak. Everything's going to be alright. Your friend, Neo.

C. S. LEWIS IN THE PULPIT, OR WHAT IS HEAVEN ABOUT ANYWAY?

NEO'S MAP WAS PERFECT, but when I arrived, I was a bit confused. What I expected to be a restaurant was actually a bar. But upon entering, I instantly knew why Neo liked it so much. There were *three* soccer games playing on three different TV screens around the room. I saw Neo standing and waving me over, and as I sat down, I was engulfed in a rather startling mix of accents and languages—Spanish, I think it was Portuguese, even some French from some African fellows at the bar.

"Wow," I said. "I always surf right by the soccer games on TV. I had no idea there were three games on at the same time though!" I said.

"No, no, no—I wish there were, but that screen there is the only live game. Those other screens are videos—that's the famous World Cup game of 1998 where France took the cup, and that one . . . I'm not sure. It's Brazil playing somebody. It's probably one of Pele's last games. For most of the world, Pele is Mickey Mantle, Babe Ruth, Joe Namath, and Muhammad Ali all wrapped up in one."

I felt a little uncomfortable. I was the only Caucasian in the restaurant, and that was an odd feeling for me. Neo made me feel a little less comfortable by asking me if I wanted a beer. I come from a long line of teetotalers, so I quickly declined and ordered a Diet Coke instead. Then he added insult to injury by ordering for himself—I'm not making this up—a beer called Pete's Wicked Ale. At least, I thought, it's highly unlikely that anyone from Potomac Community Church will come in here and see me in a bar.

Neo thanked me for the dinner on Thursday and said a number of flattering things about my family. "You're a lucky man," he said, "truly blessed."

We ordered sandwiches for lunch and talked more about soccer; then Neo turned serious. "Driving over here," he said, "I was thinking about where our conversation should go next. I feel terrible about pushing you too hard last week. I realized that I have stubbornly refused to address the original question you asked me about, and I wondered if you want to ask your questions about high school teaching."

I looked down at my folded hands and said, "No, Neo, driving over here I realized that this isn't just about my career, my future. This is about my own spiritual life—you know?—my own beliefs, my own relationship with God. I guess you could say it's about my own pursuit of truth. So if you're willing, I'd like to go right back to where we were when I . . . when I freaked out. I liked what your letter to me said, that quote from your grandmother. I think she was right. Sometimes you have to go down in the short run in order to go up in the long run. So I think we should pick up where we—"

Neo interrupted, "Where we started descending from the peak of modernity? OK. Just remember, though, often the discomfort gets worse before it gets better."

I joked: "Maybe I should order a Wicked Ale too then." (But I stuck with Diet Coke.) I nodded up toward one of the screens where a player had just scored and the crowd was going wild and the announcer was shouting "GO-O-O-O-AL!": "Let's play."

Here, roughly paraphrased, is where Neo took me. He said that he had been raised, as I had, to believe that the central story of the Bible was about saving individual souls. The gospel, as he (and I) had understood it was about getting individual souls into heaven. (His exact words were "getting my butt into heaven.") Several years earlier he had begun having some problems with this for several reasons. He borrowed a pen from me and started writing key words on his placemat.

First, it smacked of *selfishness*. Would God want a heaven full of people who wanted to be "saved" but didn't necessarily want to be good? If we pitch the whole story as, "Do you want to go to heaven or hell?" he said, we run the risk of attracting people who want salvation from hell without necessarily wanting salvation from sin. This would be a story about being chosen for elite privilege, not sacrificial service.

Second, in a postmodern context, he said, the *individualism* of this approach sounded downright evil, like using insider trading information to gain an unfair advantage over others in the stock market. A good-hearted person might respond, "I love my neighbors, and if you're offering me something that my neighbors can't have, then I don't want it." However, if it were put in the service context, so that we are chosen by God not for privilege but for service, the reverse would be true: "I love my neighbors, and if receiving God's salvation will help me help them, then I want it!" He said the difference might seem subtle, but the more I thought about it, the more I would see how profound it was. (It wasn't until months later that I agreed with him.)

Third, he said that there have to be *two dimensions* of salvation, not just one. More conservative Christians, he said, tend to focus on the eternal dimension—saving one's soul from hell. More liberal Christians, he said, tend to focus on the historic dimension—saving the human race and the planet from destruction. The biblical view of salvation was comprehensive of both, and we need to keep both alive—not only the "getting of individual butts into heaven" but also "saving the world."

He wasn't sure how this all worked out theologically, but he felt that a key component of working it out was to distinguish the *church* and the *kingdom*. I was nodding my head but not particularly engaged. He was lecturing me, I felt, and I was eager for more give-and-take.

Then he started working on a diagram. He said that most Christians see the church—represented by a circle—as identical with the kingdom—represented by another circle drawn exactly over the original circle. Some Christians disassociate the two completely, represented by two circles, one drawn on either end of the placemat, with the church being God's people now and the kingdom being reserved for some future age or dispensation beyond this life altogether. He said that he gravitated toward a different view where the church circle was a small circle mostly included in a bigger circle (not completely, he said, because there's too much stuff that goes on in the church that has nothing to do with God's kingdom). The bigger circle of the kingdom represents God's work in the world at large—God's concern for the environment, God's work with people of other religions, God's identification with the poor and oppressed, God's dispensing of artistic gifts so that artists can express beauty and glory and truth, that sort of thing. His placemat ended up looking something like this:

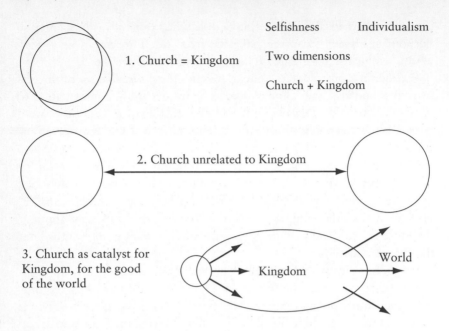

1. Church = Kingdom

Selfishness   Individualism

Two dimensions

Church + Kingdom

2. Church unrelated to Kingdom

3. Church as catalyst for Kingdom, for the good of the world

Kingdom

World

The church exists, he said, to be a catalyst of the kingdom. In other words, it doesn't just exist for its own aggrandizement. It exists for the benefit of the kingdom of God, something bigger than itself. Of course the church must grow, numerically and spiritually, but that growth matters so the church can become more and more catalytic for the kingdom of God, for the good of the world. This means that the world doesn't exist for the benefit of the church, as if the world were a mountain that we strip-mine to get ore to process in our spiritual factory, for the church's enhancement. No, the church exists for the world—to be God's catalyst so that the world can receive and enter God's kingdom more and more. I remember two particularly crisp and memorable statements from that part of the conversation: "God so loved the world that he gave it his only Son, and his Son's only church," and "God's kingdom is a reality that both inhabits history and transcends it." The kingdom, he said, is where the historical and the eternal come together.

Since then I have come to see how important that ten- or fifteen-minute conversation was, but at the time it went largely over my head. (Fortunately, that placemat was taped into my journal along with the others, so I could go back over it later.)

I was basically being polite until I could ask the question that had been churning in my brain during my car ride over to the restaurant. "Neo, getting back to other religions, like we were talking about beside the river last week, I think you kind of dodged my real question. I'd like a really straight answer from you on this: Do you believe that people of other religions will go to heaven?"

Neo gave me a look that I didn't understand at the time. I now surmise that he was disappointed because he had been trying to convince me that salvation was about more than getting people into heaven after they die but I was still preoccupied with that single issue. He paused for a while—again, looking back, I think he was trying to decide whether to answer my question or tell me I was asking the wrong question. Finally, he said, "I have an idea. One of the last sermons I ever preached before I left the ministry was on this question. I know I have it on tape somewhere. I'll be glad to get the tape to you."

From that point on, our conversation lightened up, and we watched the soccer game that was playing on the screen above the bar, and before we were done, Neo had bought me a Pete's Wicked Ale, which wasn't so wicked after all. Before we left, he invited me to a DC United game a few weeks later, a Sunday game, but late enough in the day that I could still go after church.

He also promised to lend me some books that he thought would be helpful to me.

The tape and books arrived in the mail a few days later. I put the books aside for several weeks but listened to the tape immediately, while in the car, actually two or three times, and eventually asked my secretary to transcribe it for me. Here it is. The sermon was called—Neo wasn't much for catchy titles—"Death."

DEATH

For some reason people like to tell jokes about death. For example, . . . [Note: I have omitted two jokes Neo told at this point, one about an oxygen tube and one about a dead cat. They were funny on the tape, but when written down, they sounded kind of grotesque.]

I think we like to tell jokes about death for the same reason we like to tell ghost stories on Halloween. It gives us a way to sidle up to a subject that we are nervous about confronting head on. But today I would like us to think of death as a door, and I would like us to walk up to it face on and in a sense open it and look through it together. I think a good starting point would be some words from Ecclesiastes 3 (1–2, 11): "There is a time for everything, and a season for every activity under heaven: a time to be born and a time to die. . . . He has made everything beautiful in its time."

Those are striking words, aren't they? There is a time to die, and when it is time to die, death can be, not something to fear, but something . . . beautiful. Now that statement could sound like a pathetic pile of nonsense, depending on which story you find yourself in. Let me explain what I mean by that. There are two dominant stories alive in our culture today. Worldwide, I would say there are four or five dominant stories, but only two are dominant in our culture.

Story one goes like this: Once upon a time, the universe banged into being for no apparent reason and with no apparent purpose. Someday it will end and there will be no one left to remember it ever existed. In the meantime, we live and die. And that's about it.

Story two begins with a Creator who designs the universe to produce life. The Creator cares about everything he has made, including us. The Creator reaches out to us in many ways, constantly inviting us into a relationship of trust. When we die, we enter into the Creator's presence so that in some sense this life that we now live is a prelude to a dimension of life that never dies.

Now at least one of those stories is false, and if you believe the second story is false, then no wonder you fear death. You've got to grab for all the gusto you can in life, because when life is over, you've seen your last gusto, baby. You only go around once in life, and when you die with the most toys, that's tough, because not only can you not take the toys with you, you're not going anywhere you can take them to anyway, and there's no you left and nowhere to go.

But what if the second story is true? What if, in broad outline, it describes the situation in which we find ourselves? I'm not just asking what if we pretend it's true to help us make it through the night. I'm asking you to consider, what if it is actually, really, accurately, substantially, profoundly, powerfully, definitely, unambiguously, factually, fully, and finally true?

If that's the case, then we can stop fearing death. Because the fear of death takes a terrible toll on life, but when we overcome the fear of death through believing and living by that second story, the reality of death actually yields many gifts. To illustrate, I'd like to get your help in a little thought experiment.

First, let's follow the first story through to its logical conclusions. I'll ask you to help me by periodically—when I cue you—

asking, "What's the consequence of that?" OK? First, I'm aware that I'm going to die someday. What is the consequence of that? I have to cram all the experiences and pleasures I can into the limited time frame I am allotted, and I have to fear or flee from every pain or frustration, since they are wasting precious time that I wish were being filled with pleasure. What is the consequence of that? I have just eliminated from my life all the pleasures that take a long time and all the virtues that require discipline and difficulty. And what's the consequence of that? I become superficial, hurried, maybe frantic, always disappointed, always afraid that I won't get happy and stay happy. What's the consequence of that? Well, if I am the only one living this way, it's bad enough, but if more and more people are living that way, it's not hard to imagine that you get a world very much like the one ours is fast becoming— cheapened, polluted, scarred, tense, anxious, empty, frantic. It's all meaningless in the end, so who cares? Death wipes it all away, so . . . whatever.

Now let's run through the same thought pattern living in the second story. I understand that I am going to die someday. What's the consequence of that? I realize I should focus on things that will have value not only in this life but also in the life to come. What's the consequence of that? I am able to maximize the joys of life, to slow down and really savor them, rather than rushing through them to cram the next one in. What's the consequence of that? I find myself being grateful for every small pleasure of this life, seeing it as a gift from God and seeing a preview of heaven. What's the consequence of that? I am enabled to see the hardships of life in a new perspective too, as character-building opportunities to grow and develop the sinews and muscles and backbone of my soul. What's the consequence of that? I feel that the trials of this life aren't even worth comparing to the glory that is to be revealed in the next life. What's the consequence of that? I feel a confidence and freedom from worry in the face of every trial, including the trial of death. What's the consequence of that? I do not live life in a hurry or in a desperate attempt to distract myself from a meaningless end; instead, I live life to the fullest, life as God intends it to be lived. What's the consequence of that? Well, if I live this way, it's good for me, but if I can influence more and more people to live this way, then the world will become a very different kind of place, so that in some real way we can say we are entering and experiencing the kingdom of God.

Now this doesn't mean that death will be easy. People who study death tell us that people frequently go through predictable patterns as they let go of their hold on this life and prepare themselves for the next. They often start with shock and denial and then experience anger, and then they try to bargain for a little more life, and then they feel depression, and then they reach acceptance. Others describe biological death as the last in a series of deaths, beginning with vocational death, when we can no longer work, followed by social death, when we can no longer be out and about with our friends and family, followed by psychological death, when we lose our mental capacities, followed by physical or biological death. There is often a long and difficult process of letting go. But just because the process is not easy does not mean it can't be meaningful and, in the words of Ecclesiastes, even beautiful. Listen to one of my favorite authors, Paul Tournier:

The meaning of life, its total meaning, which imparts to it its unity despite the diversity of its various stages, is obedience to God. In growing up and developing, the child is obeying God, who gave him life and its wonderful power of growth. In making his choices, the adolescent is obeying God, who granted him the liberty to choose and the responsibility of choice. In throwing himself passionately into all his creative adventures, the adult is obeying God, who has made him in his own image. And in detaching himself from particular things and ephemeral actions, and attaching himself instead to transcendent values, in accepting his human condition, necessarily fragile, temporary, limited, and incomplete, the aged person is still obeying God, who made men "strangers and exiles on the earth" (Hebrews 11:13).[1]

So nobody is saying that this process is going to be easy. But I think you'll agree that in this light and in the context of the story of the gospel, death can in fact be beautiful in its time. Now I don't think I need to remind you that this isn't just a theoretical issue for us. This is one of life's inevitables. As the great philosopher Blaise Pascal reminds us, "We are embarked."[2] In other words, if you are alive, you've already set sail. You're already moving this moment. If all goes according to normal protocols, you will grow a year older every year, and eventually you will come to the time to pass through the door of death. You will either approach that door kicking and screaming, filled with regret and

terror, or you will approach it as the nineteenth-century poet and
novelist George MacDonald does in this beautiful poem:

> Our old age is the scorching of the bush
> By life's indwelling, incorruptible blaze.
> O life, burn at this feeble shell of me,
> Till I the sore singed garment off shall push,
> Flap out my Psyche wings, and to thee rush.[3]

Well, you might ask, what shall we expect when we go through
that door? The Bible tells us that through that one door, there are
two very different experiences. The first experience is what we call
heaven. I don't know what your image of heaven is—if it's like an
eternal, boring church service or sitting in an eternal waiting room
with Muzak playing and clouds floating around. I'd like to help
you get a very different image of heaven by reading for you some
quotes about heaven by some great Christian thinkers.

According to C. S. Lewis, heaven will be above all a place of
joy: "Dance and game are frivolous, unimportant down here; for
'down here' is not their natural place. Here, they are a moment's
rest from the life we were placed here to live. But in this world
everything is upside down. That which, if it could be prolonged
here, would be a truancy, is likest [most like] that which in a better
country is the End of ends. Joy is the serious business of heaven."[4]

The fifth-century Christian philosopher Augustine described it in
words so beautiful that someone should put these words to music:
"There we shall rest and see, see and love, love and praise. This is
what shall be in the end without end. For what other end do we
propose to ourselves than to attain to the kingdom of which there
is no end?"[5] We tend to think of this life as clear, substantial, solid
and the life beyond as hazy, murky, unclear, foggy. But the Apostle
Paul said the exact opposite: "When perfection comes, the imper-
fect disappears. . . . Now we see but a poor reflection as in a mirror; then we shall see face to face. Now I know in part; then I shall
know fully, even as I am fully known."[6]

When Paul was in prison and contemplating his own death, he
described it like this: "I eagerly expect . . . that I will have sufficient courage so that now as always Christ will be exalted in my
body, whether by life or by death. For to me, to live is Christ and
to die is gain. If I am to go on living in the body, this will mean
fruitful labor for me. Yet what shall I choose? I do not know! I am

torn between the two: I desire to depart and be with Christ, which is better by far; but it is more necessary for you that I remain."[7]

And the Apostle John describes something equally wonderful—that at the sight of Jesus Christ, in the presence of his unmitigated brightness and unveiled glory, all the darkness in us will be banished: "How great is the love the Father has lavished on us, that we should be called children of God! And that is what we are! The reason the world does not know us is that it did not know him. Dear friends, now we are children of God, and what we will be has not yet been made known. But we know that when he appears, we shall be like him, for we shall see him as he is. Those who have this hope within them purify themselves, just as he is pure."[8]

Above all, according to Jesus, going through that door can be like coming home, coming to a place where you fit, a place where you belong, a place just right for you: "Do not let your hearts be troubled. Trust in God, trust also in me. In my Father's house are many rooms; if it were not so, I would have told you. I am going there to prepare a place for you."[9]

Now in contrast to this first experience, for some people, when they pass through that door, the experience will be very different. To illustrate, let me lead you on a little thought experiment. Imagine that you have just died and passed through the doorway of death. And you enter heaven. And it is a place of intense brightness, a place fragrant with goodness, a place alive with love. The presence of God seems to pervade everyone and everything, like a light that doesn't shine onto things but rather shines out of everything, everywhere. In this place, people are humble and genuinely interested in others. They are eager to serve one another, and they love to laugh and dance and be free as children. There are no inhibitions. There is nothing to hide. It is a place of true freedom, trust, and intimacy. And even though it is a place of great diversity, with people of all cultures and languages and times retaining all their uniquenesses, it is a place where no one argues, no one fights, no one hates, and no one complains—not because they aren't allowed to but because they don't want to, because they accept and love one another completely. They are fully alive. OK, do you have that picture? Think about how you would feel upon entering that place.

OK. Now I want you to imagine that someone has walked beside you through that doorway of death. And that person has lived his life cramped in hatred and fear, tight in guilt and greed, ingrown in lust and selfishness. He has spent every day of his life complaining and being bitter and blaming others and being ungrateful. He has been suspicious of those different from himself, and he has become an expert at lying and cheating and using others. He is proud, arrogant, unwilling to admit he is wrong, maybe now incapable of doing so. He is so used to getting his own way that he has never been satisfied in any situation unless he is completely in charge. These aren't just the behaviors he has practiced; these are the features of the person he has become. Now, how would that person feel?

Could it be that the very light that seems beautiful to you would seem blinding to him? Could the very warmth of the love of that place that to you is so perfect seem to him horrible? Could the acceptance and love and trust and openness that welcome you seem to him disgusting, weak, terrifying, insipid, or repulsive? Sometimes I wonder if we have it all wrong. Maybe it's not that there are two places beyond the door of death, heaven and hell. Sometimes I wonder if hell is just what heaven feels like for those who haven't learned in this life what this life is intended to teach. I believe with all my heart that God is not willing for even one person to miss out on the joys and glories of heaven. I believe with all my heart that if there is any way for individuals to be rescued from their wrong choices in this life, I believe they will be rescued and redeemed. But I also believe that we have the sober responsibility of realizing this: that, as Pascal said, we are embarked. We are becoming on this side of the door of death the kind of people we will be on the other side.

And for that reason, the reality of death gives us an important gift every day: it reminds us that we can't keep putting off the work of becoming. It tells us to prepare to meet God then by entering into a relationship with him now. It echoes the words of Jesus, "Turn, turn, turn to God . . . because the kingdom of heaven is near." Because someday it will be time to turn in our final exam. Someday the teacher will say, "Time's up. Pencils down." Someday the essay that we have written with our lives will be complete.

What we will have become on this side of the door, that we will be on the other. That fact means that we live every moment at the nexus of peril and possibility.

But I must tell you, I don't think we are ever in a position to judge others. After all, Jesus said that many who are seen as last here will be first there, and many who are first here will be last there. So I don't think it's our business to prognosticate the eternal destinies of anyone else, as a story from C. S. Lewis makes clear. In this story, a soldier has gone through something analogous to the doorway of death. This soldier has served a false god named Tash all his life, and he comes upon a great Lion named Aslan, who represents Christ.

In a narrow place between two rocks there came to meet me a great Lion. The speed of him was like the ostrich, and his size was an elephant's; his hair was like pure gold and the brightness of his eyes, like gold that is liquid in the furnace. . . . In beauty he surpassed all that is in the world, even as the rose in bloom surpasses the dust of the desert. Then I fell at his feet and thought, Surely this is the hour of death, for the Lion (who is worthy of all honor) will know that I have served Tash all my days and not him. Nevertheless, it is better to see the Lion and die than to be [king] of the world and live and not to have seen him. But the Glorious One bent down and touched my forehead with his tongue and said, Son, thou art welcome. But I said, Alas, Lord, I am no son of Thine but the servant of Tash. He answered, Child, all the service thou hast done to Tash, I account as service done to me. Then by reason of my great desire for wisdom and understanding, I overcame my fear and questioned the Glorious One and said, "Lord, is it then true, as the Ape said, that thou and Tash are one?" The Lion growled so that the earth shook (but his wrath was not against me) and said, It is false. Not because he and I are one, but because we are opposites, I take to me the services which thou hast done to him, for I and he are of such different kinds that no service which is vile can be done to me, and none which is not vile can be done to him. Therefore if any man swear by Tash and keep his oath for the oath's sake, it is by me that he has truly sworn, though he know it not, and it is I who reward him. And if any man do a cruelty in my name, then though he says the name Aslan, it is Tash whom he serves and by Tash his deed accepted. Dost thou understand, Child? I said, Lord, thou knowest how much I understand. But I said also (for the truth constrained me), Yes I have been seeking Tash all my days. Beloved, said the Glorious One, unless thy desire had been for me thou wouldst not have sought so long and so truly. For all find what they truly seek.[10]

May you live in this life, and seek in this life, so that you may approach the door of death knowing that yes, even that final departure can be beautiful in its time. Let us pray: *God, I believe in you. Although I can't be certain or prove it scientifically, the second story we considered today makes more sense to me. I want to turn to you now and not put off the work of becoming what you want me to be. I ask for your mercy, God. Please forgive me. I believe Jesus was your way of reaching out to me, and I believe that when he died, he paid for all of my wrongs. So I come to you, and ask you to accept me, just as I accept you into my life now. I want to follow you in this life and be with you forever. Amen.*

---

o

As I said, I listened to his tape several times. It both inspired and bothered me. I wasn't sure why, but I felt my theology torquing tighter each time I listened to it. We'd have a lot to talk about next time we met.

GETTING BEYOND RIGHTEOUSNESS

IT WAS A PERFECT October Sunday afternoon, October 10, 1999. (I remember the exact date because of what happened the following day, which I will tell you about in due time.) Incredible sky, clear and blue. White clouds. A bit chilly, in the low sixties, too cool for a short-sleeved shirt without a sweater. Sun so bright you'd need either sunglasses or a baseball cap to enjoy the game. Neo picked me up and showed me his cooler full of fixings for a picnic lunch before the game. We were going to meet a few of his fellow teachers, along with some students and their parents, at the stadium parking lot. He had the details all worked out—we'd find each other by using cell phones.

On the way to the game, I wanted to pick up another line of discussion from our walk along the Potomac two weeks earlier. Traffic was terrible, so it looked like we'd have plenty of time to talk.

"Neo, I listened to your tape, and I liked it."

"Why do I think a but is about to be said?" Neo asked, with a big smile.

"No buts," I said, ". . . but—" and immediately we both laughed. "OK, there is a but. I just can't imagine preaching that sermon in my church without being called a heretic and getting fired. That's the kind of thing that makes me think I should give it up and become a high school teacher."

"Please don't make it sound like high school teaching is the repository for failed preachers!" Neo said, laughing. "Some of us find it a great place to serve God and our neighbors! But seriously, what parts were most troublesome?" Neo asked.

I answered, "Well, that C. S. Lewis story, for one. It goes into that whole subject of other religions that we talked about on our long walk—which I still haven't fully recovered from, by the way."

"Recovered from the walk physically or spiritually?" he asked.

"Or from my freaking out emotionally. Either way—take your pick," I answered. "Back to the tape, it sounded like you were saying that everyone goes to the same place, heaven, but experiences it differently, when Scripture makes it clear that there two roads and two destinations, two different destinations."

Neo laughed: "Well, now you know why that was one of my last sermons! I tried to be more forthcoming on my way out! But seriously, Dan, don't you think that all of the language about heaven and hell is evocative language, not technical description? I know that moderns don't have much capacity for poetry, having been enslaved to modern technical correctness for so long. But Jesus—Jesus was allowed to be evocative in his language. Shouldn't we—or should I say, shouldn't you, as a pastor?"

"Maybe it should be that way, but I think my people would take *evocative* as *provocative!* As I said, if I talked about that sort of thing, I'd have people calling me, writing me letters, leaving the church saying I'm not biblical," I said.

Neo suddenly appeared peeved. "That's not fair! In those terms, even the Bible isn't 'biblical,' for heaven's sake! I mean, Jesus was scandalously risky with his language. He compared God to an unjust judge and an unfair boss. He held up a crooked steward as an example of the kingdom. He said that prostitutes would enter the kingdom before the Bible scholars. Where are these people coming from, calling themselves Christians but not allowing their pastors to use language in nontechnical ways? Man, no wonder you want to change professions! Spiritual realities *require* risky language, unless you think they can be reduced to little formulas and formulations. But I guess modern folk do think just that."

I asked Neo how people responded when he preached that sermon. He said, "Well, actually, exactly as you predicted. It was maddening. I remember getting four or five critical letters. But I also got a note from a woman who told me her brother and husband—church-averse people— had happened to attend church that day with her, and they talked about the sermon all week. She said it really got through to them. I had another woman come up to me in tears, telling me that she felt freer to love God after that sermon than she ever had in her life. She told me she wanted to get up and applaud when it was over. It's hard to live with the mixed reviews, isn't it?" I said, "That's for sure."

Neo continued, "And you know what frustrates me even more? By nitpicking like that, the poor people missed the whole point of the sermon! That God is real! That he is the ultimate reality we will face when we die! That we will all be held accountable—Christians and non-Christians!

And that the accountability isn't to some trivial list of petty rules but to the ultimate reality of the Being of God, in all God's glory and compassion and goodness. I mean, didn't you love that C. S. Lewis story? Doesn't that just make you want to worship God?"

I told him that it really did move me. It was ironic how many people liked to read C. S. Lewis at home, but somehow, when his ideas or approach are taken into the pulpit at church, they get nervous. We sat in silence for a few minutes. Neo turned on a classical music station—it was playing Aaron Copeland's "Lincoln Portrait," one of my favorite pieces. I felt like Neo had gotten pretty worked up and needed to calm down a bit, so I didn't say anything for quite a while longer. Then I asked him, "Why do you think church people get so tense, so inflexible? I mean, they don't start out that way."

"I gave up trying to figure that one out, my friend. What do you think?" he said.

"I guess . . . I guess they get to feeling like I felt when I blew up at you. I guess they come to religion for some certainty, some clarity, some simplicity. I guess they react when the thing they're counting on for stability starts shaking them up instead of consoling them, calming them." This was all dawning on me just as I said it. I went on: "I think a lot of them are afraid, just like I was, and actually, to be fair, they have some legitimate concerns. They're afraid of heresy and sin creeping into the camp. So they want to keep everything safe, sanitized."

Neo said, "You're making a lot of sense today, Dan. Keep talking."

"It really *is* a legitimate concern, you know. It's a real struggle for me, and for my church. How do we remain open and accepting of people, without compromising and condoning sin? We really struggle with that," I said.

"Thank God you have that struggle," Neo said, "That's the kind of struggle every church should have, because it means you're dealing with real people, real issues. Everyone isn't just pretending to have it all together."

"Yes, and that's where it gets messy," I responded. "For example, we have many cohabiting, unmarried couples attending our church, and we welcome them, even though we believe that sexual relationships should be reserved for marriage."

"So whether cohabitation is right or wrong," he said, "you agree that you have to accept them where they are, just as Jesus did. You'd agree that you have to start where they are so you can help them move on morally." I suppose he was asking me a question, although it didn't sound like it.

"Yes," I said, "but it gets pretty complicated sometimes. I tell our people that we don't expect non-Christians to act like Christians, and we don't expect new Christians to act like mature Christians, and that helps, but it's still tough to function with people playing by different sets of rules."

He replied, "I know that must be messy, but it sounds a lot like the early church. Talk about complicated, and talk about different sets of rules! You had kosher and nonkosher, vegetarians and nonvegetarians, circumcised and uncircumcised—the same kind of complexity. No wonder love is such a theme in the New Testament! Without love, they would have torn each other apart! So maybe that complexity and messiness is a sign that you're continuing in the spirit of the early church."

Neo interrupted his train of thought to point out some particularly beautiful trees in their fall colors. Then he continued, "But let's be realistic. Let's play it out. Let's say that most modern churches can't or won't handle that complexity. Let's say they won't accept anyone into their fellowship who does not already live by their moral code. Where does that lead?"

"Well, Neo, if God wants to enfold people into communities of faith, I guess he'll have to raise up new communities elsewhere."

"OK," he said, "and where will that leave your evangelical descendants?"

I almost shuddered: "Gosh, maybe a hundred years from now, the descendants of my fellow evangelicals today will be like the Amish of tomorrow, but instead of maintaining 1850s German culture, they'll perpetuate 1950s American culture. They'll still be thriving, or at least surviving, but as a kind of separated society."

"I think that's a real possibility," he said, "and although it is pretty limiting, it's not such a bad future, really. The fact is, the Amish have an important role in our society. By their very separation, they proclaim a kind of unspoken message to our whole culture."

I interrupted, "Hey, Neo, my descendants could become a tourist destination! You know—instead of 'let's go to Lancaster County to see the Amish,' it will be 'let's go to Wheaton, Illinois, or Colorado Springs or Orange County to see the evangelicals!'"

Neo joined in the humor: "That could be a very happy future for the evangelicals—perpetually preserving the 1950s, when civilization was at its highest!"

I reminded Neo that the 1950s were before my time, and he said, "Ouch, ouch!" and mimed taking a knife out of his heart. Then I got a bit more serious and said, "But Neo, you can't really mean it when you say that becoming like the Amish is 'not a bad future.' I know that you believe that Christians ought to be in touch with their times and their culture. I mean, you dance and watch MTV and drink Pete's Wicked Ale! You live as a very integrated member of contemporary society. And speaking of the Amish, you even attended an Amish Jellies concert!"

He groaned at another bad pun of sorts. "Yes, you're right. But Dan, I can still appreciate a calling very different from mine. Isn't it possible that God could have a special mission for the Amish (besides making great jellies!) and an equally special mission for people like you and me who live very differently? Does one have to be wrong and the other right? I mean, it's right there in the Bible—the sons of Rechab in the Old Testament and John the Baptist in the New served God by being total abstainers from alcohol, and Jesus served God by turning water into wine. Talk about complexity!"

I wasn't used to being around someone who was every bit as fluent in biblical references as I was. It took me a second to recall who the "sons of Rechab" were. Neo was still talking: "That's another problem with the modern view of sin: it wants to make everything simple, universal, uniform, black and white. Life isn't that simple, man. Sin isn't that simple."

"Maybe we'd better switch the radio to one of the religious stations," I said, half-joking. I tried to imitate a southern-style preacher: "Why, brother, you need a serious dose of good old-time hellfire and damnation preaching so you'll know that a sin is a sin is a sin!"

Neo didn't laugh. "Actually, Dan, I don't consider sin something to joke about. One of the most dangerous things in the world—maybe even *the* most dangerous—is to redefine sin to suit our own tastes. I hope I'm as concerned about sin as any radio preacher. The fact is, I think that our radio preacher types don't take sin nearly seriously enough."

At this point we pulled into the stadium parking lot. I was surprised how the old RFK stadium, once home to the Redskins, had gone downhill since a new stadium had been built. There was knee-high grass in the cracks in the blacktop, and kudzu vine was creeping across the parking lot from the edges. Neo pulled out his ever-present Palm Pilot from his windbreaker pocket and looked up the mobile phone numbers of his friends. It was kind of funny to watch him with his Palm in one hand, trying to read the numbers, and his phone in the other, trying to punch in the numbers with his thumb and make the calls. I made a comment about how paper and pencil might have been easier to read; he gave me a look and then went back to his calling. One by one he reached his friends and told them where to find us when they arrived—Area K, Row 9. We rolled down the windows—did I mention how beautiful the day was?—and continued talking.

"Dan, I meant what I said a few minutes ago. I think the view of sin given us by our modern Christian heritage was well-meaning and sincere but downright dangerous." I asked him for some examples. "OK. We've been talking about sexual issues. Back in the Gospel of John—and I know there's a textual issue, but let's ignore that for the moment—who was the greater sinner, the woman caught in adultery or the Pharisee holding a stone ready to execute her?"

I avoided a direct answer: "What's your point?"

"How much energy do we modern Christians put into condemning sexual sins compared to avoiding the judgmental, Pharisaical attitude of those with rocks in their hands? Who killed Jesus, adulterers or Pharisees? I'm not trying to minimize adultery—believe me, I know how terrible it is. I'm just saying that our modern preoccupations don't seem very informed by the gospel. Dan, you're a pastor, and I used to be one. We know better than most people how ugly that Pharisee stuff is!"

"You don't have to tell me." The fact was, earlier that week I had received a stunningly harsh, hurtful letter from a member of my congregation, a lifelong churchgoer who could have served as the poster child for what we were talking about. Her letter to me was hurtful enough, but since writing it she had been calling people in the congregation and was sowing a lot of discord. Rumor had it that three or four families were thinking about leaving the church because of the imbroglio. ("I'm concerned about the spiritual integrity of our leadership," "I hope you'll pray about this with me," "I just want to be sure we're anchored solidly in the Word"—I can just imagine what she said to them.)

All this was racing through my mind as I said to Neo, with sadness, "I have never been treated as badly by a single non-Christian—except the one who held me up at gunpoint once—as I have by dozens of zealous but angry Christians. In my saner moments, I realize they're just human beings and they're doing the best they can. But the religious arrogance and rigidity are . . ." I didn't finish the sentence.

Neo took off his sunglasses and rubbed his eyes. "The whole judgmental thing is so contrary to the Spirit of Christ. But I think that's just the tip of the iceberg. An even deeper problem, I think, is how modern individualism has truncated our view of sin." I asked him what he meant. He suggested that we keep talking outside the car. He wanted his friends to be able to find us when they arrived. He reached under his seat and pulled out the old faded red cap I'd seen him wear on our walk.

"Good idea, with the bright sun," I said, still thinking that the hat just wasn't him.

We were standing behind the car as he continued. "Dan, modernity had a great insight: every individual is valuable and deserves respect. But our individualism has become unbalanced, and we have lost the realization of how connected we are. Can I get a little philosophical on you?" I said sure, a soccer stadium parking lot was as good as anyplace to talk philosophy. "OK. As we cross the postmodern border, we still see individuals as important, but we don't see them as isolated monads any more."

"Monads?" I asked. "Is that a Jamaican term? Or is that a Ph.D. in philosophy term?"

Neo winked but didn't want to lose his train of thought, so he continued, "Think of it like this: a huge part of who you are flows from language, but language isn't something that you possess as an isolated monad—or isolated *individual*. It is something bigger than you, bigger than the two of us. Beyond language, our whole culture creates a fabric or canvas on which our individual identities develop, and again, our culture is bigger than all of us. The civilization, the cultures, the tribes, the families we are part of, they all define so much of who we are. The same language, the same culture runs through our veins, our circuitry. We are far more connected than we realize."

I replied, "OK, I'm with you. So what does this have to do with sin?"

"It has everything to do with sin. The only kinds of sin we want to focus on as modern Christians are the isolated individual sins committed by isolated individual monads: lying, having an abortion, indulging in pornography, taking drugs, saying naughty words. Not to minimize those things in any way, but that is far short of a fully biblical understanding of sin, and it leads to dangerous truncations of justice and compassion."

"I'm sorry, I'm not with you anymore, Neo. You lost me there."

He folded his arms, leaned back against the car trunk, and looked into the sky, thinking hard, squeezing his eyes shut. "OK. Let me try again. Let's say we've got a black teenager in the inner city who just swiped the purse of a white secretary to get money for his drug habit. That's definitely a sin, right? OK. A new kind of Christian will agree, but he won't stop there. He'll also want to look at the ways that the woman who is victimized by his crime actually contributes to the system that produces desperate teenage drug addicts. It's a systems thing."

I didn't buy it. "That sounds like a lot of liberal tripe, Neo." I imitated his accent by stretching *liberal* into three syllables. I'm not sure why I did that. Was I mocking him? "What has that woman ever done to that drug addict?"

He replied, "That's exactly my point, Reverend Poole. She hasn't done anything. Ten years ago this violent drug addict was a kid, stuck in the city with nothing to do and not much hope for the future. He was just a kid, Dan, a lot like me growing up in Port Maria or Kingston or Elizabeth. To use Jesus' words, the boy was her neighbor, and he was in need, and she succeeded in crossing to the other side of the road for all of her life. She has succeeded in being like the priest and Levite in Jesus' parable of the Good Samaritan. Everybody knows the robber is bad—but doesn't Jesus also imply an indictment on the priest and Levite? In other words, think of our line again. . . ."

He turned around and drew a line in the dust on the trunk of his car. "The priest and Levite are over here. They are 'righteous' in a superficial way. They don't rob anybody. They're not like that lousy criminal who is over here, on the bad end of the line. Do you see it? That's the line we modern Christians try to live on the right end of, but in Jesus' story the answer isn't on the line at all. The answer—again—is *up here,* moving above the line altogether. The Samaritan traveler lives on a higher level altogether. The issue isn't who is wrong or righteous; that's obvious. The issue is who is truly *good.*"

Now Neo was getting into a cadence, the same cadence I heard on his tape. Each of the next sentences got a little louder in volume, a little higher in pitch. I couldn't help it: I started saying, "Amen, amen!" and that sort of thing after each phrase. Was I playing, or was I sincere? Maybe both—it didn't seem to matter.

He continued. "To be truly good means more than not robbing people. [Amen.] To be truly good means more than being righteously religious. [Yes. Amen!] To be truly good means being a good neighbor. [That's right.] And to be a good neighbor means recognizing that there are ultimately no strangers. [Preach on.] Everybody is my neighbor! [Amen!] Everybody is my brother! [Yes, Lord!] There are no isolated monads wounded on the other side of the street! [Amen!] We're all connected!"

At that moment we spontaneously faced each other and said "Hallelujah!" and exchanged a high-five, and then started laughing so hard we both doubled over.

Eventually we stopped laughing and returned to our previous positions, leaning against the trunk, arms folded, enjoying the October sun. Neo said, "Seriously, Dan, modern Christianity has too often acted as if the only kind of righteousness that mattered was the kind of righteousness of the scribes and Pharisees—the righteousness of nice, clean, legalistic monads who managed to stay disconnected and disinfected on the other side of the street. Maybe that's better than swiping pocketbooks; I don't know.

But it's still down here on this line." He turned and pointed to the line he'd drawn in the dust on his trunk. "It it's a far cry below what Jesus is all about—up here."

Just then, three other cars pulled up full of people waving at Neo, and he only had time to add, "At least that's how I see it. I hope that a new kind of Christian will try to transcend that level of understanding of sin."

I was thinking of the place in the Sermon on the Mount where Jesus said the goodness of his followers would have to exceed that of the scribes and Pharisees. But I didn't get a chance to say anything more because Neo was already shaking hands and greeting his friends through open car windows and even a sunroof. Within a few minutes, cars were parked, tailgates were down, coolers were out, lawn chairs were set out, a CD player was booming with Bob Marley singing "Every Little Thing," and people were eating and laughing, throwing Frisbees and footballs. I went over and started joining in the party. I hadn't had that much fun in a long time. We had so much fun in the parking lot that we didn't make it to our seats until the game was well under way and DC United had scored two goals. The game was great, and United won, 7–6. I wasn't a connoisseur of soccer games, but everyone agreed it was a classic. (I wondered if it would soon be playing on videotape at the sports bar in Takoma Park.)

12

FRENCH FRIES AND THE KINGDOM OF GOD

IT WAS DARK when we reached Neo's car after the game. The moon was visible through a thin tissue of clouds. I was chilly, and it was the first time that fall that people turned on their car heaters. As we waited behind long lines of red brake lights, we enjoyed a couple of minutes of silence.

I broke it. "Neo." "Yes?" "You love those people, don't you?" "Well, I hope that doesn't seem too remarkable." "It's more remarkable than you think."

I told him that I seldom felt as comfortable with non-Christians as he seemed to be. All afternoon, I kept thinking of Jesus at Matthew's house, partying with all of the "tax collectors and sinners." Jesus seemed to extend complete acceptance toward them. Neo seemed to do the same toward his friends. I found that remarkable.

"Dan, why wouldn't I extend acceptance to them? They're people God loves, people Jesus gave his life for, unspeakably precious. They're my neighbors, my friends. I don't even think of them as Christians or non-Christians. I just think of them as people I love."

"But Neo, somehow, the way I am a Christian, the way I've always been a Christian, I think that I am always *supposed to* be thinking in those terms. You know, I wish I didn't always categorize—oh, he's in, she's out—because, as you've said, it creates a division between me and other people. But this issue, this in-out distinction, is always there, even if we don't talk about it. And when we talk about it, it only gets worse. But it's not that way with you," I said.

He replied, "It used to be. I always used to feel so tense when I was with people from outside the church. I guess there was always this threat in the air—either I was going to be pulled down by their bad behavior, or else I was going to judge them and preach to them. It was unpleasant for both sides. I felt tense, and they probably did too. I don't feel that way anymore at all, but I do know what you're talking about."

"Don't you ever try to witness about your faith to them?" I asked. "I mean, isn't there a time when friendship evangelism has to move on to the evangelism?"

"Pardon me, Daniel, but I am not too fond of that expression, 'friendship evangelism.' It can prostitute friendship, which in my mind then invalidates the evangelism. If I'm going to pretend to be somebody's friend just so I can try to proselytize them, well, I might as well be selling soap. No, it's worse than that. At least when I'm selling soap, I'm not degrading the soap by exploiting the friendship. I can't tell you how much that term bothers me."

"OK, I see your point. But Neo, won't a new kind of Christian be concerned about sharing the gospel?" I asked.

"It's funny you should say that. Remember when you were over with the Roths eating watermelon? Did you notice where I was?"

"Yes, you were talking to that woman, the one who chain-smoked, and—was that her daughter?"

"Yes, Melissa is one of my students, and that was her mother, Marita. Marita came up to thank me for something, and before you know it, we were in a deep talk about God. In fact, I'm picking them up for church next Sunday."

"Neo, I don't want to pry, but it would really help me to get an idea of how your conversation went. I'm trying to imagine what postmodern friendship evangelism—oops, sorry—looks like."

He replied, "Well, Marita thanked me for taking Melissa to the science fair finals last spring. She's a single mom and has to work weekends, and she felt terrible that she had to miss her daughter's big day, especially because Melissa won second place for a great science project on astronomy. Then we started talking about astronomy, and I said that nothing makes me feel the presence of God more than a star-studded night sky. Then she asked me if I was a 'born-again'. Then she said—"

"What did *you* say?" I interrupted.

"I never know how to answer that born-again question. Obviously, in the way Jesus used the term, I would want to say yes. But to some people, the question means 'Are you a judgmental, arrogant, narrow-minded, bigoted religious fanatic?' I remember one of my students once told me that he wanted to be a true follower of Christ, but he hoped he never became born-again. I asked him why, and he told me about another student who used to be a really nice person, but then she became a born-again, and now she is always criticizing everyone and has become so negative and stuck up, nobody can stand her. So the term has been pretty much ruined by modern Christianity."

"What does that have to do with modernity?" I asked.

"Well, I don't have to tell you this. Jesus originally used that term in a profound personal conversation with a sincere Pharisee. In that unique context, it meant a total reversal of everything Nicodemus assumed about what being religious was all about. It meant a radical humbling, a going back to the beginning, becoming a little child rather than a big religious scholar. The richness of that conversation is just mind-blowing. In fact, it's really a study in the intentional use of ambiguity. But in typical modern fashion, we turn a profound and unique image into a simple, universal, mechanical formula and a superficial slogan, and it becomes part of a slick sales pitch, and we mass market it everywhere. So now 'Are you a born-again?' means 'Have you said a little prayer at the end of a booklet?' Don't get me started on this, Dan, or you'll really get me wound up."

"It's too late for that," I said. "You're already wound up. What did you say? How did you answer her?"

He said, "I hope I answered her the way Jesus would have. I answered her with a question. I asked her why she wanted to know. She said that she was brought up going to church but dropped out after her divorce and really wanted to feel closer to God again. But her brother is a 'fanatical born-again,' in her words, and she didn't want to become a fanatic like him. I told her it was wonderful that she wanted to get closer to God and asked if I could be of help in any way. Nothing very complicated or profound. She said thanks, that she would let me know. I said that if she ever wanted to go to church with me, I'd be glad to take her. And she immediately asked for the time and where she should meet me."

"Why didn't you share the gospel with her?" I asked.

"Oh, boy. I don't think you're going to like this, Dan," he answered. I gave him a kind of shrug, which invited him to go on. "OK, you asked for it. Dan, I don't think that most Christians have any idea what the gospel really is." He paused, and I saw it coming: "For example, how would you define the gospel?" I said something about accepting Christ as your personal savior and justification by grace through faith, not by our works, based on the finished work of Christ on the cross, and he said, "Yes, that's exactly what most modern Christians would say." I protested, and he said, "Does it bother you that Jesus never defined the gospel in this way? And does it bother you that no Christians in history ever used the phrase 'accept Christ as your personal savior' until a few decades ago? Does it bother you that our little gospel presentations are really just modern sales pitches that reduce the gospel to modern dimensions—laws, steps, simple diagrams, complete with a sales close?" I felt a bit embarrassed and intimidated; this was the closest Neo had come to being pushy since our walk along the Potomac. My tone was intentionally calming: "OK, then, how would *you* define the gospel?"

Neo said that it couldn't be reduced to a little formula, other than the one Jesus used, which was "The Kingdom of God is at hand," and he didn't recommend using that exact language today. I asked why not.

"Dan, everything is contextual. No meanings can exist without context. Language only works in a context, since words mean different things at different times. In Jesus' day, the biggest issue was that the Jewish people were subordinated to the Roman Empire. This was agonizing for them: How could good people who truly believed in the One True God be under the heel of bad people who believed in a pathetic pantheon of little false deities? Jesus' use of the expression 'kingdom of God' in that context is so dynamic and full of meaning that even though I see only a little sliver of it, I can hardly put it into words."

We were finally out of the parking lot traffic jam and onto the highway. I asked him to keep going. "OK. The biggest, most powerful reality in those days is the regime of Caesar. Jesus comes along and basically says that Caesar is no big deal at all; the real big deal is the regime of God, the empire of God. And not only that, he says that the kingdom of God is right here, right at hand." I told him that in all my readings, I had never heard it put that way. "Of course not," he said. "Remember, modernity only wants abstract principles, universal concepts, and disembodied absolutes. So we take an expression like 'the kingdom of God' and try to give it meaning without any context. Postmodern theology has to reincarnate; we have to get back into the flesh and blood and sweat and dirt of the setting, because as I said, all truth is contextual. If the Bible teaches anything, it teaches that. After all, there's no 'First, Second, and Third Trinity' or 'Book of Moral Absolutes' or anything like that. Instead, there are letters and prophecies, all with a specific address, a specific time, a specific context. The word of the Lord always comes to a specific somebody, in a specific somewhere, at some specific time. But with the kingdom, we've only scratched the surface of all the meaning that's there."

Neo had taken an exit and pulled into a McDonald's. "Do you want to go in or eat in the car?" I preferred going inside, so we continued our conversation over quarter-pounders. I asked him to get back to the stuff about the kingdom. "Dan," he said, "by using that expression as the centerpiece of his teaching, Jesus was also doing something very risky. He was playing with the expectations of the people. Remember—John says that once the people wanted to make him king by force? He was flirting with all of their dreams for a great superhuman deliverer who would fight the Romans, expel them with a show of force, and reestablish the security, fortune, and status of the true people of God. Jesus walks right into the middle of their expectations and just blows those expectations to pieces."

I had unconsciously moved to the edge of my seat. I jumped in: "You're right. Maybe that's why Peter is so upset when Jesus wants to wash his feet—that's no way for a great king to act. And maybe that's why he pulls out his sword there in the garden. Maybe he assumes it's finally time for the showdown between the forces of King Jesus and King Caesar."

Now Neo was on the edge of his seat too. He started talking with his hands. "Yes, Dan, and that's why, I think, that Matthew, who is writing most specifically for a Jewish audience, decides to alter the language. Instead of talking about the kingdom of God, he uses a different expression, 'kingdom of heaven.'"

"Oh, I get it. Matthew is emphasizing the spiritual nature of the kingdom."

"Yes, but no, well . . . context is everything. We hear 'kingdom of heaven' and we think 'kingdom of life after death.' But that's the very opposite of what Jesus is talking about. Remember—he says repeatedly, the kingdom of God, the kingdom of heaven, has arrived! It's near, here, at hand, among you! It's not just about after you die; it's about here, now, in this life!"

Neo's enthusiastic volume was drawing stares, and we both laughed. He lowered his voice. "It's perfect. The kingdom of God is not about geography. It's like the air. Remember, the word for heaven back then meant, among other things, 'above the ground,' as in 'the birds of the heavens,' another phrase Jesus used. It's a kingdom that transcends all earthbound geography, all human borders. It surrounds us like the air, the wind; it's unseen but real. To exclude it is like a two-year-old holding his breath in a temper tantrum. To receive it is as simple as . . . receiving it. I mean, it's beautiful!"

At that moment, sitting there in a McDonald's, with the glossy bright yellow and red and white paint around us, with the grease of french fries on our fingertips—at that moment I had one of those revelations that come a few times in life, if you're fortunate. "Kingdom of the heavens—a kingdom that is higher than the earth. Neo, it's just like your line in the dust! The Kingdom of God transcends the normal level of discourse. I get it! It's up here"—I started circling with my hand, palm down, a foot above the table—"not down here!" I said, drawing a line of french fry grease on the table. Now I was the one almost shouting, and again the stares came from the nearby tables, and again Neo and I shared a moment of slightly embarrassed laughter. We lifted our chocolate shakes in a toast and laughed like little boys.

When we got in the car, I felt a kind of sustained elation. It was a feeling of fullness. It was as if I had become a Christian all over again, as if I were "getting it" for the first time. I don't know why, but there was one question on my mind, which I raised as we pulled out onto 95: "So Neo, how will you explain the gospel to this woman, what was her name, Melissa?"

"That's the daughter. Marita is the mother. Well, we'll see what happens. I'll introduce her to the church, and she'll experience some degree of Christian community—because that's an important dimension of the gospel. Maybe we'll invite her to come on the short-term mission trip we're planning, and through it all, we'll engage in conversation, and I'm sure God will lead the whole thing along. It's a natural process, really."

"You'll talk to her about the kingdom of God, then?" I asked.

He shrugged: "That depends. I mean, I'm not trying to say that kingdom language is the only right language to use. The fact is, if Jesus were here today, I'm not sure he would use that terminology at all. Maybe, since commerce is a bigger deal in the postmodern world than governments, maybe he would talk about the 'enterprise of God.' Or maybe, with the whole Internet revolution, he would talk about the 'web of God' or the 'network of God.' Or maybe he would emphasize the idea of family—you know, the 'family of God.' Or maybe with the rise in film and music as the dominant art forms, it would be the 'story of God' or the 'adventure of God' or the 'music of God.' Probably he would do a little bit of all of these. That's the wonderful thing about life: it's hard to escape images and metaphors for spiritual realities. After all, the whole show is God's creation. It's all God's idea, God's work of art. And don't worry, Dan, at some point I'm sure we'll talk about justification by grace though faith too, along with the atoning death of Christ and all the other doctrines our good evangelical brothers and sisters think constitute the whole gospel. Because obviously they are important parts of the story. But the story itself is bigger and more important than any doctrine or theory we lift out of it or impose on it. As long as the conversation continues, I'm sure we'll explore more and more dimensions of the many-faceted gospel."

"You use the word *conversation* a lot," I observed.

"Actually, if there's one thing I wish I could tell every Christian about evangelism in the postmodern world," he replied, "it would be about that word. I would say to stop counting conversions, because our whole approach to conversion is so, I don't know, mechanistic and consumeristic and individualistic and controlling. Instead, I'd encourage us to count conversations, because conversation implies a real relationship, and if we make our goal to establish relationships and engage in authentic conversations, I know that conversions will happen. But if we keep trying to convert people, we'll simply drive them away. They're sick of our sales pitches and our formulas."

Stop counting conversions and start counting conversations, I mused to myself. I thought about the gospels, which are not a series of sales pitches but a series of unique conversations. I thought about the elation I felt at "getting" the idea of the kingdom of God, maybe for the first time in my life, even though I'm a pastor. I thought about what it would be like to help others get it. And then I thought, *How ironic. I'm a pastor, and in spite of all my talk, talk, talk, I feel like I've never really gotten it myself, much less helped anybody else.*

Too quickly, we were in front of my home. It was late, and everyone inside was asleep.

As I opened the car door to get out, Neo said, "Oh, no!"

"What's wrong?" I asked.

"My Palm Pilot. It's not in my pocket, and it's not under the car seat. I think it must have fallen out at the game. Gosh, I can't afford another one, and all my information is in there. I need it for school tomorrow. I'll have to go back for it. Shoot."

I offered to go with him, but he insisted it wasn't necessary: "You preached two sermons this morning. Get some sleep. You deserve it." So he sped off, and I said goodbye. That was the last I saw him.

SPIRITUAL PRACTICES: SECRET AND SHARED

IT WAS MONDAY AFTERNOON, October 11. Jess got a ride home from school with a friend, so she arrived earlier than if she had taken the bus. I was sitting at the computer in our home office, answering e-mails. I heard the predictable after-school rhythm: front door squeaks open and slams shut, books hit floor, voice announces "I'm home!" But instead of "I'm home," I heard, "Dad, Dad! Where are you?" When she came into the office, she was out of breath. "Dad, did you hear about Dr. Oliver?"

"No, what, honey?"

"He's gone. He had to leave the country or something. I heard he went to Syria or somewhere. Mr. MacIlvine is taking over the soccer team. I don't think Dr. Oliver's coming back."

"That's crazy! I was just with him last night. What happened?"

"I don't know, but our whole season is down the tubes. I can't believe this is happening!"

I called his home number. No answer. I rummaged around and found his cell phone number. Two rings and then an answer. "Neo, where are you? My daughter is really upset—she said you're gone for the rest of the year or something."

"Dan, I'm at O'Hare in Chicago. I'm going to Seattle, where my parents live—where my mom lives. Dan, my father died last night, I guess while we were at the game, and my mother has Alzheimer's disease. Without him to take care of her, well, I'm the only one who can pick up and be there for her. My brother lives in California, and he has kids and . . . I'm more upset than anybody about having to leave so suddenly. I can't believe this is happening. I didn't get home last night until nearly four in the morning—never did find my Palm—and the call from the hospital was waiting for me. I haven't slept all night. I got a six o'clock flight out of BWI. I'm barely keeping it together." Then there was something like a cough or maybe a muffled sob.

We talked for a few more minutes while he waited for his connecting flight. I spend a lot of time at O'Hare myself, so I could picture right where he was as we talked—near the Starbucks at the C gates. He sounded like he was on the verge of tears. I tried to offer some comfort. I asked some questions and listened. Then they called his flight. "I've got to go," he said. "But Dan, I want to keep our conversation going. I've got my laptop. We can communicate by e-mail. My address is neoliver@fdrhs.edu. Send me a message and I'll respond. OK?" I said OK but was a little surprised he was thinking about staying in touch with me at a time like this.

It took a few days for him to get affairs settled. By Thursday the funeral was over and he was learning how serious his mother's illness was. Meanwhile, Neo and I had established contact online, and e-mail became our new mode of communication.

When Neo responded to my initial e-mail, it was as if our relationship instantly went to a deeper level. I was intrigued by this: as soon as he was so physically distant, we seemed to get closer. Somehow it seemed unavoidable to be more personal and open with each other via e-mail. It was as if the educator-Ph.D.-mentor took off his gray suit and Oxford shirts and started conversing in a sweatshirt, gym shorts, and bare feet. I'm sure part of it was the emotional vulnerability of grief that softened him, but I'm also sure that part of it was the medium of e-mail.

In one of our first exchanges, for example, Neo told me that in the previous few months I had become one of his best friends. In my response, I told him the same. It felt like a long time since I had said to anyone, "You are my friend." Maybe since I was a boy. I felt closer to Neo at this time than I had when he was across the table from me or walking along a path or standing a foot away leaning against the trunk of his car. I guess we moved beyond being rational conversation partners talking about theology and ministry to being two men in the middle of life with all its craziness and grief too.

Early the next week, Neo asked me if I'd go to his townhouse and handle some of his loose ends there. He sent me a key by overnight mail so I could pick up his mail, forward his bills and his financial files, and maybe help him find a renter to move in. During that time, we were online two or three times a day. Since he was taking care of his mother all the time, and since she slept a lot, and since he had little use for TV (and since he didn't have his Palm Pilot to fool around with), I think he lived at his laptop during all his free moments. I was glad to help him, really glad. I felt that somehow I was having the chance to repay him for the positive effect he was having on my faith and my life.

I had never gone through anyone else's personal and financial papers before. It was a strange feeling. One of the things that struck me was Neo's generosity. His teacher's salary was decent (I was finally getting those details I had originally wanted about teaching!), but the number of organizations to which he sent money—beginning with a full 10 percent of his gross income going to St. Tim's, and that was only the beginning— was to me beyond all proportion. Along with the money he sent, it became apparent that he had visited many of the organizations he supported financially; his files were full of personal notes and expense reports from his travels. It was as if he had this secret life going: on the surface, Dr. Neil Oliver, mild-mannered science teacher, but behind the scenes, international philanthropist with connections to an orphanage in Guatemala, a Christian care facility for drug addicts in New Hampshire, a new church being planted in Moscow, a Seattle-based organization trying to liberate children from the most horrible kinds of prostitution in Bangkok, and several more.

I made a remark to him about his financial generosity in one of our e-mail conversations, and I asked him how he could afford to give away so much. He said that when he was very young, in his Brethren assembly back in Jamaica, he had made a vow to God to tithe—give 10 percent of his income—to the church he attended. But through the years he would find himself pulled toward supporting additional charitable endeavors, and so year by year the percentage had crept up. (My estimate was that he was living on about 70 percent of his salary, giving away about 25 percent, and saving 5 percent.) He said that giving was one of his greatest joys in life. When I made some comment that I wished I had more people like him in my church, he sent me a long e-mail urging me to preach on giving more, to really challenge people to give, for their benefit, and for the benefit of the world. He knew that I would feel hesitant to do so because it seemed self-serving for a pastor to ask people to give more, but he told me to get over that. He told me that if he ever went back into the pastorate (this was the first time I had heard him say anything like that), he would lose all of his inhibitions about talking about money because he felt that generosity was one of the most important spiritual disciplines and that greed was one of the soul's worst poisons.

He said that if the new kind of Christianity we had been dreaming about wasn't radically generous, it was a waste of time. I responded by saying that it seemed like an overstatement to me, but he was adamant: "We live in the most affluent culture in the most affluent period of human history. If we can't discipline ourselves to learn the joys of generous living, I think we're an embarrassment to the gospel."

Outside of this brief foray into our beliefs about financial stewardship, all of our e-mail contact during October and November was of a personal nature. I learned a lot about him, more about his marriage and divorce, more about his experiences as a youth pastor and then as a solo pastor, more about the kinds of questions that led to his resignation and departure from church ministry—things I understood all too well, as they mirrored my own misgivings, questions, doubts. He told me how he decided to return to graduate school to study philosophy. He told me more about his favorite philosopher, Polanyi, and made me promise to read him—something I still haven't gotten around to doing.

He wrote often about his love for teaching and how his singleness had allowed him to give more to his students and the whole school community than he could have otherwise, and he was grateful for that, even though he always had hoped to remarry.

Although he never mentioned it directly, it was clear to me how disappointed he was that he heard so little from his fellow teachers and students at Franklin Roosevelt, and his friends at St. Timothy's too. He asked me about the girls' soccer season (I made it to nearly all of Jess's games, thankfully)—and I thought it was sad that he had to ask me for this information. It's strange to have a person you've seen in a kind of two-dimensional way—a teacher, an intellect—begin to take on three dimensions. I might as well admit that on several occasions, his grief, homesickness, and loneliness came through his e-mails so acutely that sympathetic tears fell onto my keyboard.

By early December, Neo seemed eager to resume our theological conversation, as is reflected in the following thread of messages. Let me apologize in advance for the relative incoherence of my e-mails compared to Neo's. For me e-mailing is always squeezed in before or after something else, so it's always rushed. That's my only excuse. When I wanted to talk to Neo in depth, I'd be more likely to reach for the phone than the mouse.

To: danrpoole@backspring.com
From: neoliver@fdrhs.edu
Date: December 3, 1999
Subject: Resuming the Conversation

Good day, Daniel! It's actually sunny in Seattle! Thanks for asking about Mother. She recognizes me about half the time. The rest of the time, she either thinks I'm my dad or she looks at me strangely and seems irritated that I'm here. I had a real time taking her to the doctor yesterday. She wet herself on the way, and I had to come back and dress her all over again. It is truly bizarre having to undress and dress your own mother. When she walks, I have to hold her up because she's so unsteady. The doctor told me she has had a few minor strokes over the last year—my dad never told me about this at all. She sleeps a lot during the day and then gets up and wanders around at night, which is dangerous for both of us. I'm going to have to rig up some kind of bell on a string or something so that when she gets up at night, I'll wake up. Enough about me. How are you doing? What theological mountains are you climbing up (or skiing down!) these days? I miss our talks. Let's resume the conversation!—Neo

To: neoliver@fdrhs.edu
From: danrpoole@backspring.com
Date: December 3, 1999
Subject: Re: Resuming the Conversation

Neo, good to hear from you. All's well here. Been doing some writing—trying to capture some stuff we've talked about. Mainly trying to expand those ten descriptors you gave me—kept all those restaurant placemats! Good stuff. Maybe I'll try to get something published. Others need to hear this. OK with you? Listened again to your tape on death the other day while driving somewhere. Don't want my thinking to shrink back to where it was before meeting you. So glad to "resume the conversation." Don't stop stretching me!

You asked what questions are on my brain. Here goes: How will our way of being Christians change in years ahead? What will new kind of Christian look like? What changes, what remains same? You're the closest I've ever come to seeing a new kind of Christian, so I wonder what you think? I remember what you said about financial generosity, but what other areas of change are coming?

BTW, Carol tells me I haven't been sighing so much lately. Not taking as many mental vacations to New Mexico either!—Dan

To: danrpoole@backspring.com
From: neoliver@fdrhs.edu
Date: December 4, 1999
Subject: Update

I just got in from another trip to the doctor. Mom couldn't breathe very well, so I rushed her to the clinic (open Saturdays) and they did an X-ray. They say her heart is slightly enlarged. What next? I managed to get her into Depends before we left, after her accident the other day. Good thing. Sorry to bore you with this sort of thing, but this is my life now.

Regarding your questions—to be honest, I'm a little worried about how you want to keep pushing aside the issue of money. Let me say one more thing about that, so you know why the subject of generosity is so important in my mind. The early Christians had to live in Caesar's world, and Caesar always demanded top allegiance. You know, I'm sure, that the early Christians were killed not for being Christians but for being unpatriotic: they wouldn't worship the gods of Roman civil religion (including Caesar). Have you ever wondered who or what our Caesar is? In my mind—and I feel quite certain about this—it's our economy of consumption, greed, materialism. I think there are many people who are rendering to Caesar everything that is Caesar's, and they are also rendering to Caesar much of what they think they are rendering to God.

Let me give you an example. I am on the mailing list of a Bible college that a graduate from my church's youth group attended back in the '90s. I get all the annual reports and financial appeals. The world is going through a revolution, and this college is in a time warp—stuck in the 1940s or '50s. Why is this? The only conclusion I can come up with is because, really, it is a hostage to money. The institution ultimately exists for two reasons, whatever its mission statement says. It exists first and foremost to keep its staff salaried and to keep its donors satisfied. Whatever they do for students and for the church and for the world must be secondary to that, because if they really cared about their students and the church and the world, they would be doing things very differently. I'm sure they pray, they teach the Bible, and on a personal level they are utterly sincere, but I think they're held captive to Caesar. I don't condemn them for this, but I see their situation as a mirror for my own self-examination.

If that scenario doesn't make sense to you, think about religious broadcasting and all the other organizations that raise money by direct mail. (As you've seen by sorting through my mail, once you get a reputation as a generous person, you end up on a million appeal lists.) Do their priorities reflect the real needs of the real world? Of course not. Their priorities generally reflect what raises money—issues that appeal to fear and guilt, various short-term crises, conspiracy theories about imaginary enemies, simplistic projects that promise a big bang for the buck—or, if they fail, blatant appeals to self-interest. ("Give to our organization THIS MONTH and you will receive back TEN TIMES as much! Glory to God!"—that sort of thing.) Perhaps you will think I'm being too harsh. OK. I'm stepping down from my soapbox.

Other than that, I think we've already talked about the most important areas of change: our understanding of the Bible and how we follow it, how we let it work on us, our posture in relation to other religions, and our understanding of Jesus not as IN the way, keeping people away from God, but AS the way, bringing people to God; our releasing of the ways in which our faith has been enmeshed with modernity, so we can discover what a Christian can be in a postmodern context; our exploration of theology free of the constricting, reductionistic categories of modernity; our escape from the narrowing of the gospel to an individualistic story only about saving souls to a missional, communal, and global story about saving the world.

The only other area I think we haven't talked about much is spirituality, spiritual formation. So important! Somehow I think we have to discover a form of authentic spirituality that is broader than our modern pietism. Do you have any thoughts on this?—Neo

TO: neoliver@fdrhs.edu
FROM: danrpoole@backspring.com
DATE: December 6, 1999
SUBJECT: Hi and 'Bye!

Neo—Sorry for delay. Swamped at church, no time for e-mail. If you have anything urgent, call me by phone, OK? Sorry. Things should slow down soon.—Dan

TO: danrpoole@backspring.com
FROM: neoliver@fdrhs.edu
DATE: December 6, 1999
SUBJECT: No Apology Needed

I forget that the rest of the world has things to do other than change their parent's diapers, cook meals, take occasional trips to the doctor, and write e-mails! My mother sleeps a lot—she's been napping all afternoon today. So I really am living a life of relative ease—except when she's awake, of course. Then my life is like the parent of a toddler's—never a dull moment! So no need to apologize for having a normal life!

I've been thinking more about the subject of spirituality and spiritual formation. I'm reflecting on how I was "discipled" in a conservative evangelical context and what has stayed with me through the years and helped me and what has proved either useless or counterproductive.

One of the first things that strikes me is this: whatever made me more "religious"—by which I mean whatever made me more identified and isolated as a member of a religious subculture—those elements have not served me well in the long run.

The things that helped me connect with God are the things that helped me most. For example, a counselor at a Christian summer camp taught me how to keep a journal—his five-minute explanation sitting on the front porch of a camp cabin enriched my life forever. I think you keep a journal too, right? Journaling and all other spiritual practices done "in secret" seem to me to be essential, especially for people like you who make a living by talking about God.

A tangent—talking about God for pay always threatens to work against really loving God, I'm sure you will agree. The people who talk the most about God are the ones most in danger of taking him for granted, of letting God become just a comfortable word in their lexicon, a piece of furniture, rather than a reality, a friend, a constant surprise. The people who talk the most about loving God are the ones most in danger of being PROUD of how much they love him. The people who speak most vehemently against sin are the most in danger of feeling superior to those whose sins they excoriate, thus falling prey to an even more horrible, subtle species of sin. And since they preach so hard against sin, they are also the most in danger of yielding to the temptation to hide the sins they themselves commit.

So getting paid to love God can make it hard to love God. That's why I believe that whatever new kinds of Christian spirituality and spiritual formation may be about, they should focus us on the practices "done in secret" that no one sees.

One other thought, and then I should go wake up Mother (otherwise she'll be up all night). Since—as we've said before—postmodern is post-Protestant, I think that our forms of spirituality and spiritual formation will be more like the ancient and medieval church and less like the modern church. I think we may welcome back tradition and saints and liturgy and holy days. Does that make any sense? Must go—sounds like Mom is waking up.—Neo

TO: danrpoole@backspring.com
FROM: neoliver@fdrhs.edu
DATE: December 6, 1999
SUBJECT: P.S.

A quick follow-up to the previous note, which I had to finish prematurely.

I just had a most wonderful experience with my mother. I fed her dinner—she keeps asking for mangoes now, something you just can't get in December in Seattle! After dinner, she asked me if we could sit on the front porch. It seemed like a strange request for this time of year, but I decided to indulge her, since I couldn't fulfill her request for mangoes. It was a mild evening for December, in the mid-50s, rainy (of course) and foggy. For a half-hour or so, we sat bundled up in a blanket on the loveseat where she and Dad used to sit, watching the cars go by, watching the rain fall in the cone of light beneath the street lamp, savoring the smell of wet leaves on damp streets in late autumn. She reached over and took my hand and began singing an old hymn, one I haven't heard since I was a boy, an old Brethren hymn called "Abba, Father, We Approach Thee." She remembered the words to all four verses. I joined in where I could remember. By the last verse, though, even if I had remembered the words, I couldn't have sung them. Tears were streaming down my face, and I felt the presence of God there with us. When she finished singing, she said, "I'll go to bed now, Frank," and that was it. The window of clarity and memory were gone.

I found the words in one of her little old leather-bound hymnals. Here they are:

Abba, Father! We approach Thee
In our Saviour's precious name;
We, Thy children, here assembling,
Access to Thy presence claim.
From our sin His blood hath washed us;
'Tis through him our souls draw nigh;
And Thy Spirit, too, hath taught us,
"Abba, Father!" thus to cry.

Once as prodigals we wandered,
In our folly, far from Thee;
But Thy grace, o'er sin abounding,
Rescued us from misery.
Thou Thy prodigals hast pardoned,
Loved us with a Father's love;
Welcomed us with joy o'erflowing,
E'en to dwell with Thee above.

Clothed in garments of salvation,
At Thy table is our place;
We rejoice, and Thou rejoicest,
In the riches of Thy grace.
"It is meet," we hear Thee saying,

"We should merry be and glad;
I have found My once lost children,
Now they live, who once were dead."

Abba, Father! All adore Thee,
All rejoice in heaven above;
While in us they learn the wonders
Of Thy wisdom, power, and love.
Soon, before Thy throne assembled
All Thy children shall proclaim
"Glory, everlasting glory,
Be to God and to the Lamb!"[1]

It struck me as I sat there listening to my mother's frail voice singing that old hymn—she knew (or knows) something about spirituality (a subject of my last e-mail) that goes beyond anything I know.

I wanted to mention another area of spirituality that I think we must rediscover, something I failed to mention before: creation spirituality. I got an e-mail yesterday from one of my students who is so excited because she is going to Mexico over Christmas vacation, and she plans to swim with dolphins at a special park that is set up for that purpose. Why will swimming with dolphins be such a meaningful and unforgettable experience for Sherri? It will go far beyond science (although she was one of my best science students and wants to be a marine biologist). I think it will be a spiritual thing for her. It's part of the reconnection that is at the heart of true religion: we reconnect with God, with our own soul, with our neighbor, and with all of God's creatures—brother sun, sister moon, and brother dolphin too.

Modern men and women have lost their connection with creation. We're always insulated from it by shoe leather, cotton-polyester, glass, metal, plastic, HVAC, and screens of many kinds! One of the things I most cherish about Jamaica was the joy of living with open windows, with birds singing, with spiders building their webs, with lizards darting across your path, getting wet when it rains. These are gifts from God, and I can't help but believe our souls are starved for the company of God's creatures.

If I could live another life, I think I would devote it to ecology, because I also believe that this is a truly spiritual and Christian work. Genesis begins with our mandate to take care of God's creation, and never has our failure to do so been more acute than now. Learning to live as caretakers of creation and friends to our fellow creatures must be at the core of a new kind of Christianity. That probably sounds odd to you; as I recall, you weren't very fond of the beautiful garden spider we saw on our walk along the river!

From the sublime to the ridiculous: Mr. Remko hasn't paid the rent yet. Would you check into it for me next time you stop by to pick up mail?—Neo

To: neoliver@fdrhs.edu
From: danrpoole@backspring.com
Date: December 8, 1999
Subject: Townhouse and Other Stuff

Glad I was able to reach you by phone this morning. After, spoke to Remko. Everything OK—he had check ready—just forgot to send it (or so he says). Furniture looks fine. Seems to be taking good care of place. Not to worry.

Very interested in your thoughts on spirituality. Personally, have felt negligent in this area. Was raised on two or three assumptions about spirituality, which I question now. Feel like I've put those assumptions on a shelf but haven't come up with anything new to replace them. Never tried to talk about this to anyone, so it might sound a little fragmented, but here goes. . . .

Staple of evangelical spirituality in my experience was "the quiet time": get up each morning to read the Bible and pray. Hard to be against Bible reading and prayer! But here's my problem: the whole quiet time endeavor seemed to be about quantity. The more of Bible you read or studied, the better. The more you prayed (how many minutes?), the better. I remember for many years almost hating to read the Bible and pray, because as soon as I finished, the only thought in my mind was, "I should be doing this so much more than I am."

Looking back, really does seem "modern" eh?—wanting more information (knowledge is power), quantifying everything, reducing to formula and mechanism ("if I pray this much, I get these results"), making everything measurable. How can we keep prayer and Bible reading as key to our spiritual lives without turning spirituality into spiritual techniques, duties, and legalisms—still more to feel guilty about?

In recent years, spirituality focuses more on public worship, where we sing "praise and worship" choruses not as doctrinal treatises about God but as intimate love songs to God. I'm certainly not against this! Some of most wonderful moments in my life have come during times like this. But sometimes I feel uncomfortable with the lyrics—it's all about "me." How Jesus makes me feel, what he does for me, how he loves and forgives me.

The language is almost erotic—he holds me close, embraces me, and so on. Again, nothing wrong with this, but I wonder—does this represent a kind of narcissistic and overindividualized spirituality? Reading Isaiah other day (having quiet time!), I was struck by how global his visions were. God's reign pertains to whole world, not just little me and how I feel.

What do you do with all this? Prayed for you and your mom today. Beautiful story about her singing. Agreed with what you wrote about creation but still don't like spiders!—Dan

To: danrpoole@backspring.com
From: neoliver@fdrhs.edu
Date: December 8, 1999
Subject: Spirituality

It's strange to realize that your e-mail said 4:01 p.m. when I received it, and you'll have this response coming back to you the same day saying 2:30 p.m. This Pacific Time Zone is hard for me to get used to!

I resonated with what you said about our spirituality being so oriented around guilt. I remember feeling uncomfortable about this when I was preaching. I would listen to sermons sometimes on the radio and say to myself, "They're all about the same thing. They're about how the people aren't doing enough." I promised myself I would do better (but I probably didn't). I felt that most preachers didn't preach good news about grace; they preached bad news about inadequacy and pressure. One week would be you need to read the Bible more. The next week, pray more. The next week, give more. The next week, witness to your faith more. The next week, serve more. It's a wonder people can stand coming to church!

I remember learning something after my first few years of teaching science that might help us figure out a solution to this whole mess. I remember thinking, "Why do I give so much homework? Is it really to help my students, or is it because I think good teachers give homework?" For a few years I stopped giving homework. Instead I tried to make every minute of the class useful. Instead of preparing students to do homework, I in a sense had them do their homework in class. Eventually, I went back to giving some homework, but I think those couple of years really taught me something: instead of telling people to go do something at home, we do them a favor by helping them do it now.

That suggests to me that we would make our church services less about preparing to do something spiritual at home on their own and actually doing something spiritual here and now. I suppose that's what the worship experiences you talked about are supposed to do. They allow people to have an old-fashioned quiet time all together, all in the same place. That's why people close their eyes and raise their hands—they're each drawing near to God and doing so together. I think that's good, as you said.

Your point is well taken about us becoming so privatized and personalized. That probably reflects consumerism—as in "I want to feel good!"—and individualism—"this is all about me!"—two facets of modernity that we are having a hard time getting beyond.

How do we develop a more holistic, balanced spirituality in people, Dan, without a boatload of guilt? Something for you to think about!—Neo

To: danrpoole@backspring.com
From: neoliver@fdrhs.edu
Date: December 10, 1999
Subject: Haven't Heard from You

I noticed you haven't answered my previous e-mail. That means either that you are still excessively busy or that you are stumped by my question about spiritual formation. Well?—Neo

To: neoliver@fdrhs.edu
From: danrpoole@backspring.com
Date: December 11, 1999
Subject: No Excuses

No excuses—just terribly busy! Carol's sick on top of everything else. I haven't touched the computer in days. That's why I'm in the office on Saturday morning. OK, some thinking on spiritual formation . . .

I look back over my years in ministry and ask what has really helped people change and deepen spiritually: (1) youth retreats, (2) short-term mission trips, (3) some small groups (I say some—others were a waste of time), (4) many one-to-one relationships, (5) getting people involved leading something or serving somewhere.

I look over this list and wonder what they have in common. The biggest thing—intensity. Odd: we try to make our spiritual formation experiences routine, and that maybe guarantees they become less effective. The more intense and less routine the educational experience, the greater the impact—at least that's what strikes me as I look over my list.

Oops—listening to sermons is not on the list! I do believe in preaching, but maybe in preaching as a front door that invites people into other, more intense experiences. Maybe it creates a "field" (like a magnetic field in science) where spiritual experiences happen. Speaking of preaching, have to get back to sermon prep. Talk to you soon, my friend.—Dan

TO: danrpoole@backspring.com
FROM: neoliver@fdrhs.edu
DATE: December 11, 1999
SUBJECT: More on Spirituality

A quick thought about your last e-mail. I remember writing to you awhile back that I think our future approaches to spiritual formation will be more akin to ancient ones. That's exactly the case with the list you sent me. For example, what are youth retreats but a short-term monastic experience? People live together in simplicity (no TVs and such) and in community and practice spiritual disciplines together—prayer, Bible study, solitude, that sort of thing.

What are short-term mission trips but modern examples of the missionary journeys of Paul and his entourage or of the Celtic monks' adventures? In a way, they are also like pilgrimages—journeys undertaken for a spiritual purpose.

What are small groups and one-to-one mentoring relationships but echoes of ancient training methods, before we slipped into the modern misconception that the best education takes place via theoretical monologue in sterile classrooms? Small groups and mentoring—filled with give-and-take, personal as well as intellectual interaction, formation as well as information—recall the old images of the apprentice training with his master or the disciples following Jesus throughout the land.

And what is getting people involved in lay ministry—which we both agree is the REAL ministry—but an echo of the many biblical stories where God taught people to swim by throwing them into the deep end? I think of Moses, feeling so inadequate, or even the disciples being sent out two by two, after only several months of training, to learn by success and failure the lessons that can only be learned by doing, not just listening or studying.

That's not to say that people don't need information, knowledge, facts, history, theory. But information of that sort is now easier to come by than ever. I think my students and your kids (for whom the Internet will be as much a part of life as indoor plumbing is to us) can process information so much faster than we can deliver it by lecture. So my guess is that teachers of the future will spend less time giving out information and more time helping students learn how to find what they need when they need it. Sorry for rambling on about this, but obviously, education is a subject close to my heart. I hope your schedule is calming down. You need to enjoy Christmas!—Neo

14

IT'S NONE OF YOUR BUSINESS
WHO GOES TO HELL

It was late on Saturday night. I had finished writing my sermon and reading it through aloud to check its length. Twenty-eight minutes. That meant
it would be about thirty-five minutes the next morning (I always speak
more slowly in the pulpit). I thought about Neo and felt bad for not having enough time to respond to his e-mails. I looked at my watch—almost
11:00 P.M.—and decided to give him a quick call since it was only 8:00
P.M. in Seattle. Our conversation was short as his mother was still awake.
Neo was trying to play Yatzhee with her. His mother seemed to enjoy
rolling the dice and picking out the matches. It was good to hear my
friend's voice, even for a few minutes. The next afternoon I had another
long e-mail waiting for me.

To: danrpoole@backspring.com
FROM: neoliver@fdrhs.edu
DATE: December 12, 1999
SUBJECT: Life in Seattle

Thanks for your phone call last night, and thanks as always for asking
about Mom. I wish I could have talked longer, but I know you understand. Sometimes she is so funny—I mean, not to laugh at her, but just to
watch her act like a little child. It's almost cute. For example, yesterday, I
made dinner, and she got so mad at me for serving her applesauce. I said,
"Mom, you love applesauce. It's one of your favorite foods." She said she
has always hated it. So I got really firm, as if I were her father, and I said,
"Young lady, you have to at least try it," and she's very compliant when
I'm firm with her like that, so she put a spoonful in her mouth. Then she
got this big smile on her face and said, "Oh, that IS good! I'll have some

more, Frank." (She thought I was Dad again.) She ate almost half the jar! She went on and on about how much better applesauce is now than it used to be. She was like a little girl who had just discovered a new kind of candy. I just laughed and laughed, and she looked at me and broke out laughing too. Then she said, "My, Frank, you certainly do get excited over applesauce!" Which made me laugh even more. It's hard to explain, but in spite of the disease, we do have some wonderful moments together. I keep thinking of her holding me as a baby in her arms, changing my diapers, putting me to bed—to do the same for her now is an unspeakable honor.

Sometimes, of course, it is pure sadness to look at her and think about how much she has lost. I mean, her husband has died and she doesn't even realize it. Whenever she calls me Frank, I feel a little pang.

I stayed up late last night watching religious television. Pretty weird stuff. I heard one chap going at it about hell. It brought me back to some of our discussions along the Potomac. You seemed abnormally fixated on the subject! Seriously, though, I understand why: it's a subject about which modern Christianity entrenched itself in some very ugly positions, and I think a new kind of Christian will handle the subject very differently. That TV show bothered me so much, I had a new thought. Remember the line I used to draw, and—I liked this term of yours—the higher level of discourse? Here's how I picture the various doctrines of hell (I hope this comes through OK):

| Universalism | Inclusivism | Exclusivism |

Pluralism/Relativism

Universalism (of the Christian variety—obviously there are other forms) says that Jesus is the only way and the Savior of the whole world and that everyone is already saved regardless of whether they believe in him.

Exclusivism, at the other extreme, also says that Jesus is the only way, but he is the Savior only of those who choose (or are chosen) to believe in him. Only they will go to heaven.

Inclusivism says that Jesus is the only way and the Savior of the whole world and yet affirms the possibility of rejecting the grace of God. Salvation from hell extends to everyone who in some way (known only to God) accepts the grace of God and is withheld only from those who reject the grace of God in whatever way it presents itself to them, whether or not they have heard of and believe in Jesus.

I yoke pluralism and relativism together because pluralism alone can mean many things. (For example, when it means acknowledging that there are many different cultures, many different approaches to religion, pluralism must be a positive thing. After all, it means that we are beginning to see the world more the way God has always seen it!) Yoked together, the terms for me refer to a popular approach to questions of heaven and hell that says, "There may or may not be a God, a heaven, a hell, and so on, but there are many beliefs about each, and all are valid for those who hold them. No one belief has superiority over the others." I placed this approach below the line because it is often more a mood than a logical position. But if you pinned it to the ground and forced a confession of faith about hell, I think it would say that since no one can prove anything one way or the other, you can choose whatever belief you want as long as you accept others' rights to do the same.

This approach at first glance feels very tolerant. But ultimately, it may be the least tolerant position of all, since behind the scenes it must admit that every other position's claim to legitimacy is bogus. The only ones who really have it right are the pluralist/relativists—which is a kind of exclusivism all over again. To me, pluralism/relativism is more of a late-modern option—trying to hold itself aloof from personal commitment, trying to be absolutely objective, trying to avoid believing anything that can't be rationally and "absolutely" proved. It's certainly very popular, although I consider it a seduction into apathy.

The big question you're asking is, I know, what's ABOVE the line? And although I don't have a name for it, here's what I think that higher position says: "It's none of your business who does and does not go to hell. It is your business to be warned by it and to run, not walk, in the opposite direction! It is your business to love God with all your heart, soul, mind, and strength, to love your neighbor as yourself, to have confidence in Jesus Christ and live as Jesus lived. Let the imagery of hell remind you that life is serious business, that there are real consequences to how we live and believe, that justice and injustice ultimately matter more than most of what people worry about. Now stop speculating about hell and start living for heaven!"

I guess if I had to give this above-the-line position a name, I'd call it predicamentalism, since it refuses to let anyone speculate about other people's eternal fate but instead focuses you on your own. It's the same approach Jesus took twice in Luke 13, when he responded to similar theoretical questions about who is to be saved. Or it's the approach he took when Peter asked him (at the end of John's gospel) about John. ("What about him?" Peter asks, and Jesus responds, "Hey, none of your business! What about YOU?") I remember us talking about in-grouping and out-grouping once. I think Jesus does everything he can to steer us away from that. (But of course, we manage to do it anyway!) So when we try to in-group and out-group regarding heaven and hell, I think we're disappointing the Lord, who would rather we concentrate on our own predicament.

Watching that TV show got me thinking about hell, and so I did some research on the Web—just to get an idea of what different groups have to say about it. I was checking out the Website of one of your evangelical magazines and caught an article about hell and the "exclusiveness of Christ." The tone of the article, which seemed to delight in defending the assertion that many (or most) people would be eternally damned (in spite of the atoning work of Christ), struck me as quite odd, if not heretical. I thought to myself, True, Jesus was demanding. He called people to a path of radical, wholehearted discipleship. But Jesus didn't get crucified for being exclusive; he was hated and crucified for the reverse—for opening the windows of grace and the doors of heaven to the tax collectors and prostitutes, the half-breeds and ultimately even Gentiles. Right? Do you ever think your friends may be off the track with that kind of talk? No need to answer that—it's just a rhetorical question, and not a very nice one at that.

There's a lot more we need to learn about how the doctrine of hell developed. I have a feeling that if we knew more of the historical background of the concept of hell, we'd have a very different understanding of Jesus' statements on it. The same goes for heaven.

Speaking of heaven, I wouldn't be surprised if my mother goes there soon. It's kind of a double hit for me—losing Dad and at the same time having Mom slip away mentally even while her body is still here. On top of her dementia, she's not breathing right, and the doctors want to see her again tomorrow for a chest X-ray.

Right at this moment, she's talking up a storm in the other room, and of course no one is there. I'd better check on her. Talk to you later.—Neo

To: neoliver@fdrhs.edu
From: danrpoole@backspring.com
Date: December 13, 1999
Subject: Reply

Neo, I've been promising to devote serious time to sit down and respond to your e-mails. Meanwhile, a couple of long-term parishioners have been driving me crazy. Suspicious, cynical attitude, and so on. How much time to spend with them? Just ignore it? I've noticed these situations follow a pattern. Parishioners experience some personal offense—loss in power, hurt feelings about something. This causes withdrawal. They begin keeping a mental notebook, noting all additional offenses. "Demerits" add up, and a conspiracy theory develops. They can't help but talk about it, and "concern" spreads. If I don't address it, they drift away, and their leaving adds a demerit in the mental notebooks of others. Helping usually requires huge amounts of listening, and sincere listening at that, plus long hours responding to concerns. Maybe what I say matters little in comparison with the fact that I give them time and attention, filling up their empty emotional tank. The pattern becomes cyclical unless I do more than respond to complaints; I must also challenge them not to get into demerit–offense notebook mode in the future and to get beyond that to real productive involvement.

Anyhow, this is a busy time of year, so every hour I spend with these folks simply adds work to my life. (Meanwhile, Carol and the kids haven't seen enough of me lately. Plus with three kids in fall soccer, it's a crazy schedule!) There is nothing more distracting or draining than a "believe the worst" suspicion. Yet I love these people! Very often they're our most loyal long-term members. So what else can I do? I must try to help them reconcile to whatever and get on track again.

So there's my long and elaborate excuse for not answering your e-mails or even reading them with care they deserve. Maybe after Christmas? Sincerely sorry. But look, you have time on your hands, so keep writing! I profit by it now or later and am archiving everything to go back and reconsider later. I know what you're thinking—I need to slow down. But you know how Christmas season can be.—Dan

To: danrpoole@backspring.com
From: neoliver@fdrhs.edu
Date: December 13, 1999
Subject: Re: Reply

Dan—no apologies necessary. And don't worry about me being bored. I'm carrying on several other conversations online, some of them almost as intense as ours! One person in particular I want you to meet sometime— Casey B., the youth pastor at St. Tim's. We've been getting into some pretty interesting stuff lately.

Hey, something to celebrate—remember Melissa and Marita? (You met them at the football game last month.) I've been carrying on an e-mail conversation with Marita, and she told me that she and Melissa are going to become members at St. Timothy's next week. She is making a public commitment to live as a follower of Christ. Good news! I guess in your terms we'd say she has been "saved," although as you know, I don't like that term myself.

OK, I'm imagining you asking why. You encouraged me to ramble online, so here goes!

The way you modern evangelicals use the word "saved" is, I think, terribly unbiblical. (How's that for throwing down the gauntlet?) The way you talk about salvation suggests that the only thing that matters in life is getting your butt into heaven, being saved from hell, getting eternal life for yourself. (We talked about this once, right?)

Here's a question: Is getting individual souls into heaven the focal point of the gospel? I'd have to say no, for any number of reasons.

Don't you think God is concerned about saving the whole world? I often think that we are more Platonic than Christian, and here's a case in point. We seem to think that the only thing that God really wants to save is "souls." But to me, the biblical vision is never a disembodied soul floating in or out of space. No, it's the redemption of the world, the stars, the animals, the plants, the whole show. I feel that especially when I read Revelation. It's like this wonderful dream where there are streets of gold and gates of pearl—not literally, of course, but the imagery is of something real, substantial, not ethereal. In this dream there are strange creatures full of limbs and eyes and horns and manes—composites of all the animals, as I interpret the vision, telling us that even the animal kingdom will be redeemed. And don't forget the plant kingdom and the environment as a whole—there are trees, and there are cities with rivers of crystal-clear (not polluted!) water flowing through. And even human culture is redeemed—with human languages being spoken and human songs being sung. Wow! So there's this paradox of continuity and discontinuity between earth and heaven, and I think we tend to emphasize the discontinuity, probably thanks to Plato. (But that's another story. Ask me about our doctrine of the Fall sometime.)

To: danrpoole@backspring.com
From: neoliver@fdrhs.edu
Date: December 13, 1999
Subject: Part 2

Sorry, my mother called out and I hit "send" by mistake.

The preoccupation with being saved sometimes strikes me as strangely selfish. I think we've talked about this before: Do you think that God would want a heaven filled with people who cared more about being saved from hell than saved from sin? Who cared more about getting their butts into heaven than being good? Who cared more about having their sins forgiven than being good neighbors? Who in fact became worse neighbors precisely because they became so religious in their concern about their own personal souls?

I think our definition of "saved" is shrunken and freeze-dried by modernity. We need a postmodern consideration of what salvation means, something beyond an individualized and consumeristic version. I may have a personal home, personal car, personal computer, personal identification number, personal digital assistant, personal hot tub—all I need now is personal salvation from my own personal savior. I hope I'm not offending you—but this all strikes me as Christianity diced through the modern Veg-o-matic. (Are you too young to know what a Veg-o-matic is?)

The way conservative Christians talk about "personal salvation" seems to me to try to persuade by exclusion. In other words, the argument says, "You, the 'unsaved,' are on the outside and I'm on the inside. I'll tell you how to get inside if you want." I think we would be more in line with the spirit of the gospel if we invite by inclusion, saying, "God loves you. God accepts you. Are you ready to accept your acceptance and live in reconciliation with God?"

Similarly, I also think the standard definition of salvation breeds passivity. It's like a line in the sand, and we say, "The most important thing in life is to be on the other side of this line." OK. People cross the line. What then? They try to get other people to cross the line. OK. What then? I see a huge contrast between crossing a line in this way, and following Jesus on a journey. It's as if we have taken what is for Jesus a starting line and turned it into a finish line. Sounds like another case of modern reductionism—going for the greatest efficiency, the most measurable results, the least common denominator.

Here's a thought that just hit me as I was writing. What if "being saved" was like data being saved on a computer? In other words, when God pulls the plug on the universe, will the data and software of our lives be saved, so our "program" can still run? Or will it be "lost"? This gets more interesting the more I think about it. I think of that verse from somewhere in the Bible, where God says our sins and lawless deeds he will remember no more. Interesting. What if forgiving our sins is actually the same thing as judging them? (I know—you're saying, "What?") Try this: What if some people do so little good and so much bad in their lives that when God forgives and forgets all their sins, there just isn't much left to remember?

One other thing: the scope of salvation in the Bible is so much bigger than my little soul. We have talked before about the grandeur of the visions of Isaiah and the other prophets. I was thinking about how when Jesus came, he was essentially saying to his people, "Your view of salvation is entirely too narrow. It is nationalistic. God's vision is global. It will extend beyond our nation to all nations." He was trying to reignite in them a global vision more like Isaiah's—that the God of the Jews had a plan for saving the whole world. But then we get hold of it for a few thousand years and in a sense we shrink it even smaller than the nationalistic vision of the first-century Jews. For us today, it's not the salvation of a nation that God cares about; it's only the salvation of individuals. Forget the Jewish nation, and forget the nations of the world, and certainly forget the world itself. We need a strong dose of the prophets' grand visions of God as Savior of the whole world. Because Jesus' vision is equally global.

That's all for now. You might be convinced my faculties are departing as fast as my mom's! But seriously—how about helping me here, Daniel? If you agree that our modern definition of salvation is somewhat deficient, what would an alternative look like? Any ideas? It's far too easy to criticize without constructing an alternative.—Neo

To: neoliver@fdrhs.edu
From: danrpoole@backspring.com
Date: December 14, 1999
Subject: Responses

Hey, Neo. Wow, pretty intense thoughts. I'm not as shocked as you might imagine. I have felt my thinking shifting in this direction already, from our face-to-face conversations. I also remember reading something similar in book by Newbigin you lent me (I still have it. Haven't finished. Sorry!). I'm sure some of what I'm about to say will be from him and some from you!

OK. Let's say that salvation means becoming part of the solution rather than part of the problem.

Let's say that heaven is a by-product, not the main point.

Let's say that the goal is the glory of God, the pleasure of God, so God's universe turns out the way God dreams—all ways of saying "the kingdom of God" that we're supposed to seek first. (I remember our talk at McDonald's—just last month, but it seems like an age ago.)

Let's say that the essence of our identity as people of God isn't that we're an elite, saved for privilege, but ordinary people saved for service, for responsibility. As you said, it's not about God giving us privileged "insider trading information." God recruits us to the mission of spreading the good news and love to the whole world. In fact, maybe the real enemy isn't hell but instead living out of harmony with God, disconnected. So salvation is joining God's mission instead of trying to live by our own selfish personal agenda.

(Wow, this just struck me as I wrote that—frightening—we could want personal salvation as part of our personal agenda, so evangelism = appeal to spiritual selfishness—ugly!)

So maybe salvation isn't something we "get" and then consider the option of joining God in his grand mission. Salvation is what we experience and spread in the process of joining God in his grand mission. Of course this is not a works/earning/self-justification thing—it's all about God's grace from start to finish. But the focus moves from me to God, from my plan for myself to God's plan for whole world (not just "wonderful plan for my life"?!).

Also, then, salvation isn't exclusive. The way God brings salvation to others is by giving it to some, recruiting them as agents of salvation to others. So he blesses the whole world by blessing one nation, the Jews. They become God's agents in world. Then, at just the right time—this is a huge part of what Christmas is about, eh?—God breaks out beyond national boundaries, recruits agents in every nation. Same idea: God wants to bless the many through the few. He doesn't want to bless the few to the exclusion of the many. I'm not sure how this all pans out, but this feels healthier.

Now, the real issue isn't an emotional crisis or the stereotypical experience of being "saved" or "born again" or of "crossing a line" and then stopping there. The issue isn't signing on to a new set of beliefs alone. The issue is following Jesus, joining him in his adventure and mission of saving the world and expressing God's love. If a person isn't moving ahead on that journey, then no matter how many aisles he walks down and cards he fills out and "sinner's prayers" he says, whether or not he is going to heaven (yes, you've convinced me, it's none of our business to make pronouncements!), there is still no way we can say in any meaningful sense that he is experiencing salvation.

How does that sound to you, Neo? I can think of a hundred preachers who would think it sounds like a whole different religion from what they preach. And maybe they're right.

One other idea inspired by your last e-mail: modern gospel constricts, narrows, reduces biblical gospel by neglecting the role of the Christian community. I was struck by how your relationship with Melissa and Marita led them into a Christian community and how much their commitment to Christ is integrated with their integration in St. Tim's.

That's a dream I have for my church—that it would increasingly become a community of communities, a place full of little "villages of Christ" where people really connect, really care, really make their faith visible through love. A place where we help people believe and become by helping them belong. Sometimes I'm discouraged about this, and sometimes I'm hopeful.

BTW, I'm finally starting to get into the Christmas spirit—finally. The unhappy campers at church are doing better. I'm preaching on the names of Jesus—Prince of Peace, Son of David, Immanuel. I love the gospel, Neo! What an honor to preach it! I'm so glad I didn't retire to New Mexico. Do you ever think you'll return to the ministry? Moses went back, you know, even at an advanced age!—Dan

P.S. Stopped by townhouse to see the renter. He told me to tell you that if you ever want to sell it, he wants to buy it, furniture and all. I told him I think you'll be back in a year or less. Just FYI.

To: danrpoole@backspring.com
From: neoliver@fdrhs.edu
Date: December 15, 1999
Subject: Advanced Age?!

My dear Dan, I am successfully fighting the temptation to take offense at your comment about "advanced age." Nor will I take offense at your last question, even though it implies that teaching high school and now caring for my mother do not qualify as ministry. Come on, man, you know better than that! But I know what you meant, and actually, I had never thought about it even once until that day you and I went walking along the canal (in spite of the unhappy end to that conversation). I love teaching high school, but the intensity of that conversation—it really tempted me to go back. But it's not just that. It's you, Daniel. Our friendship is reducing my cynicism about "paid professional ministry," which is what you really meant when you asked about me going back, right? But I don't know.

A practical matter: Do you know a Realtor? I think you told me a friend of yours sold you your house. I think we can go ahead and draw up the papers for my renter to buy my townhouse. I'm glad he wants to buy my furniture, too. The only thing I'll need to get when I fly out is my papers and my personal stuff—my books, artwork, music, that sort of thing. If he wants to close the sale fast, I might have to hire a company to come in and pack it up and ship it to me. I'll let you know. For now, I'm literally trapped here, always on duty. I can't even take a long shower. Thanks again for handling this power-of-attorney stuff.

Merry Christmas! I went out and bought a tree, and Mom seems to like watching the lights. If I can just let go of my memories of what she was, what she is is still pretty wonderful. My brother and his family are coming up for Christmas. I haven't seen my nieces and nephews for years. (They didn't come up for Dad's funeral.)

Will you send me some of your sermon tapes? I haven't figured out a way to get to church yet here in Seattle, but I will. Right now, you and a few others are my virtual church, I suppose. By the way, I agreed with everything you wrote in that last e-mail. Right on.—Neo

To: neoliver@fdrhs.edu
From: danrpoole@backspring.com
Date: December 15, 1999
Subject: Townhouse Sale?

Neo—I'm confused. Why would you want to sell your townhouse? What's going on?—Dan

To: danrpoole@backspring.com
From: neoliver@fdrhs.edu
Date: December 16, 1999
Subject: Re: Townhouse Sale?

Sorry for the confusion, Dan. When my dad died, I received a pretty big inheritance. When my mother dies—and the doctors have told me that she is a prime candidate for a stroke or heart attack, so they say it could be anytime—her house here is paid off, and it's worth even more. So when I come back, I think I'll need to put some money into a larger house. That's one of many options though. I'll keep you posted. But will you ask your Realtor friend to call me? I'll get her to draw up the papers. Thanks again for all your help. I know you're already so busy.—Neo

15

BEGINNING THE JOURNEY INTO TERRA NOVA

WHEN I CHECKED MY E-MAIL on December 19, there were two messages waiting for me from Neo.

TO: danrpoole@backspring.com
FROM: neoliver@fdrhs.edu
DATE: December 19, 1999
SUBJECT: URGENT NEWS

Dear Friends,
I am so sorry to send you this news in a mass mail way, but my mother passed away last night. She went peacefully in her sleep. The funeral director just left with the body, and I will go over to the funeral parlor now. I am broken-hearted and exhausted, as you can imagine. But how relieved I am that I made the decision to come out here to care for Mother. I thought I might have two years to care for her, but it wasn't even two months. I will never regret this time with her. The funeral will probably be held December 23. Details will follow. Thanks for your prayers.—Neo

TO: danrpoole@backspring.com
FROM: neoliver@fdrhs.edu
DATE: December 19, 1999
SUBJECT: Request

Daniel—Will you call my rector over at St. Tim's and let him know about Mother? Father Scott is not on e-mail yet. I cannot deal with a lot of phone calls right now. Thank you, my friend.—Neo

I called Father Scott, and he told me he would check into flights to be there for the funeral. Flights would be hard to come by Christmas week, I thought. He asked me if I wanted to travel with him, and I said yes—but then realized that I had so many duties at the church, there was just no way. With his assistant available to preach for Christmas Eve and Christmas Day services, he was free to go. "Our liturgy runs along whether I'm there or not," he said. "Getting away is much harder for you non-liturgical folk."

Of course, we sent flowers, and I sent a card, and then another card, but that Christmas will always carry a pang of regret in my memory because I really wish I could have gone out to support my friend.

I received only one more e-mail from Neo, after the holidays, perhaps the most surprising message of all. Here it is.

To: danrpoole@backspring.com
From: neoliver@fdrhs.edu
Date: January 2, 2000

We Made It!
Good morning, Dan. It's 2:45 a.m. here in Seattle as I write.

Well, we made it—through the memorial service and burial . . . and through the Y2K hype too. Father Scott carried your greetings. He was truly sorry that you were unable to get away. Thanks for the flowers, the letter, and the cards. You are a true friend, Daniel.

Everything is going well enough here. I spent the last week cleaning out Mother's house, working each day from 7:00 a.m. to nearly midnight. I hope to have the house listed with a Realtor by week's end. The market here in Seattle is very active, so I am optimistic for a quick sale at a good price.

With all those hours alone, packing boxes, throwing out things that were precious to my parents but of no value to anyone else, cleaning (so much dust!), carting clothes to a homeless shelter downtown, donating food to the Presbyterian food pantry, finding a used furniture company to take the furniture, canceling Dad's magazine subscriptions and Mom's remaining doctor's appointments—with so many details and so much physical labor, my hands have been busy and my mind free to think. I am not used to thinking about myself, my life, my future, day after day. But somehow, packing away old photographs, smelling my father's scent on old shirts, boxing Mother's old jewelry, discovering a box that included a red metal toy car I remember playing with on our patio in Port Maria, all this has made me think about my life.

Last night I finished emptying the first floor. I turned on Mother's old stereo and loaded a stack of LPs—Mozart, Glenn Miller, Segovia (Father's favorite), John Coltraine, Bob Marley, the Smoothtones, even the Beatles (Father loved them too)—I just grabbed whichever disks didn't look too warped. The room was empty—all the furniture gone except the stereo and an old Shredded Wheat crate full of LPs that I couldn't bear to throw away yet. I sat on the wooden floor and drank a Wicked Ale and prayed some and cried as I haven't cried in years. The music made me cry, the scratches on the records made me cry, and I guess most of all, I finally felt the loss of both my parents in so short a time. I'm a grown man, but I truly felt like one for the first time only last night. When your parents die, you suddenly realize that now there's nothing left between you and death but time. It's like being in a cold Northwest rain and having your umbrella taken away, and the cold sinks into your bones.

When the needle followed the last groove toward the center of the last record and the arm clicked up and over and came to rest, I got up and went to my journal at the kitchen table. I have no one to talk to, I thought, except God. So I've been writing in my journal and crying and praying for a few hours now and feeling so lonely, and then I realized that I could share all this with you.

Two feelings have come over me tonight, Dan, urges that have arisen with me with such force that I don't know whether to be afraid of them or excited by them. First, I feel a compulsion to travel. I cannot imagine leaving here and returning to the East Coast, Roosevelt, science lab reports, soccer practices, and the Beltway—much as I love them all (well, not the Beltway). All I can picture for my immediate future is this: boarding a plane and heading west across the Pacific. You know from handling my papers that I have connections to people around the world through my charitable work. When the rest of the world wakes up, I'm going to call a travel agent and see about one of those open tickets that would let me travel anywhere within a certain time frame.

In my imagination over these last few hours, I take this journey: I visit my old friend from seminary who is in New Guinea, I visit an orphanage I have supported in North India, I go to Europe and Africa, I go to South America and indulge my scientific interest by visiting the Galápagos Islands, and eventually I come home and see you, Father Scott, the Curtises, and other friends from St. Tim's, my many friends at FDR . . . and that's where a second powerful feeling has overtaken me tonight. In these hours it feels as though my passion for teaching has drained away. At this moment I can't imagine going back to the classroom. This is frightening for me, because with all the uncertainties of life, for the last ten years my passion for high school teaching has been the one constant, but tonight it is gone, evaporated.

And here is the real surprise, although it may surprise you less than it does me. In its place, Daniel, I feel a pull—stronger than I can explain to you—to come back to the pastorate. It's as if a door has opened and I know I must go through it.

That, of course, is why I am writing you at this odd hour. I feel I must thank you, Daniel. When I met you, I felt I was meeting myself back at the most difficult juncture of my life. I felt that somehow I might be able to give you the help that I so wish I had received when I came to the end of the gangplank, so to speak, and had to step beyond modernity into what was for me, then, a frightening void. Last fall I felt that I was watching you face the challenge that I ran away from years earlier. That's why I pushed you so hard, Daniel. I didn't want you to give up, because I knew that if it weren't you, it would be someone else who would have to pass through the same rough territory, because we both know, this thing must be done, this passage must be pioneered.

This morning, I think it was about 2:00 a.m., I still had the music playing in my mind, even though the old stereo had clicked off long before. And I said to myself, "I'm going back. I have a few decades of strength left in me. I'm going to work with Daniel and everyone else we can find to pioneer what it means to be a new kind of Christian in a new kind of church in the uncharted terra nova that lies ahead of us."

I had a dream a few nights ago. I hardly ever remember my dreams, and I am certainly not claiming anything revelatory, but the dream involved you, and it related to all this, so I want to tell you about it. In the dream, you were exhausted and worn to the bone, struggling to shape a church that was meaningfully expressing the gospel in this new world we've been talking about. I asked God why you were so tired, and this answer came to me: there are so few working at this exploration of faith in postmodern territory, and all of those who are are exhausted because it is so difficult. It seemed like God's heart was pained at how few are exploring beyond the edges of our modern maps and at how exhausted those few are. When I woke up, the dream felt so real, and I felt that it posed a very personal and pointed question to me about what I am doing with my time and energy—do I need to be in the struggle in the local church again somehow? Tonight, or I should say this morning, I feel flooded with an affirmative answer to that question. No, actually, it is not just a practical answer to a question—it is a flood of personal passion to join you in a mission we both know will be difficult.

Of course, a million practicalities come to mind. Fortunately, with my inheritance, money is not a problem. And Reedman has a long-term sub for me to finish out the school year, the soccer season is long over, and (thanks to you) the sale of my townhouse and furniture to Remko is almost complete. If I can prevail upon you to help me with some final details there, I find the way is clear and I am free to launch a new chapter in my life.

I wrote to you awhile back about spiritual formation and how pilgrimages, journeys, and such have been such an important part of the spiritual life of people. I suppose I'm going off on a pilgrimage of my own.

I wanted to tell you all of this "live" by phone, but I didn't want to alarm you and Carol by phoning so early in the day. But I hope you will call me here when you read this. I'm also wondering if you could come out to Seattle for a few days. I would gladly buy your ticket. There is a coffee shop near here with the best Jamaican coffee and New York–style bagels you have ever tasted. Just the smell of the place gives one a religious experience.

I hope you preach a good sermon later today!—Neo
P.S. Have you heard any Amish Jellies music lately?

It was 8:00 P.M. Sunday night. when I next checked my e-mail. Of course I called Neo immediately. I couldn't get away to visit him, much as I wanted to. He left Seattle for New Zealand four weeks later, on January 31. Before he left, we talked almost daily by phone, mostly about the sale of his townhouse and the storage of his personal belongings here but also about his travel plans. He planned to go from New Zealand to Australia, then up to Papua New Guinea and India, then to Europe, then to Jamaica, then to Ecuador, and then home. Quite an itinerary! He hoped to be home either by September or by year's end.

Here's the last e-mail I sent him.

TO: neoliver@fdrhs.edu
FROM: danrpoole@backspring.com
DATE: January 31, 2000
SUBJECT: READ THIS BEFORE YOU LEAVE!

Neo—It's after midnight here, but I had to send you this quick note. I hope you get this before you leave Seattle. I've tried calling, but your phone is already disconnected.

I just got back from addressing a young adults group not far from here—mostly college students, but some in their late twenties too. I tried to share some of the things you and I have talked about. I know I blew a few members of the audience away (as you did me on several occasions—but fortunately, nobody came after me with sticks!). But there were two conversations that I must share with you.

After my talk, one young man came up to me and said, "This was a very significant night in my life. You see, my dad is a pastor, and for several years I have felt this calling from God that he wants me to be a pastor too. But I couldn't stand the thought of becoming like my dad. Tonight, as I listened to you speak, something inside me went, like, BING! This is it! I can't be a pastor like my dad, but I could be a pastor like this guy. I mean, you really came across as down-to-earth and real. And accepting. And no less committed to Christ than the people who are forced and judgmental. Thanks."

As soon as he said that, I thought back to that night at the Amish Jellies concert where our conversation first began, and I remember telling you how I felt less than real—the same word this fellow used. In whatever ways I was able to help this guy, Neo, you have helped me in the same ways. I wanted you to know that.

Then I find myself standing in line at the refreshment table, and I'm standing behind a young woman with a lot of earrings and I say something to her and she turns around and seems startled and says, "Whoa, you're the speaker, aren't you?" And then her eyes fill up with tears, and she says, "I started crying during your talk tonight. You are the first pastor I've ever met who admitted that Christianity didn't own God."

Actually, I hadn't said that, at least not in those words. Then she says, "I want to serve God somehow with my life. I think at heart I'm like a missionary or something. But here's what I know: whenever I get to know individual non-Christians—I mean really get to know them—I am completely convinced that I find God already there and at work in their lives. It doesn't matter if they're way-out New Agers or even atheists. So it's clear to me that God doesn't limit himself to working in Christians' lives. We try to serve God, but we don't own him, and deep down I have always known that, but you're the first member of the clergy who was, like, real enough to say it. Somehow, hearing you talk about God working outside the context of the 'saved,' I really felt validated."

Again that word—real—and again this feeling that the spark I sensed in you has begun to glow in me. I can't tell you how good I feel about what I am becoming, thanks to you. Thanks, my friend. I thank God for you. Have a great trip, and remember you have friends waiting for you when you return.—Dan

P.S. Carol is standing here reading over my shoulder. She says thanks too.

I've never been sure if Neo got that message, because I never received a response. I hope he checked his e-mail one last time, because that note was the closest I ever got to adequately thanking him for his impact on my life.

As I write these words, it's late August, and I still haven't heard word one from him. I've worried at times—anything could have happened to him. But my guess is that at this very moment he's having a ball watching elephants in India or sipping cappuccino at a sidewalk table in some piazza in Italy or scuba-diving with sea turtles in the Caribbean or visiting old friends in Port Maria. Or maybe he's on his way home even as we speak.

He told me he wouldn't write, and he kept his word. But it's been almost seven months! With the new school year not far away, I keep expecting that he'll be back and that I'll bump into him at back-to-school night. I half expect him to show up at my door any day, smiling in his old red cap, inviting me out for coffee or a walk along the river. I'm waiting. He'll have some great stories to tell, I know, and I still have a lot of questions. I've been thinking about offering him a job on staff at Potomac Community Church. Maybe the two of us together could . . . well, it's probably not worth thinking about.

In our last phone conversation, several days before I sent that last e-mail, I asked Neo three questions:

Could I have his permission to document our conversations in a book? Without hesitation, he said yes but asked me not to include the personal details he shared in his e-mails about his marriage and divorce.

Would he be willing to read the manuscript and critique it for me when he got back? Again, yes, of course, if he got back in time.

Would he be willing to write one section of it—a section where he tried to tell the story of the gospel as he understood it? To this one he said maybe. He wasn't going to bring his laptop (he told me he was sure he would break it or lose it somewhere), so e-mailing it was out of the question. He had my address, and if he could get time to write, he would send it to me via snail mail.

I began writing and compiling our conversations immediately. I still haven't received his story of the gospel, and it looks like this manuscript will have to go to the publisher without the benefit of Neo's own comments.

Back in early February, we were hit with a major snowstorm here in Maryland. Snowstorms are a special gift to the Washington, D.C., area, which tries to live at the speed of light, not the speed of life. Snow is a blessing, because even an inch brings the city to a standstill. No one can drive, no one can work, and the whole city and its environs grows quiet, peaceful, calm. A snowstorm is our city's only Sabbath.

One Tuesday evening, as the snow was falling down, I asked Carol if she would take a walk with me. We bundled up in our winter coats, hats, gloves, and boots and walked around our neighborhood, something we hadn't done in . . . ever, actually. For a long time we didn't talk, beyond mentioning the beauty, the quiet, the peace. There was only the sound of our own breathing, the gentle crunch of snow underfoot, the rustle of winter clothing.

I told Carol that I had reached a decision about my future. She kept looking down at her boots shuffling through the snow.

"Carol, before, I saw only two alternatives: either keep up the status quo, and feel less and less honest about it, or try to be honest about my thinking, which meant leaving the church altogether to avoid a big meltdown. But Neo has helped me see a third alternative, one that would be more courageous, more honest, and more pleasing to God. I thought this would be impossible before, and maybe it is, but now I wonder if I could become a new kind of Christian and I could try to lead Potomac Community Church in that new path too. It won't be easy. I know how much I have struggled, and I know this will mean struggles for others too. I have to expect that people will sometimes lash out at me just as I lashed out at Neo, because to talk about change like this . . . well, it's agonizing and threatening and terrifying. But deep down, it's what people need, and it's what the church needs. And I guess it's what the gospel is about. Besides, as Neo said, sooner or later this has to be done, and I'd hate to die and think I shrank back from my chance to help. So I'd like to take the risk, if . . ."

Carol was still looking down, but I think I could detect a smile at the corner of her mouth. I continued, "I don't want to try this unless you feel good about it too. I don't know where this path will lead. It's like we've come to the edge of the map, and all familiar paths are behind us, but a new world is out there ahead of us. I feel this urge to try to find other people who are at the edge of the map too, and maybe if we travel on together, we can make some new discoveries, and help each other, and—"

Carol stopped walking and looked up toward the next street light. "It's kind of like the snow tonight, isn't it, Dan? There aren't any footprints to follow, but there's light ahead, and there's a certain beauty in it all."

16

NOTES ON CHURCH LEADERSHIP FROM ONE CERTIFIED NOBODY TO ANOTHER

THE DECISION THAT WE MADE that February night left me feeling a bit like I did after proposing to Carol eighteen years earlier: *I know this is what I wanted, but what have I gotten myself into?*

I felt this desperate need to talk with Neo. Virtually all of our conversations had been about theology, theory, concepts—but few were about what our theories would look like worked out in a living Christian community. How can I help Potomac Community Church go through this transition without blowing it up? How will people let go of Christianity as a modern construct when a better alternative has not fully presented itself? How can people let go of the trapeze they're holding on to if the next one isn't yet within reach—do they take a leap into nothingness, clutching at air? Is that faith—or insanity? How can a church hold together through the turbulence unleashed by these sorts of questions? How far do we go with this rethinking, and how far is too far? Am I the only pastor thinking these kinds of thoughts, or are there others?

With these questions simmering in my mind, in late July, when I was reading through the e-mail archives from which the last few chapters were gleaned, I came across the name of the youth pastor from St. Timothy's Episcopal, someone Neo said he hoped I would meet. I decided to try to find him. Maybe he and Neo had discussed some of these issues.

The only name that Neo had given me was "Casey B." When I called St. Timothy's, I found out three things: Casey B. had left St. Tim's in June, his full name was Casey B. Curtis, and . . . "he" was actually an African

American woman. Everyone called her Casey B. because her father, who still attended St. Tim's, was Casey C. Curtis. I called Casey C. and learned that his daughter was working for the summer with an interdenominational youth ministry called Life Unlimited—in Poland! Fortunately, Casey B. had e-mail access, and Casey C. had his daughter's e-mail address.

Casey B. turned out to be a delightful young woman—energetic, passionate, bright, confident. "Watch out," her father had told me, "she's high voltage!" and he was right. No wonder Neo had been so impressed with her, first as her Sunday school teacher and then as her youth leader at St. Tim's in the early '90s. She became his top student leader and his protégée, and after her graduation, he encouraged her to study youth ministry at a Christian college near Chicago. In fact, I learned from Casey C. that Neo had covered her tuition. In 1998 she returned to St. Tim's as their first—albeit part-time—paid youth pastor, and Casey C. suspected that Neo had funded the first half of her salary, hoping the church would pick up the second half.

"Neo was my MENTOR," Casey B. wrote, "so OF COURSE I printed out everything he sent me online and saved it. He also had this CON-STANT habit of drawing little diagrams on restaurant placemats and stuff, and I kept all of those too. They're TREASURES." She kept all her "Neo stuff" in a binder—which was in her room back home. She e-mailed her father and asked him to bring me the binder when she heard I was writing this book.

Like me, she hasn't heard anything from Neo since January. Like me, she worries about him—more as the months pass with no word from him.

This final chapter contains several of Casey B.'s e-mails from Neo, written during the time I was getting to know him. You'll notice there's some repetition and overlap in our conversations, which is what you'd expect, since they occurred around the same time. I figure that anything repeated often by Neo would bear repeating.

Unfortunately, Casey did not save her e-mails to Neo, so the conversation here is one-sided. However, in most cases, Neo's responses imply the questions or issues raised by Casey.

What meant so much to me in reading their conversation was this: some of the very questions I would have asked Neo—questions to help me figure out what to do next at Potomac Community Church—were exactly the questions he had addressed for Casey B.

To: cbc@youthnet.net
From: neoliver@fdrhs.edu
Date: September 21, 1999
Subject: Seminary Recommendation

CB—I really have mixed feelings about answering your last e-mail! You know we'd hate to lose you at St. Tim's, and I would miss you more than anyone, except the youth group members themselves, of course—and maybe their parents! I know the part-time salary isn't sufficient. Losing you would be another example of the high cost of being cheap. But knowing you, it's not the money that is making you consider moving on.

Having said that, I think you'd make a great pastor or rector. You know that personally, I think working with teenagers is generally more important and more strategic than working with adults, but if you feel a call to move from youth ministry to adult leadership, I'll back you wholeheartedly. I'm your biggest fan, CB, you know that.

Now as to your specific questions—remember, this is just my opinion—you asked for it, so here it is.

I wish I could recommend a good seminary for you to finish your studies. Of course there are a lot of good seminaries out there, but nearly all are working on the modern model, more or less, and you know that I think that model is pretty outdated already. For someone as young as you, it would be so good if there was a seminary that was preparing you for ministry in 2040, not 1940. Oh, well. Maybe that will change soon. Maybe it is changing already and I just don't know about it.

If you do decide to pursue church planting, you may need to change denominations or go nondenominational. If you're going to start from scratch, you really should find a context that would give you the most freedom to experiment, explore, and innovate. That would mean either going independent or finding a denomination that would offer you good support without a lot of strings attached. If it were me, I'd start a new church, and I'd build my core with as little baggage as possible. Of course, our denomination is really generous financially when it comes to starting new churches, but sometimes the strings attached aren't worth the price you pay for them.

Hope that helps, my young friend!—Neo

To: cbc@youthnet.net
From: neoliver@fdrhs.edu
Date: September 25, 1999
Subject: Re: Seminary Recommendation

You're right. I was referring to the fact that most Protestant seminaries fight with vigor the battles of yesterday, largely oblivious to the issues of today, hardly thinking of the issues of tomorrow. They still preoccupy themselves with fighting the Protestant Reformation and the liberal-fundamentalist debates. (Somebody tell them those wars are over, OK?) As for your other comments, yes, I'd be glad to clarify.

When I said that seminaries operate on the modern model, I meant (among other things) that they put theory before practice and that they assume that knowledge (not character, skill, experience, know-how, passion, and so on) is power. In the postmodern world, I think we'll interweave theory and practice (which will mean that education will be lifelong, not pushed to the beginning of one's career), and we'll believe that power in ministry flows from character, know-how, experience, relationships, spiritual disciplines, passion, AND knowledge (and probably some other things too). The dethroning of theoretical knowledge will require something far more radical than rewriting seminary curricula; it will require reinventing the whole idea of professional ministry training. (It might even make us deconstruct the idea of "professional," but that would be another subject for another time.)

Yes, I do believe established churches can change. Later tonight or tomorrow, I'll write up some thoughts on how I think churches can transition to postmodern ministry. You'll keep in mind that most of what I say would be classified as "hunch," not experience-born insight.

Today I'm going on a hike with the father of one of my soccer players—pastor of Potomac Community Church. Have you heard of it? This fellow is just entering into this whole postmodern conversation. I feel for him. I'm not certain if he's genuinely curious or just testing me. You know what I'm talking about. I haven't told him about my first career yet. Do you think I should?—Neo

To: cbc@youthnet.net
From: neoliver@fdrhs.edu
Date: September 25, 1999
Subject: Too Tired Tonight

CB—I'm tired! What an intense day I had with the pastor fellow I told you about. Not only did he ask questions, questions, questions—and tough ones, too—but he walked me ten miles, I'm sure, and for a minute there at the end, I thought he was going to hit me with a stick! I'll tell you about it when I see you at church.

So needless to say, I'll work on the church transition issue tomorrow afternoon. I'm going to bed early tonight.—Neo

To: cbc@youthnet.net
From: neoliver@fdrhs.edu
Date: September 26, 1999
Subject: Church Transitions

CB—Sorry I missed you at church this morning. No, I wasn't kidding about the stick. And yes, I think I pushed him too hard. You know what that's like! I'll tell you about the whole incident next time I see you.

Here are my thoughts on the church transition question you raised. As I said, much of this is hunch, although my pastoral and lay leadership experiences certainly come to bear.

My guess is that out of one hundred churches, maybe ten would say they want to transition. Most are happy as they are, or they'd rather die than change.

My guess is that out of the ten churches who say they want to transition, probably only two or three really do, meaning that they are willing to pay the full price.

My guess is that of those two or three, one or two could actually do it, but it would be far more difficult than they imagined.

This next hunch is going to be counterintuitive—but I would guess that churches that "missed" the traditional-to-contemporary transition (à la Willow Creek or Saddleback) might have a better chance of transitioning to postmodern ministry than ones that became contemporary. (I know you will ask why, so . . .) Why? Contemporary churches are happily modern, and their numbers (attendance, budget) are probably sufficient so that the pain of changing would be greater than the pain of not changing. Of course, there are some amazingly smart contemporary pastors out there—Rick Warren and Bill Hybels and others. So I'm sure there will be exceptions to this. At any rate, traditional churches are generally less happy, "successful," and secure in their modernity, so they may be more willing to change. Not only that, but the contemporary shift generally made churches more antiseptic—it purged them of ritual, liturgy, symbol, and so on. I actually think that these things will be assets for the postmodern church. (Many contemporary churches painted themselves into a corner by saying that ritual, liturgy, symbol, and all that were wrong or evil and such, and that might make it hard for them to change. But some will face the music, I hope, and reverse their rejection of all things historic and traditional.)

The traditional churches will have to do one thing about their traditions, if they want to retain them: they will have to relativize them. They won't be able to enforce them as being right, necessary, or biblically mandated; they will rather simply offer them as elements of their church culture that have meaning for them. And if they don't work, they will feel free to drop them in favor of new practices that will work. (For example, I would not require people to make the sign of the cross, but I'll bet if people really considered what that tradition could mean, they would want to incorporate it into their faith.)

I used to think that the liberal churches might navigate the postmodern transition more gracefully than the conservative ones. But as I think about it, the liberals are generally more free in their thinking and more rigid in their methodology, liturgy, and such. Conservatives are generally rigid in their thinking but more free in their methodology. Their passion for evangelism drives them into the world (which is populated by a lot of postmodern folks), and that evangelistic encounter always has the potential to transform the evangelizer as well as the evangelized. (For example, remember our Bible study on Peter and Cornelius in Acts 10? And remember the short-term mission trip I took you on to Guatemala back when you were seventeen? You kids—along with yours truly—were transformed more by that experience than any of the Guatemalan children we went to minister to.) For that reason, I now think that liberals and conservatives have about an even shot at seizing the postmodern moment. (Of course, maybe neither will, and God will raise up some other new movement to do so.) In any case, be sure you don't get yourself into some situation where the church you pastor (or plant) runs in deep ruts of modernity! That would be a terrible waste and a definite step down from youth ministry.

When it comes to bringing change, you have two options. First, you can push down the status quo—scare people, help them see that things aren't as copasetic as they believe them to be. Second, you can lift up a vision—inspire people, help them see that things could be so much better. There's a place for both, but without the second, the first is only a short-term, quick-fix tool for change. Knowing you, you should plan to lead by no more than 25 percent status quo redefinition and at least 75 percent vision inspiration.

The other big decision in bringing about change anywhere, but especially in a church, is whether to move incrementally or innovatively. Incremental changes (improving little by little) are great when your basic system is sound, when your basic philosophy and "business plan" make sense. But whether we're dealing with public schools (I know too much about this!), churches, or seminaries, incremental change is the worst enemy of true innovation. Innovation means introducing a bold new system, a new philosophy, a whole new plan. It's like being a travel agent or stockbroker in the age of the Internet: Do you keep improving your services, or do you jump to a new way of doing business entirely?

Maybe you do both—create incremental improvement of your existing services and at the same time innovate by creating new ways of "doing business." What that would mean in church transition would be this: you would lead a revolution by addition, not subtraction. You wouldn't change the "services" (you can read that with either meaning) so loved by your dominant group. But you would add new worship and spiritual growth experiences for new people—completely new ways of doing things. It reminds me of back in the early '70s (I guess before you were born) when gas stations had to provide two kinds of gas, leaded and unleaded. Eventually, the leaded was phased out, but you couldn't bring in the new without continuing to serve the old, because all of the existing cars needed the leaded fuel. Do you follow me? I think for the next decade or two (or more), we'll need to have modern "leaded" church services (again, in both senses of the word) as we add postmodern "unleaded" ones. Maybe a better example from your lifetime would be the use of cassettes and CDs. Are you in the cassette business or the music business? The question becomes even more important with the rise of MP3, Napster, and other new ways of acquiring recorded music. The whole process will be tricky. But change always is.

One other thing—I would lean toward maximizing rather than minimizing discontinuity. In other words, don't try to underestimate how significant the changes are to the people. Instead, tell them, "I'd like us to consider making some really major and difficult changes in the way we do ministry around here." If I were assigned to a struggling church, I might propose that they actually shut down the church but stay together as a core group to plan a new beginning. Then I'd help them choose a new name, symbolic of a whole new philosophy of ministry that we would develop. I would also bring in a lot of outside consultants. Outsiders have so much more power than insiders—another counterintuitive reality I've discovered.

I realize I'm writing this as if you've already made your decision to become a "grown-ups'" pastor instead of a youth pastor. Are you sure that's what you should do?—Neo

To: cbc@youthnet.net
From: neoliver@fdrhs.edu
Date: September 28, 1999
Subject: Re: My Decision FOR NOW

CB—Yes, I'm relieved. I think it could be a good thing, but there aren't many youth pastors as good as you are. I will keep praying with you about this. I know you'll end up where you belong.

I love the questions you ask, Casey. But please don't consider yourself a Nobody. But then again, Nobodies change the world. The Somebodies in Places of Power tend to exercise their power to maintain the status quo or to improve the status quo. But when it's time to move from status quo to terra nova, that's usually the job of Nobodies from the powerless places at the margins. Think of Moses, Esther, Nehemiah, Jesus, Paul. Think of Martin Luther King Jr. or Nelson Mandela.

So in that light, here are the thoughts from one certified Nobody to another on your two excellent questions:

You asked what my "dream seminary" would be like. This is something I have thought about a great deal. My seminary experience was so formative and positive—even though I sometimes sound like I'm seminary-bashing, really, I love seminaries. But I think that seminaries will become amazingly different in the future. Thinking back to my last message to you, they'll have to decide they're not in the cassette or CD business but in the music business. In this case, they'll realize they're not just in the certification business or even just the theological education business but in the Christian leadership development business. So with that in mind, my ideal seminary would be one part monastery, one part mission agency, and one part seminar. Here's what I mean.

By monastery, I would want the seminarians to live in community of some sort, to experience a real sharing of life and of "the offices," of shared spiritual practices. This would contribute to spiritual formation, and it would weed out sociopathic types who are attracted to ministry because they like power or they like being right or they need attention but they don't love or serve people much. As a youth group leader, you've often told me—and I agree—that more spiritual formation takes place in a weekend retreat than in six months of weekly meetings and that more spiritual formation takes place in a week of summer camp than in a year of weekly meetings. It strikes me that a retreat is simply a short-term monastic experience. It's intense—and intensity is an undervalued key to spiritual growth—and it's holistic: it's not a matter of just adding some Bible onto a busy, fragmented life. This would be an essential part of my ideal seminary. Whether people lived in this sort of community for a year, a semester, a quarter, a month, or a weekend out of every month (kind of like the Army Reserves), I know it would be a good thing for them.

The mission agency part is closely related. In my mind, while modern Christianity was fixated on systematic theology, the erection of a conceptual cathedral that would comprehend all truth, so postmodern Christianity will focus on mission, on our role as agents of God's kingdom. We will be God's people for the world. For this reason, I would want my seminarians to spend a lot of time traveling and experiencing places where mission is happening. This would mean internships in churches, soup kitchens, youth centers, refugee camps, church-planting projects, employment centers, small enterprise development projects, care facilities, hospitals, community organizing and community redevelopment initiatives, orphanages, and summer camps. This would weed out all who were really interested in comfort and safety rather than adventure and compassion. I'm thinking of the Celtic monks who loved to go on journeys—my seminarians would be sent out on several missionary journeys during their apprenticeship. Does that sound vaguely biblical?

The seminar part would be different from a traditional school, which assumes that people learn best by listening. We both know (extroverts that we are) that most people learn best while talking. So my seminary would be based on seminars, not lectures, meaning that students would read or experience something (a book, a CD, a movie, a conference, an interview, a retreat, a Website, an art exhibit), and then they would discuss it with their fellow learners, with a teacher present. The teacher would make sure that needed content was conveyed and understood, but in the context of conversation, not just monologue. Information transmission should be handled in the most efficient way possible—through film, reading, lecture, Websites, interviews, whatever.

By the way, as a teacher, I've learned that instead of me giving all the lectures, I can assign my students various readings and then let them teach various parts of the material to one another. They learn more by having to teach it, and learning then becomes collaborative, turning the classroom into a knowledge acquisition team. I'm around to make midcourse corrections and keep the process moving, kind of like the team coach. That's what I mean by seminar. This makes sense especially in the training of pastors, whose bread and butter is teaching. Why not give them all the study, teaching, and preaching practice we can during their education?

We wouldn't stop with information transmission, of course; that would only be the beginning. More important would be integrating that information into our understanding of the story.

By story, of course, I mean the story of God's work in the universe and, in particular, the story of God's work in the human community. When I teach science, I teach it this way—as the story of the development of science or the story of the development of the galaxy or the story of the evolution of life or the story of the development of a fetus or whatever. That's something Polanyi taught me. For me, everything finds meaning in its place in a story.

Hope that's helpful, my friend! Thanks for asking me to dream.—Neo

To: cbc@youthnet.net
From: neoliver@fdrhs.edu
Date: September 29, 1999
Subject: Re: You Forgot My Second Question!

CB—You're right, I forgot to answer your second question. You realize my thoughts on this are only guesses. When I was a pastor, I never succeeded at helping a church transition into a new form or philosophy of ministry. Even as a layperson at St. Tim's, we've only begun to grapple with some of the issues of postmodernity. We're still very early on in the learning curve. But since you asked—twice—here are my thoughts.

If I were going to transition a church from a modern model (whether traditional or contemporary—and as I said, I think contemporary models would actually be harder to change in many cases), I'd really focus on process. I would begin by self-reporting—telling my key leaders what I was thinking about, questions I was having, struggles I was dealing with. I wouldn't say, "The church needs to do something," but rather, "I am changing in my thinking about some things." This is what the systems thinking people call "self-differentiation," and it's essential in the early stages of a transition; the leader is reporting on the fact that he is moving ahead himself, and this alerts the rest of the organization that change may be coming for them too.

Then I'd develop a proposal—a proposal for the organization to move into a new beginning or a new chapter. As I said, my bias is to maximize the change I am proposing to the organization, rather than minimizing it in people's minds; I've found that minimizing the change (to avoid fearful reactions) is counterproductive. The proposal would be a multiyear transition plan (I think the longer the time frame included in the plan, the more likely the plan will actually work), clarifying what the change would involve, why it's important, and how it would be achieved. It would begin with a major celebration to acknowledge the past, thank a lot of people, and seek to inspire people about the future, with a lot of prayer to be sure that people are moving ahead "in the Spirit."

The plan would include an implementation phase and a lengthy assessment phase too, which would allow the church to address the questions "What if it works?" and "What if it doesn't?" That's important, because if the transition works, a whole new range of problems can be anticipated, so change will unleash more change. And if the plan doesn't work, the organization will face a whole new set of decisions (including whether it needs to find a new pastor!).

As part of my plan, I would include a list of consultants—outsiders we could call for input, problem solving, and other needs. I have a huge respect for consultants—as the Proverbs tell us, we grow wiser and plans succeed more often with many of them. I would be especially sure to have a conflict resolution consultant on board as part of the plan—so that we had someone to come in when (I didn't say "if") conflicts arise, as they always do during times of change (for a whole bunch of reasons). Wouldn't it be great if there were a cadre of wise consultants who specialize in guiding churches through the postmodern passage?

Ultimately this transition is not about changes in musical style, preaching style, liturgy, or architecture, although all of those things may change if we go through the transition. At heart, it's about attitude, theology, and spirituality. People talk a lot about "seeker-sensitive services," but I think the real issue is "seeker-sensitive people" with "seeker-sensitive attitudes"—all of which would flow from a more missional theology and spirituality. If the attitudes change, the stylistics are not only easier to change, but they will also "want" to change. Maybe that's why the traditional-to-contemporary change was so disruptive—too often we tried to change exteriors without changing our attitudes, theologies, and spirituality. Am I making sense here, CB?

I feel a bit uncomfortable with what I've just written. It feels kind of technical, and in the end, church leadership was for me a matter of the heart—a love affair, not just a technical bag of tricks. It's a lot about who we are as leaders. Do people trust us? Have we really earned the right to be heard, trusted, followed? If you became a pastor, I know you would lead sensitively and strongly.

Two key qualities for leaders in transition—both of which you have in abundance—would be compassion and patience. Here's an analogy that comes to mind. We modern Western Christians have been living in a beautiful old Victorian mansion for generations. It's comfortable; it's full of memories; it's quaint; it's home for us. On the walls hang the portraits of our ancestors. The floorboards show the paths worn by thousands of feet—our grandparents, our cousins, ourselves as children. Each room holds special memories. Now someone tells us that the civil engineers have just come by. They say that our house lies on a fault line and that recent tremors have begun to crack our foundation and the house is certain to crumble—we just don't know how soon. Or maybe they say that our home has been infested with termites and the walls and floor joists are about to give way.

We look around, and we can't believe what they're saying. Everything looks as it's always looked. Sure, there are a few cracks in the plaster, and the floors and the walls have some gaps between them—that's typical of old houses. But the engineers are insistent. We ask, "Well, if we have to leave, where do we go?" And they say, "We're sorry, but the new house isn't built yet. In the meantime, we have set up some pup tents in your front yard. For now, please box up all your belongings and photographs—eventually you'll be able to hang them in your new home again, but for now they'll have to go into storage."

Or, to try a different metaphor, the church is being urged to flee the collapsing modern regime. But we have grown comfortable with modernity. Why face the hardships and dangers of becoming a refugee? Is the collapsing regime really so bad? Is there a better place to go to?

Do you see why I say we need to be patient and compassionate with people who face these choices?

Now I find myself thinking, "Maybe you should go in this direction." Because as important as youth ministry is, without good, strong local churches on the other side of this postmodern transition, the Christian cause is stalled in midair. I think you could be an architect of a new kind of faith community, Casey. I firmly believe that the top question of the new century and new millennium is not just whether Christianity is rational, credible, and essentially true (all of which I believe it is) but whether it can be powerful, redemptive, authentic, and good, whether it can change lives, demonstrate reconciliation and community, serve as a catalyst for the kingdom, and lead to a desirable future. That drama must be played out on the local level, in communities of people who live by the gospel. I've seen you build that kind of community among teenagers; I know you could do it among adults too.

As I wrote that last sentence, a third option dawned on me. Maybe you could work with youth but consider your youth work part of a fifteen- or twenty-year subversive plan to locate and train a new generation of church planters and pastors. On the surface you look like a typical wild and crazy youth worker, but underneath you're an agent of radical change in the church. Not a bad way to spend a decade or two!

I want to write more about the importance of mission in all of this, but that will have to wait. I have a monumental backlog of e-mail to read and respond to. This technology is a blessing and a curse, isn't it?—Neo

To: cbc@youthnet.net
From: neoliver@fdrhs.edu
Date: October 3, 1999
Subject: Re: Thanks, Coach!

CB—Thanks for your kind words. I meant everything I said. I'm so glad it was helpful.

Yes, I would be honored to speak to the youth group this Friday night. I haven't been invited to do so in quite a while. But are you sure you want me to speak on the whole science-faith debate? You know I'm going to tell the kids that I think evolution is one of God's coolest creations, and that's going to get some of the parents upset, if not some of the kids. I'm glad to help, eager to help—but just be prepared to get some phone calls. Remember, I went through this once already at FDR!

I'm having some interesting conversations with the pastor fellow I told you about. I'm really starting to like the chap. He reminds me of you—full of questions, sincerely desiring to be "real." As we'd say in science, he wants to be true to the data.

I told you I had some thoughts on mission. I haven't shared any of these thoughts with my pastor friend. I don't think he could handle them yet. He's pretty entrenched in a modern model of doing ministry, with all the attendant assumptions—church is ultimately a consumer or customer satisfaction project, modern stuff like that.

In my thinking, church doesn't exist for the benefit of its members. It exists to equip its members for the benefit of the world. To do that, it is about three things: community, spirituality, and mission—kind of a triangle, where each point is connected to the other two. (Can you picture this? Maybe someday it will be easier to insert drawings into our e-mails!)

Community means that we create a place of belonging where people can learn to believe the good news, belong to a community that is learning to behave (or live) by it, and become (together) a living example of it. I think of the beautiful phrase in our Nicene Creed: "I believe in one holy, catholic, and apostolic church." This is the "one . . . catholic" part. We are unified, connected to one another, maintaining the humility and gentleness necessary for unity to flourish. And we are catholic, meaning that we accept anyone whom Christ accepts. We don't show favoritism, screen out, or judge.

Spirituality focuses on the "holy" part. But it is not just about individual spirituality (as was the case in modernity, where everything was privatized, atomized, individualized). The spirituality itself is communal. True, the "done in secret" part is important, but what we experience with God in secret must be brought to the community and shared like a common meal. So we read the Bible as a community, always listening for the insights and input of others. We pray as a community, our individual prayers merging with those of our brothers and sisters. We fast and study and celebrate and worship and rest together. In these ways, through private and communal spiritual disciplines, we become unique, holy people.

But in my thinking, both spirituality and community flow into mission. Mission is the "apostolic" dimension of the church—"mission" and "apostolic" simply being Latin and Greek ways of saying that we are sent.

I know that in the modern era, we interpreted "apostolic" as meaning "based on the teachings of the apostles," which of course I agree with, but oddly, in classic modern fashion, we seemed to think we could be founded on the teachings of the apostles without sharing the identity of the apostles as people sent into the world on a mission. Jesus said it: "As the Father has sent me, so I send you"—which means that we are sent not to "be served" but to "serve," and that we are sent not to "the healthy" but to "the sick" (profound new thoughts for many people—that the church exists for the world, not its members, and that we are on a mission to the irreligious, not the religious).

If the triangle is moving (and it should be, right?), it is moving behind the "point" of mission. And as you know from all of our Bible studies back in high school, in my thinking, our mission is simply seeking, receiving, and manifesting the kingdom of God, the reign of God, the reality of God's will being done on earth as it is in heaven. In that mission, the church is the catalyst, not the goal; you know I believe the kingdom is much larger than the church, and the more successful the church is in mission, the more expansive the kingdom. This includes evangelism but is not limited to it, because in a sense evangelism is in the service of the larger mission of the kingdom. Our mission is comprehensive—so that every Christian, "clergy" and "lay" (troublesome terms themselves), is equally sent—to a classroom, a factory, an office building, a highway, a jungle, whatever—to be an agent of Christ, an agent of the kingdom. (Paul called them "peace ambassadors of Christ.")

One of the ways modernity captured Christianity was in this area of mission: our mission evaporated (except in the narrow slice of church life that we called "missions"—whose very existence unfortunately legitimized the largest part of church life not being mission-oriented). We became purveyors of religious goods and services, seeking a clientele, competing for market share, complete with brand names and all the rest. If you want useful plastic kitchen articles, you go to Wal-Mart. If you want low-cost, high-fat food in generous portions, you go to Taco Bell. If you want a standard, scripted vacation, you go to Disney World. If you want a fizzy, sugary drink, you go to Coca-Cola. And if you want a spiritual pick–me–up, you go to church. This put us in a situation exactly opposite to— as I see it—Christ's intent.

For Christ, his "called ones" (which is what the Greek term for "church" really means) were also to be his "sent ones." He trained those whom he called to follow him as apprentices so that they could be sent in his ongoing mission to teach his good news. In this line of thinking about the church, we don't recruit people to be customers of our products or consumers of our religious programs; we recruit them to be colleagues in our mission. The church doesn't exist to satisfy the consumer demands of believers; the church exists to equip and mobilize men and women for God's mission in the world.

Thankfully, his mission isn't to make more and more people more and more religious! His mission is much bigger than an individualistic or even human project. How big is it? Well, I guess you'd have to read Isaiah 2:1–5; 9:2–7; 25:6–9; 35:1–10; 58:5–12; and 65:17–19 to get a feel for its full dimensions.

That, to me, is a vision of the future that informs a mission for the church. That's something I can be excited about for the new millennium.

Sorry to preach. I get pretty excited about these matters.

Speaking of preaching—Father Scott had a good sermon today, didn't he?

Did your dad tell you I took him out to breakfast yesterday morning? He is so proud of you! And so am I. See you Friday night.—Neo

TO: cbc@youthnet.net
FROM: neoliver@fdrhs.edu
DATE: October 10, 1999
SUBJECT: Re: Complaints Coming

CB—I'm so sorry my talk at the youth group last night caused so much trouble. I warned you. Thanks for warning me too. I haven't received any phone calls yet. I'm not surprised that Groves and Miller complained. They didn't waste any time, did they? Poor Father Scott—when did they call him, midnight last night? He must be used to it, the poor guy. There's the downside of pastoral ministry!

When Father Scott asked me to preach for him that Sunday last spring (when he was hospitalized for, what was it, appendicitis?), Darby Groves ate my lunch after the service. He didn't like something I said about hell, as I recall—so he gave me a dose of it! Anyhow, then he wrote an angry letter to Father Scott—and addressed it to him in the hospital! Can you believe that?

Poor Jennifer and Jason must feel torn, because I know they love you and me too, but their dad is relentless in his defense of every modern system he inherited from his fundamentalist forefathers. His loyalty is admirable, but his vehemence can be quite ugly, as you have now experienced. If he leaves the church (as he also threatened to do last spring), just remember: it is not your fault, and it is not about you. He's trying to defend a shrinking territory, and the world to him must look like it's spiraling right down the toilet. No wonder he's afraid and angry. Not only that, but he was "discipled" to be angry. My upbringing was very similar to his: the more "mature" you are, the angrier you are, the more negative, the less gracious, the more suspicious. Being mean isn't a sin in his Bible. (I keep thinking of a guard dog—protecting, defending, growling, snapping!) Hard to believe but true. I'm sure in his own mind he is trying to do what is right.

As to your question, when people draw a small circle that excludes me or those I love, I try to draw a bigger circle that includes them. That's what we have to do with the Groveses and the Millers too. We can't stop loving, being gracious, opening our hearts, trying to be sympathetic. Somehow I know that Darby, at least, still respects Father Scott, so maybe he won't leave. But even if he does, it's not the end of the world—although I know you'd miss Jen and Jason greatly, and they would lose so much by leaving St. Tim's.

As for Darby's accusation, Casey, there is no way you can understand what the word "liberal" means to someone like Darby Groves. Remember, he grew up in the era of the Cold War, when liberal and conservative meant bad and good. He grew up in a time when evangelical Protestantism still knew what it was protesting against: medieval Catholicism and modern liberal Protestantism. Meanwhile, we have those in our denomination with the opposite bent. They grew up in the era of the McCarthy trials and the Ku Klux Klan, and for them liberal and conservative have exactly the opposite meanings. Where does that leave us? We run an interesting gauntlet, don't we? To some we're too liberal and to others we're too conservative!

As for his comments about my treatment of the Bible, well, I would just say that there is more than one way to "kill" the Bible. You can dissect it, analyze it, abstract it. You can read its ragged stories and ragamuffin poetry, and from them you can derive neat abstractions, sterile propositions, and sharp-edged principles. (One wonders why God didn't just give the abstract system instead of all the stories and poetry!) You can sanitize the text of all evocative language, paradox, multiple perspectives, and interesting, three-dimensional people to end up with cute little morals, simple two-dimensional systems, and flat, boring prose that reads like a legal code or assembly instructions for a bicycle. As a result, the Bible itself begins to vaporize, to disappear, leaving the desired residue of systematic theology, which is all you ever wanted anyway.

Or if you prefer, you can also kill the Bible by demythologizing it. You can read it like an engineer and dismiss anything that doesn't fit your modern, Western, rationalistic, reductionistic mind-set. You're left with a pickled specimen, a hollow shell, a stuffed tiger this way too, through a kind of expert theological taxidermy.

What a relief to have a third alternative—to read the Bible as a pre-modern text, emerging from a people who believed that truth is best embodied in story and art and human flesh rather than abstraction or out-line or moralism. We relieve the biblical writers of having to conform to modern expectations. Instead, we join them in our common human pre-dicament as "angels and demons trapped in meat" (didn't Merton say something like that?), whose little three-pound brains can't hope to con-tain the wonder of one grain of wheat or sand, much less the Creator of the universe!

According to the Bible, humans shall not live by systems and abstrac-tions and principles alone but also by stories and poetry and proverbs and mystery. And best of all, instead of lending us moralisms that we must try to impose on followers of different stories (consider the story of Western civilization), it calls us to live as part of its own story, the story of a lov-ing Creator who started something wonderful and beautiful that in spite of our many failures he will surely bring to a good completion. As we live by that story, we find followers of other stories interested in ours because our story, rightly understood, has plenty of room for them and for their stories too.

According to the lower-right corner of my screen, it's 2:00 a.m. already. I suppose I felt, with you "under attack," that you might need a little extra encouragement when you wake up and log on. Remember, you can call me at any time if you need to talk IRL. Maybe I'll see you at church for a moment. I wonder if Groves and Miller will seek me out. Thank-fully, I have to leave right after the early service. I'd love to avoid them. I don't look forward to another scolding from either of them.

Did I tell you that I have tickets for the DC United game at RFK later today? I'm taking along my new pastor friend. It should be a great game. We'll talk soon.—Neo

For the next few weeks, Neo's e-mails to Casey focused on practical matters in the aftermath of his father's death. Since Father Scott wasn't on e-mail, several of the e-mails involved Casey getting messages through to him. There was considerable discussion about the controversy stirred up by Neo's talk on evolution at the youth group, just before he left town. It was a shame, as he was grieving his father's death, that he had to deal with a somewhat petty church controversy back in Maryland. Because Casey was having to deal with this controversy (which involved, I gather, at least one call for her to resign), along with an important career deci-sion, Neo said very little to her about his daily life and routines in Seat-tle, caring for his mother and all that. Rather, his focus was entirely on her and the questions she was asking.

To: cbc@youthnet.net
From: neoliver@fdrhs.edu
Date: October 22, 1999
Subject: Re: Super Ticked Off

CB—No apologies necessary. I can't blame you for being angry.

You wrote: "The church is NOT about self-aggrandizement for its own sake. Maybe that's what turns me off about these guys. They always want more members, more members—and for what? It's like they're human vacuum cleaners, sucking people out of neighborhoods, so all their energies can be sucked up by the church. That sucks! Their SUCCESS comes at the expense of the world around them, and I keep wondering when they start GIVING BACK."

Well put! You know I agree with your sentiments. But there are two cautions I wanted to offer.

First, you wrote: "Why even TRY when UPTIGHT white snipers can take you out with one shot?" While I understand your frustration, I think the name-calling goes over the line. Think of how you'd feel if they said something about you being an "uppity black woman." So watch that. You don't want to abandon the teaching of Christ ("Blessed are . . ."; "Do unto others . . .") in trying to serve Christ, although I know it is tempting sometimes.

Second, your words "why even TRY" scared me. I've never heard you even hint at quitting before. Please don't let critical people like the Groveses and Millers make you decide to leave your ministry. Don't let their criticism give you an excuse for cynicism. I felt that cynicism coming through when you wrote, "It's a nice ideal, but I worry that it will never HAPPEN. You know I love St. Tim's, but even here, the forces that pull us away from being missional are so STRONG. A few well-placed critics can TOTALLY DERAIL a whole lot of hope." I share both your love and your worry regarding St. Tim's, but we can't let that worry paralyze us and seduce us into surrender, defeat, cynicism.

Remember, Jesus went all the way, and that meant patience, and that meant suffering. It's sad when much of your suffering comes at the hands of your brothers and sisters, but being humans, we should expect that. Right now you need to feel your feelings, blow off some steam—and then get ready to get back in the battle with a good spirit, a humble attitude, "patient when wronged," as Paul said to Timothy.

Oh, my. I just had one of those "shiver moments" that you talk to the kids about. I just realized that I'm asking you to do something I wasn't able to do myself. It was situations like this that made me quit years ago. I hope you can do better than I. I'm almost shivering as I write.—Neo

TO: cbc@youthnet.net
FROM: neoliver@fdrhs.edu
DATE: October 24, 1999
SUBJECT: Re: The Latest

CB—It sounds like you're handling this really well. I'm glad you feel that the vision of the church we've been dialoguing about "REALLY ROCKS." If you do decide to become a pastor, help develop this kind of church, OK? One that "really rocks." As you said, "It is so much EASIER to be a point or a line than that triangle of yours." Hard indeed.—Neo

TO: cbc@youthnet.net
FROM: neoliver@fdrhs.edu
DATE: October 27, 1999
SUBJECT: Re: Definition, Please

CB—Sure, I'd be glad to try to define the term "theology." For me, it's not so much a list of beliefs or an outline of beliefs. It's more of a story, the story of how people have sought and learned about God through the centuries. Like any human story, it's got a lot of ups and downs, glories and embarrassments, but that's because it's a human story. Of course, God is involved—shown both in the glories and the embarrassments, the glories giving us glimpses of God's own glory, and the embarrassments giving us glimpses of God's mercy, patience, and compassion.

But actually, another whole dimension of "theology" comes to mind. In a way, theology isn't just about God. It's about the universe. In some ways, theology is about generating models of the universe that flow from our understanding of God and the story we find ourselves in. Does that make any sense at all?

God can't ever really be an object to be studied. He refuses to donate tissue samples for our microscope slides or to lie down on our dissection tables (although that might be an interesting understanding of the cross—it's what we do with a living, loving God—tack him down like an insect in a display case or a frog in a dissection tray).

I wonder if theology in the new millennium will be more like scenario creation. If God is like this, what would the universe be like? If God is like that, what would the universe be like? And it would go the other way too: if the universe is like this, then what might that tell us about God?

Even though we all live on the same planet, we live in different universes—depending on the kind of God we believe in and on our understanding of the master story we are a part of.

I guess things bring me back to that question you asked me about a few weeks ago, about my ideal seminary. At the spirituality point of the triangle, I'd have students study historical theology—as much like a story as possible, focusing on how various theological systems produced various universes or models of reality. I would have them integrate the theology of an era with its art, architecture, liturgy, spiritual disciplines, economics, science, forms of community, and family life. I'd want them to see how human beliefs literally create a way of life. That way of life is what I mean by spirituality.

Then we'd try to face today's world and challenges, and drawing from the Bible, with twenty centuries of "Christian universes" to learn from, we'd help students construct their own model of reality, their understanding of the universe and story we find ourselves in. And—this is SO important—we'd teach them that their model isn't reality; it's just a model. It must always be open to correction, adjustment, improvement, even revolution. Otherwise, we stop being disciples and become know-it-alls. We stop being seekers and become defenders (and you have had some firsthand experience lately of what defenders can be like).

To keep our imaginary seminarians in the seeking mode, we'd spend a lot of time studying contemporary culture. We'd have to. I'd send the students out to exegete movies and art galleries, concerts and sports events, shopping malls and bars, video game parlors and campgrounds, synagogues and mosques. We'd come back from these adventures and talk about what we've seen, what's going on, what it means to be a Christian in our world.

Indulge me in a little more dreaming. Libraries and classrooms would be optional (especially with the Internet); experiences, journeys, and mentors would be required. I might even require seminarians to hold down jobs during part of their training. Six months in a McDonald's might build more spiritual maturity into a young man or woman than sixty credits of hamartiology, soteriology, and all the rest.

That's the kind of seminary I would wish for you, Casey—two or three years of experience, exposure, practice, reflection, dialogue, mentoring, serving, friendship, adventures, co-learning, co-teaching, reflection, tears (no doubt), and laughter.

And actually, I would hope that it would not end after two or three years. I would hope that you would periodically be able to "retreat" into this kind of renewing and enriching experience many times throughout your career—whether you focus on serving youth or adults. Why? Because in the postmodern world we disabuse ourselves of the myth that theory precedes practice.

When I wrote that last sentence, a new idea popped into my mind. Perhaps what we really need is not a seminary that one attends but a lifelong learning community, perhaps like the Catholic orders, that one joins—for life. What would you think of that?

Thanks for asking about me. Really, I'm doing amazingly well. And no, I'm not holding things back. It's just that my days are pretty quiet here taking care of Mom, so there isn't much to say about my day-to-day life. I do miss you guys so much. I've been listening to Father Scott's tapes, so I feel in touch in many ways, and I do exchange e-mails with a few other folks—the Hanleys, the Denimals, the Whites. The pastor I told you about has become a real friend. He's not very good online, but he calls regularly and pastors me by phone. And Father Scott also calls faithfully on Tuesday mornings. He has lifted the word "dependable" to the level of an art form. So thanks for your prayers and your concern. I'm really doing fine.—Neo

TO: cbc@youthnet.net
FROM: neoliver@fdrhs.edu
DATE: November 7, 1999
SUBJECT: Re: Postmodern Theology

CB—Good questions. Actually, I sometimes wonder if there will even be a postmodern systematic theology. I wonder if your generation will focus more on the creation of Christian cultures that embody our faith in ritual, art, liturgy, community, and mission—maybe more like the Celts in the first millennium or like parts of the African American church in the last century. That's not to say that we don't need theologians to work with words, but it is to say that believing as we do that the Word became flesh, the focus of our words should be the creation of communities that embody our good news—in dance, in cooking (remember the Passover?), in crafts (maybe quilting will come back—or perhaps Web pages will be our modern quilts!), in forms of community, in mission endeavors, in music, in painting and sculpture, in architecture and landscape design, in friendship, in solidarity with the poor and forgotten. It's exciting to think about, isn't it?

Regarding your second question—yes, I think the changes in leadership style will be huge. We'll have to talk about this sometime. Be sure to ask me about how postmodern leadership is embodied by Dorothy in "The Wizard of Oz."

CB, I must say I'm jealous of you. I was watching the Weather Channel, and it looks like you're having gorgeous weather back in Maryland. We haven't seen the sun here in Seattle for seventeen days! I miss you and the whole St. Tim's family, especially on Sundays.—Neo

To: cbc@youthnet.net
From: neoliver@fdrhs.edu
Date: November 9, 1999
Subject: Re: UNBELIEVABLE NEWS!

CB—A miracle! Frame that letter! That's the first time I've ever heard of Darby Groves apologizing to anyone. I think that's just great. The Holy Spirit is working!

It's funny—these ugly things in church, like the "inquisition" you've just been through, often become the occasion for the best things. Good for Darby. That was a good letter. Thanks for typing the whole thing out for me. I'm just smiling and smiling and cheering for God. I'm sure that Father Scott had to spend a lot of hours helping both Groves and Miller get to this point. Let Father Scott know that I would give him a high-five if I were there, OK? I'd give you one too, because it was your graciousness under fire that made it impossible for Darby to stay in attack mode.

I guess this is your first big trial in ministry. You have handled things really well. I think again of Paul's words to Timothy about being kind to all, patient when wronged, determined to gently teach those who argue. You've done all that beautifully. Again, echoing Paul to Timothy, no one could "despise your youthfulness" because you set such a wonderful example in speech, behavior, love, faith, and purity.

Casey, whether you stay in youth ministry or become a pastor, church planter, or bishop for that matter, what you've learned in the last month or so will be extremely valuable to you. My friend, as your father says, you are "high voltage!" You are one of the brightest young women I have ever met, and if the only thing I do in my life is to encourage you to soar and fulfill your potential as a leader in Christ's cause, I'll feel that my life has been well spent. Whichever path you choose, go to the front edge, the curl of the wave, the wild frontier, and throw your life and efforts there. That's where we need you!—Neo

AFTERWORD

HAVING READ THESE REPORTS of my friendship with Neo—a short friendship, really—perhaps you realize why I feel this story is worth telling.

Neo is a hard character to explain, impossible to forget, and defiant of nearly all categories. That's why I have to use this rather clumsy description of him: *a new kind of Christian.*

He would probably quarrel with that description. He would probably say that he is on a search, trying to learn what a new kind of Christian will be. But I think that's the first qualification for being one.

He would probably argue that what we've been talking about isn't really so new. But our conversations have opened up so much that's new for me that I would keep the phrase anyway, even though I would see his point.

Beyond that, he would probably be nervous about creating any kind of label that could be used for in-grouping and out-grouping. But I'm quite certain that "a new kind of Christian" is too awkward a term to be used for that purpose.

But it's got a certain ring to it. Kind of like "the Amish Jellies."

NOTES

INTRODUCTION

Thanks to all my colleagues at Leadership Network and the Terranova Project, who have been traveling partners in this journey of faith. Thanks as well to Cedar Ridge Community Church and especially its leadership team and staff, who have courageously accepted the challenge of embracing the postmodern world to transform it with the message and love of Christ.

1. P. M. Senge, "Learning for a Change," *Fast Company,* May 1999, p. 178.

2. B. D. McLaren, *Reinventing Your Church* (Grand Rapids: Zondervan, 1998), pp. 13, 35–36. Revised, edited and retitled as *The Church on the Other Side* (Grand Rapids: Zondervan, 2000), pp. 14, 37-38.

3. B. D. McLaren, *Finding Faith* (Grand Rapids: Zondervan, 1999).

CHAPTER ONE

Thanks to Chuck Smith Jr. for the insights into fundamentalism. He once told me, "Remember, Brian, charismatics are just fundamentalists with a different set of practices," which got me thinking about fundamentalism in a new way. Thanks to Tim Ayers for "the Amish Jellies." Thanks to Doug Koenigsburg for the crisp term "agents of Christ."

CHAPTER TWO

1. P. M. Senge, *The Fifth Discipline: The Art and Practice of the Learning Organization* (New York: Doubleday, 1990).

CHAPTER THREE

Thanks to Dieter Zander for the beautiful phrase "falling into God."

CHAPTER FOUR

Thanks to Dr. John Franke and Dr. David Dunbar of Biblical Theological Seminary for inviting me to team-teach a course on postmodernity in 1998. Many of the insights of this chapter came through that team-teaching experience. Thanks to Neil and Renea Livingstone for many good conversations—and for the C. S. Lewis quotes.

1. C. S. Lewis, *The Discarded Image* (Cambridge, England: Cambridge University Press, 1964).
2. Ibid., pp. 219–220.
3. Ibid., pp. 98–100.
4. Ibid., p. 221.
5. Ibid., p. 222.
6. Ibid., pp. 222–223.

CHAPTER FIVE

Thanks to Dr. Len Sweet for the omelet analogy. Thanks to Steve Tuttle for the analogy of the horse and buggy.

CHAPTER SEVEN

Thanks to Dr. Nancey Murphy for introducing me to the concept of the web of belief in her excellent book, *Beyond Liberalism and Fundamentalism* (Valley Forge, PA: Trinity Press, 1996).

CHAPTER NINE

Thanks to Gerry Eisely and the Washington Arts Group for hosting the Ugandan Dance Troupe (many years ago) described in this chapter. Thanks also to the organizers of the Promise Keepers "Stand in the Gap" event, through which I met the Native Americans on whom the fictionalized story in this chapter is based, and to the "brothers from the res" themselves. Thanks to Jose Torres for the comment about the Bible's most unsettling parts often being most important for us. Thanks to Chris Seay for the idea that Christianity began as an Eastern religion.

CHAPTER TEN

Thanks to the late Lesslie Newbigin for the concept of election to responsibility, not just to privilege. This is one of the most powerful new ideas of my adult life. Thanks to Chris Seay for Neo's choice in beer.

1. P. Tournier, *The Adventure of Living* (New York: HarperCollins, 1965), p. 238.

2. B. Pascal, *Pensées,* 418.

3. G. MacDonald, *Diary of an Old Soul: 366 Writings for Devotional Reflection* (Minneapolis: Fortress Press, 1994).

4. C. S. Lewis, *Letters to Malcolm* (Orlando: Harcourt Brace, 1963), pp. 92–93.

5. Augustine, *City of God* 22:29.

6. 1 Corinthians 12:9, 12.

7. Philippians 1:20–24.

8. 1 John 3:1–3.

9. John 14:1–3.

10. C. S. Lewis, *The Last Battle* (New York: Collier, 1956), pp. 164–165.

CHAPTER ELEVEN

Thanks again to Lesslie Newbigin for the insights about modernity being excessively individualistic.

CHAPTER TWELVE

Thanks to Os Guiness for once telling me over lunch, "Most evangelicals don't really know what the gospel really is," and for challenging me to think about the "gospel of the kingdom." Thanks to Dallas Willard for guiding so many of us deeper and higher into the kingdom of God/kingdom of heaven.

CHAPTER THIRTEEN

Thanks to Dallas Willard for the thoughts on intensity.

1. James G. Deck, "Abba, Father, We Approach Thee." From *The Believers Hymn Book* (London: Pickering & Inglis, circa 1900), Hymn 1.

CHAPTER FOURTEEN

Thanks to Dr. John Franke for his insight that pluralism (recognizing the world's many diverse religions) means seeing the world more the way God has always seen it.

CHAPTER SIXTEEN

Thanks to Rabbi Edwin Friedman for his insights into self-differentiation, in *Generation to Generation: Family Process in Church and Synagogue* (New York: Guifford, 1986). Thanks to the Gospel in Our Culture Network for insights into mission and consumerism, in *Missional Church* (Darrell L. Guder, Ed., Grand Rapids: Eerdman's, 1998). Thanks to Mike Regele for his analysis of the ways that liberals and conservatives vary in change aversion. Thanks to Tom and Christine Sine for celebrating the global missional vision of the referenced passages from Isaiah. Thanks to Dr. Stanley Grenz and Dr. John Franke for their expanded definition of theology, found in their important new book *Beyond Foundationalism: Shaping Theology in a Postmodern Context* (Philadelphia: Westminster John Knox, 2000). And thanks to Mark Driscoll for the fascinating idea that a postmodern systematic theology may not be encoded in books but rather in art and ways of life.

THE AUTHOR

Brian D. McLaren, born in 1956, graduated from the University of Maryland with degrees in English (B.A., summa cum laude, 1978, and M.A., magna cum laude, 1981). After several years of teaching and consulting in higher education, he left academia in 1986 to become founding pastor of Cedar Ridge Community Church, an innovative, nondenominational church in the Baltimore-Washington region.

Brian has been active in networking and mentoring church planters and pastors since the mid-1980s. He is a popular speaker and lecturer for conferences, seminaries, campus groups, and retreats, nationally and internationally. His public speaking covers a broad range of topics including the spiritual search, faith and doubt, postmodernism, Biblical studies, evangelism, apologetics, global mission, leadership, pastoral survival and burnout, church growth, church planting, and the integration of faith with literature, film, music, visual arts, and ecology.

He has written two books, *The Church on the Other Side: Doing Ministry in the Postmodern Matrix* (Zondervan, 2000), and *Finding Faith* (Zondervan, 1999), and has published articles in numerous periodicals and e-zines. He is coordinator of the Terranova Theology Project, an initiative within the Dallas-based Leadership Network, and is active on several non-profit boards.

Brian is married to Grace, a corporate consultant in teambuilding and human resource development. They have four children, one of whom is a cancer survivor. His personal interests include wildlife, hiking, fishing, and the arts.

ABOUT LEADERSHIP NETWORK

The mission of Leadership Network is to accelerate the emergence of effective churches by identifying and connecting innovative church leaders and providing them with resources in the form of new ideas, people, and tools. Churches and church leaders served by Leadership Network represent a wide variety of primarily Protestant faith traditions that range from mainline to evangelical to independent. All are characterized by innovation, entrepreneurial leadership, and a desire to be on the leading edge of ministry.

Leadership Network's focus has been on the practice and application of faith at the local congregational level. A partner with Leadership Network, the Leadership Training Network uses peer learning and interactive training to accelerate the equipping church movement through gift-based team ministry.

Established as a private foundation in 1984 by social entrepreneur Bob Buford, Leadership Network is acknowledged as an influential leader among churches and faith-based ministries and a major resource to which innovative church leaders turn for networking and information.

For additional information on Leadership Network, please contact

Leadership Network
2501 Cedar Springs, Suite 200
Dallas, Texas 75201
800-765-5323
www.leadnet.org

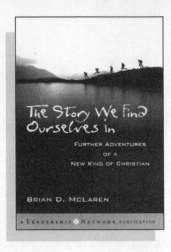

The Story We Find Ourselves In

Further Adventures of a New Kind of Christian

Brian D. McLaren

$21.95 Hardcover
ISBN: 0–7879–6387–9

"A blessing of a book that can alter your view of yourself, your church, and your world."

—LEN SWEET, Stanley E. Jones Chair of Evangelism, Drew University; visiting professor, George Fox University; and chief contributor, Preachingplus.com

AFTER MANY YEARS as a successful pastor, Brian McLaren has found, as more and more Christians are finding, that none of the current strains of Christianity fully describes his own faith. In *The Story We Find Ourselves In*–the much anticipated sequel to his award-winning book *A New Kind of Christian*—McLaren captures a new spirit of a relevant Christianity, where traditional divisions and doctrinal differences give way to a focus on God and the story of God's love for this world. If you are searching for a deeper life with God—one that moves beyond the rhetoric of denominational and theological categories—this delightful and inspiring fictional tale will provide a picture of what it could mean to recapture a joyful spiritual life.

Brian McLaren's witty and wise characters take on difficult, faith-busting themes, from evolution and evangelism to death and the meaning of life–and reveal that the answers to life's pressing spiritual questions often come from the most unlikely sources. Dan and Neo (and some new characters as well) invite reflection on the story we find ourselves in—that is, the narrative of God's presence and meaning in the world now and in the future. In doing so they encourage each of us to live as a new kind of Christian. *The Story We Find Ourselves In* ultimately provides inspiration for revitalizing Christian spiritual life and offers Christians everywhere a new story of their faith's relevance in today's world.

BRIAN D. MCLAREN is the founding pastor of Cedar Ridge Community Church in the Washington-Baltimore area. He is the author of four previous books on contemporary Christianity, including *The Church on the Other Side: Doing Ministry in the Postmodern Matrix* (2000) and *A New Kind of Christian: A Tale of Two Friends on a Spiritual Journey* (Jossey-Bass, 2001), which won a *Christianity Today* Award of Merit for Best Christian Living title, 2002.

[Price subject to change]